New Horizons in the Study of Language and Mind

This book is an outstanding contribution to the philosophical study of language and mind, by one of the most influential thinkers of our time. In a series of penetrating essays, Noam Chomsky cuts through the confusion and prejudice which has infected the study of language and mind, bringing new solutions to traditional philosophical puzzles and fresh perspectives on issues of general interest, ranging from the mind–body problem to the unification of science.

Using a range of imaginative and deceptively simple linguistic analyses, Chomsky argues that there is no coherent notion of "language" external to the human mind, and that the study of language should take as its focus the mental construct which constitutes our knowledge of language. Human language is therefore a psychological, ultimately a "biological object," and should be analysed using the methodology of the natural sciences. His examples and analyses come together in this book to give a unique and compelling perspective on language and the mind.

NOAM CHOMSKY is Institute Professor at the Department of Linguistics and Philosophy, Massachusetts Institute of Technology. Professor Chomsky has written and lectured extensively on a wide range of topics, including linguistics, philosophy, and intellectual history. His main works on linguistics include: *Syntactic Structures; Current Issues in Linguistic Theory; Aspects of the Theory of Syntax; Cartesian Linguistics; Sound Pattern of English* (with Morris Halle); *Language and Mind; Reflections on Language; The Logical Structure of Linguistic Theory; Lectures on Government and Binding; Modular Approaches to the Study of the Mind; Knowledge of Language: its Nature, Origins and Use; Language and Problems of Knowledge; Generative Grammar: its Basis, Development and Prospects; Language in a Psychological Setting; Language and Problems of Knowledge;* and *The Minimalist Program.*

NEIL SMITH is Professor and Head of Linguistics at University College London. He is the author of *An Outline Grammar of Nupe; The Acquisition of Phonology; Modern Linguistics: the Results of Chomsky's Revolution* (with Deirdre Wilson); *The Twitter Machine: Reflections on Language; The Mind of a Savant* (with Ianthi Tsimpli); and *Chomsky: Ideas and Ideals.*

New Horizons in the Study of Language and Mind

Noam Chomsky

Massachusetts Institute of Technology

PUBLISHED BY THE PRESS SYNDICATE OF THE UNIVERSITY OF CAMBRIDGE
The Pitt Building, Trumpington Street, Cambridge, United Kingdom

CAMBRIDGE UNIVERSITY PRESS
The Edinburgh Building, Cambridge CB2 2RU, UK   www.cup.cam.ac.uk
40 West 20th Street, New York, NY 10011–4211, USA   www.cup.org
10 Stamford Road, Oakleigh, Melbourne 3166, Australia
Ruiz de Alarcón 13, 28014 Madrid, Spain

Aviva Chomsky and Eric F. Menoya as Trustees of the Diane Chomsky
Irrevocable Trust
© Foreword: Neil Smith 2000

First published 2000

Printed in the United Kingdom at the University Press, Cambridge

Typeset in 10/12 pt Plantin   [G C]

A catalogue record for this book is available from the British Library

Library of Congress Cataloguing in Publication data

Chomsky, Noam.
    New horizons in the study of language and mind / Noam Chomsky.
      p.   cm.
    Includes bibliographical references and index.
    ISBN 0 521 65147 6 (hardback) – ISBN 0 521 65822 5 (paperback)
    1. Language and languages – Philosophy.   2. Philosophy of mind.
    I. Title
    P106.C524   2000
    401–dc21   99–36753 CIP

ISBN 0 521 65147 6 hardback
ISBN 0 521 65822 5 paperback

Contents

Foreword

Neil Smith

Chomsky's position on the world intellectual scene is unique. He was the leading figure in the "cognitive revolution" of the 1950s and 1960s, and he has dominated the field of linguistics ever since. His theory of generative grammar, in a number of different forms, has been a guide and inspiration for many linguists around the world and the point of comparison for almost everyone. You may not agree with Chomsky's work, but it would be both short-sighted and unscholarly to ignore it.

Chomsky graduated from the University of Pennsylvania in 1949, with an undergraduate dissertation about Modern Hebrew, that was later revised and extended as his master's thesis. However embryonic, that work inaugurated modern generative grammar. The issues he touched on then have burgeoned to define a field of inquiry to which he is still contributing fifty years later, and which is in large part the product of his genius. Yet this intellectual odyssey has taken only half his time. The other half has been devoted to political activism, exposing the perceived lies of Government and the hidden agenda of the corporate establishment. This has involved him in giving seemingly countless lectures around the world, and has resulted in the production of about fifty books, hundreds of articles and thousands of letters. There may be little connection between the strands of his work, but his fame and in part his influence are the joint product of both. (Chomsky's output is prodigious; for a recent overview and discussion of a representative subset of his work, see Smith (1999).)

His foundational work on language has had widespread implications not only for linguistics but also for several other disciplines, most notably philosophy and psychology. The present volume of essays concentrates on this third strand in his thought, dealing especially with metaphysical issues arising from his research, and clearing some of the underbrush of confusion and prejudice which has infected the philosophical study of language. In so doing he brings new solutions to traditional puzzles and new perspectives on issues of general interest, from the mind–body problem to the unification of science.

The core of these articles is an extended meditation on Chomsky's "internalist" interpretation of the human language faculty. Much of the philosophical tradition has concentrated on language as a public construct of which individuals have partial knowledge. This view is preoccupied with the relation between language and external reality: the word–world relation which underpins standard theories of referential semantics. In opposition to this tradition Chomsky defends at length, and with a series of imaginative linguistic analyses, the view that knowledge of language is individualistic, internal to the human mind/brain. It follows that the proper study of language must deal with this mental construct, a theoretical entity that he refers to with the neologism "I-language", an *internal* property of an *individual*. A corollary of his view is that the lay (and philosophical) concept of "language", according to which Chinese (as spoken in Hong Kong and Beijing) or English (as used by Shakespeare and us) is not a domain about which one can construct coherent scientific theories.

His concentration on an internalist view of language brings Chomsky's work into the domain of psychology, and ultimately biology: human language is a "biological object". Accordingly, language should be analysed by the methodology of the natural sciences, and there is no room for constraints on linguistic inquiry beyond those typical of all scientific work. Although this methodology is most fully developed in and characteristic of physics, it does not follow that linguistics is reducible to physics or to any other of the "hard" sciences. It has its own laws and generalisations that cannot be described in the language of "quarks and the like". "Naturalism" in this sense is central to all of Chomsky's work, and explicitly excludes dualist demands that the analysis of language must meet criteria different from or in addition to those of chemistry or bacteriology. The measure of success for linguistics, as for any empirical discipline, should be the explanatory insight and power of its theories, not their conformity to the strictures of philosophy.

A number of consequences follow from his naturalistic thesis: there is no justification for the common assumption that natural languages ought to be treated like the invented formal languages of logic or mathematics; for the demand that the rules of language that we ascribe to individuals should be consciously accessible; for the requirement that the mental be reduced to the physical.

His rejection of this philosophical dualism is seen most strikingly in Chomsky's treatment of the mind–body problem. A perennial problem in philosophy has been to account for how the mental can affect the physical, how something which is by definition insubstantial can cause changes in spatially located entities: in other words, how the mind can move the body. Chomsky has cut the Gordian knot by emphasizing a more fundamental difficulty: the mind–body problem cannot even be formulated. This is not, as generally supposed, because we have too limited an understanding of the mind, but because we don't have criteria for what constitutes a body. In a typically radical attempt at clarification he points out that, as Isaac Newton's insights led to the demise of contact mechanics, the Cartesian notion of body was refuted and nothing since has replaced it. In the absence of a coherent notion of "body", the traditional mind–body problem has no conceptual status, so no special problems of causality arise. More generally, there is no special metaphysical problem associated with attempts to deal naturalistically with "mental" phenomena (such as knowledge of language), any more than there are metaphysical problems for chemists in defining the "chemical".

A further implication of this argument is that common notions of reduction in science are inappropriate. We obviously want to integrate our theories of the mental – including in particular linguistics – with our theories of the brain and any other relevant domain. However, despite the example of the reduction of biology to chemistry brought about by the revolution in molecular biology, unification does not have to take the form of reduction. More importantly, the assertion that the physical or the physiological has some kind of priority is misconceived: theories in linguistics are as rich and make as specific predictions across a wide domain as do theories of chemistry or biology. Trying to reduce linguistics to neurology in the current state of our understanding is then unlikely to be productive. Consider the specific example of understanding the implications of electrical activity in the brain, as measured by "event-related brain potentials" (ERPs). Linguists have a reasonable understanding of different kinds of "deviant" linguistic structure, where deviance is defined in terms of departure from principles of grammar, and it now appears that such differences correlate with particular patterns of electrical activity in the brain. Such correlations have been taken to suggest that linguistic facts can be explained in terms of neurology. But here, and in a range of other cases, it is linguistics that enables us to make any sense at all of the results, as there is no relevant electrophysiological theory in existence. It is as impossible to express interesting generalisations about language in terms of the constructs of cells or neurons, as it is to express generalisations about geology or embryology in terms of the constructs of particle physics. In both cases demands for reduction go too far.

In some areas, scientific unification, let alone reduction, may be impossible in principle. This is not simply the truistic claim that we are incapable of understanding some domains, but the more subtle point that there are aspects of our make-up that are inherently inaccessible to our intelligence. We do not doubt that rats are intellectually incapable of dealing with notions like prime number, and we should not doubt that our genetically determined make-up has resulted in an organism which is similarly incapable of understanding some domains. As Chomsky puts it, the intellectual world is divided into "problems" and "mysteries". The former may (or may not) succumb to our theorising; the latter never will. Our Science Forming Faculty may enable us to get some theoretical understanding of vision, language, genetics and so on. It doesn't follow that all domains will be so amenable, and some issues – like that of free will or the correct characterisation of consciousness – may lie beyond our intellectual abilities and remain mysteries, just as prime numbers are presumably a mystery for the rat. The claim is not that we can get no insight into these areas, but that we can (perhaps) get no scientific insight, and will need to rely on the genius of novelists or poets for greater understanding.

One area where Chomsky is pessimistic about the reach of scientific understanding is the characterisation of our use of language as opposed to our knowledge of language. His work over the past half century has opened up the study of our "competence" (to use the term now replaced by "I-language"), but how we put that competence to use in our performance is still largely a closed book, perhaps a mystery. This is not to deny that we have made progress in understanding how humans process the sentences they hear. All of the following have provided some understanding: experimental and theoretical studies of language perception and language production; insights from language acquisition and language change; and the analysis of brain function in normal and pathological subjects. There are even preliminary insights into how we interpret particular utterances in context, but we are still as far away as René Descartes was from knowing why someone chooses to react to a picture with *how beautiful*, or *it reminds me of Bosch*, rather than by silence.

This collection is called "New Horizons", but many of the topics discussed above are ones that have been the focus of attention for many years. Since his early foray into the history of ideas in *Cartesian Linguistics* (1966), Chomsky has shown a striking ability to put his ideas into a wider historical and general scientific perspective. His historical scholarship serves not only to make possible the tracing of intellectual antecedents, but also to illuminate developments in linguistics by comparing them with those in the traditional sciences, especially the history of chemistry. At the same time he relates these developments to ongoing work in psychology, philosophy, mathematics and the cognitive sciences more generally.

There are two aspects to what is new. On the one hand, there are new kinds of evidence for old positions; on the other, there is now the possibility to ask questions which it was previously impossible even to formulate. We do not yet have answers to these questions, but the ability to pose them is itself an exciting advance.

The first of these can be illustrated by reference to a claim for which Chomsky has long been famous (or notorious): namely, that a substantial part of our knowledge of language is genetically determined, or innate. That something linguistic is innate is self-evident from the fact that babies do – but cats, spiders and rocks do not – acquire language. Much of Chomsky's work of the past 40 years has been devoted to spelling out the technical detail of precisely what we have to attribute to the "initial state" of the human-language faculty to explain that elementary fact. Advances in linguistics and related disciplines have given rise to a situation where there is now a "distant prospect" of adducing evidence from the brain sciences and genetics to show how this determination takes place and, therefore, of unifying this part of linguistics with other sciences. Such unification is not central to Chomsky's own work, but the sophistication of his linguistics has made it a feasible enterprise.

The second aspect is the possibility of relating our knowledge of language to an account of the rest of our cognition. To explain how this might come about requires an outline of a little recent history. Current generative linguistics is dominated by two strands: the theory of "Principles and Parameters" – as spelt out in *Knowledge of Language* (1986) – and Minimalism – as seen most clearly in his book *The Minimalist Program* (1995c). For many years Chomsky and his followers devoted considerable effort to devising formal mechanisms adequate to describing the vast complexity of natural languages, a complexity that becomes ever more amazing the more one looks at individual languages. Some of these formal devices, in particular transformations and the notions of deep and surface structure were remarkably successful, and achieved a certain common currency outside linguistics, among philosophers, psychologists and even the lay public. The trouble with this stage of the theory was that the resultant complexity made it look as if languages were unlearnable: how could a child master this dramatic complexity in the few years during which first language acquisition takes place?

Chomsky's response was that much more of our knowledge of language is innate than had been previously suspected. Specific languages like English or Japanese could obviously not be innate – as witness the environmentally triggered differences between them – but the course of normal language acquisition makes it equally clear that a huge amount must be innate. It is not just that there are constraints on the kind of hypothesis the child learning its first language can entertain, all the core properties of language are built in from the start. That is, the child does not need to learn from scratch the properties of the language to which it is exposed; rather it merely selects particular options from an antecedently specified set. For instance, languages are either "head-first" (with the verb preceding the object, as in English) or "head-last" (with the object preceding the verb, as in Japanese). The child is born knowing that there are these two alternatives, and what it has to do is equivalent to throwing the switches of a switch-box to "fix the parameters" of the language it is learning. It is significant that this resolution of the tension between description and explanation mirrors developments in other sciences. In immunology, an "instructive" theory of antibody development was replaced by a "selective" theory in which the presence of antigens, even artificially produced ones, called up antibodies which were already present in the organism before it was exposed to external influence. The parallel with language acquisition is striking.

The theory of Principles and Parameters which has been developed over the last two decades is probably the first really novel approach to language of the last two and a half thousand years. It is conceptually so different from previous accounts of language, either traditional or generative, that for Chomsky this is the first time that linguistic theory might justify the description "revolutionary", more usually accorded to his work of the 1950s. The current version of Principles and Parameters – already substantially different from the version of the early 1980s – is embedded in the Minimalist Program of the 1990s. This is a radical attempt to rethink the foundations of the discipline, eschewing all constructs which are not conceptually necessary or forced by empirical necessity: the usual requirements of science. This rethinking has meant abandoning much of the descriptive machinery of earlier versions of generative grammar – even such successful innovations as the levels of deep and surface structure – and has forced a search for new explanations.

Chomsky is careful to stress that "Minimalism" is not yet a theory; it is just a program defining a certain kind of research endeavour. Any theory of language must of necessity provide a link between sound and meaning, between representations of the pronunciation and representations of the logical properties of words and sentences. Accordingly, a grammar – the I-language – must define two levels of representation, called PF for "Phonetic Form" and LF for "Logical Form", and specify the link between them. Ideally, there should be no other levels and the complexity of this link should be minimal. This suggests two questions which it had previously either been impossible to address seriously or perhaps even to formulate. First, how good a solution to this conceptual problem of linking sound and meaning is a human language? Is it right to suggest that the grammars of natural languages are in some sense optimal? Second, what are the relations between the language faculty and other systems of the mind/brain? In particular, can any perceived deviations from optimality in the first be attributed to conditions imposed by the second?

Chomsky addresses these issues in terms of the question: "how 'perfect' is language?", with the answer, surprising for a biological system, that it is very close to perfect. What this means is that any deviations from conceptual necessity manifest by the language faculty (that is, the I-language) are motivated by conditions imposed from the outside. Chomsky calls these "legibility conditions": conditions imposed by the need for other systems of the mind/brain to use representations provided by the language faculty. In particular, this refers to the need for the articulatory and perceptual systems to exploit PF representations, and for the conceptual system to exploit LF. Against such a background, movement or "displacement" processes of the kind seen in the different positions occupied by *Clinton* in *They elected Clinton* and *Clinton was elected* appear to be conceptually unnecessary. Why do natural languages exploit such devices which are completely foreign to the artificial languages of logic and mathematics? One tentative answer is that displacement may plausibly be motivated by the need to structure information for optimal communication. If this is, indeed, the correct account then it looks as if a property of the language faculty is imposed from outside the system, from another part of the mind/brain.

Chomsky does not stop there, but attempts to link this apparent imperfection of language to another. Natural languages are full of phenomena that give rise to problems for second-language learners, and irritation for philosophers. There are morphological complexities like declensional paradigms and irregular verbs, which appear to have no real meaning of their own and to be semantically useless. They are another imperfection, necessitating the postulation of uninterpretable features; that is, features with no semantic interpretation. However, current syntactic theory makes systematic use of such uninterpretable features: their function is to drive the movement processes that we have just seen to be motivated from outside the language faculty. If such conjectures are on the right lines, they allow the interesting possibility of reducing two kinds of apparent "imperfection" to one. In fact, if the argument is correct, the imperfections are, indeed, only "apparent". Given the constraints that other systems of the mind/brain impose on solutions to linking sound and meaning, there may be no other alternatives, so conceptual necessity explains the form of the grammar overall.

Finally, I turn to the individual essays. The opening chapter "New horizons in the study of language" (Chapter 1) is a succinct and generally non-technical introduction to Chomsky's current thinking on the nature of the language faculty, setting his ideas in their historical and intellectual framework: the Galilean and Cartesian traditions. It shows his now familiar flair for taking simple examples and drawing out deep consequences from them. If a library contains two copies of Tolstoy's *War and Peace*, and each is taken out by a different person, did they take out the same or a different book? Either answer is appropriate depending on whether we are viewing the book as a material or as an abstract entity. This may seem self-evident but, as Chomsky goes on to show, there are serious implications for the philosophy of language. A further striking observation is that our knowledge that objects such as books can be viewed in these different ways seems to come to us largely independently of experience. Accordingly, we have a poverty of the stimulus argument for the innate determination of such knowledge. Much of the essay should be accessible to the layperson, but it also has a great deal to offer the expert.

"Explaining language use" (Chapter 2) is a critique of the views of externalist philosophers, especially Hilary Putnam, and a defence of naturalism in the investigation of language. Chomsky provides a long series of new examples to substantiate the view that the most successful treatment of language is in terms of computations over internal, mental representations. This, of course, is the domain in which his greatest technical contributions reside, but the discussion presupposes no expertise in syntactic theory. Part of his exposition involves a generalisation of the internalist notion I-language to the epistemological domain, invoking the notion I-belief. Again, the thesis is illustrated by simple but striking examples of the depth and detail of our knowledge of common lexical items like *house* and *near*. In *John is painting the house brown*, we know – apparently without instruction – that it is the external surface of the house that is being painted, rather than the inside. But the meaning of *house* cannot be restricted to its external surface. If two people are equidistant from the surface, one inside and one outside, only the one outside can be described as "near" the house. Again, as demonstrated in practical experiments, even very young children seem to know such facts, suggesting that the knowledge is in some sense antecedently available to the organism.

"Language and interpretation" (Chapter 3) takes these ideas further and, in particular, elaborates his arguments against Willard Quine, Michael Dummett and others on such issues as the indeterminacy of translation, public versus private language, the nature of tacit knowledge and the status of linguistic "rules". Chomsky takes simple syntactic examples which have featured widely in the technical literature and uses them to argue for a range of philosophical positions. Consider the interpretation of *Mary expects to feed herself* (Where *Mary* and *herself* are taken to refer to the same individual), as opposed to the partially identical *I wonder who Mary expects to feed herself*, where this coreferential construal is impossible. Chomsky spells out a number of implications of such examples and their analysis. They belie the Quinean claim that there is "no fact of the matter"; they can be used to support an analytic–synthetic distinction; they raise problems for any notion of meaning holism; and they point to the independence of our language faculty from other aspects of our belief system.

"Naturalism and dualism in the study of language and mind" (Chapter 4) returns to the attack on the philosophers for their tacit adoption of the "bifurcation thesis": the view that the study of language should be subject to standards and conditions additional to those which hold for the natural sciences in general. Beginning with the observation that the term "mental" simply picks out some aspect of the world that we wish to subject to naturalistic enquiry, Chomsky proceeds to give a succinct history of ideas – especially as they pertain to the study of language – from Descartes to the present, drawing analogies especially from chemistry and the study of vision. The implication of the exercise is that the mind–body problem is unstatable; the putative role of consciousness in defining what constitutes knowledge of language is unmotivated; and that only an internalist construal of linguistic knowledge is capable of providing any explanation for our abilities.

"Language as a natural object" (Chapter 5) returns to a number of the same issues, but with the focus more directly on language and knowledge of language. Linguistics is one of the natural sciences, and Chomsky traces his intellectual antecedents in an erudite and informative summary of the history of science. Despite this repeatedly justified claim about the "scientific" status of linguistics, Chomsky is acerbic in his treatment of reductionist attempts to reduce language to the physiological or the physical. What is needed is unification, and reduction is only a rare case of such integration. The scope of current linguistics includes the problems of how children learn their first language, and how adults use it. Here Chomsky makes two surprising observations. First, if languages really are learnable, that would be a surprising empirical discovery; second, that languages appear to be in part unusable, as is evident from the fact that performance systems often fail. The essay ends with a sobering discussion of the limits of intuition. Intuition or linguistic judgements are central to argumentation in linguistics, but Chomsky points out that we can have no comparable intuitions when it comes to the technical vocabulary of mathematics or philosophy, and that the philosopher's reliance on appeal to intuitions about Twin-Earth, for instance, is systematically pernicious.

"Language from an internalist perspective" (Chapter 6) addresses some of the same issues but with different examples and with a lengthy discussion of the difference between naturalistic scientific investigation and what is often called "folk science". The relation between the two is not self-evident. In physics one does not expect folk views to inform the expert's theory construction, and while ethnoscience is itself an interesting field of inquiry, there is no reason to assume *a priori* that the concepts and constructs of pre-scientific debate should carry over unchanged into formal theories of I-language. More particularly, there is no reason to impose conditions of accessibility to consciousness on the rules that characterise our language. If a child says *I rided my bike* we have no reason to deny that she is following the regular rule of past-tense formation and still less reason to assume that she is aware of the fact. As always, deep and sophisticated conclusions – about the sterility of externalist conceptions of language and the necessity for internalist ones – follow from simple examples.

The last chapter, "Internalist explorations" (Chapter 7), continues the exposition of his internalist perspective, providing both new examples and arguments, and extending the criticisms to a wider range of targets, in particular aspects of Twin-Earth. In addition, it ties the discussion in more closely with his recent work in the Minimalist Program, and ends with a sustained discussion of the scope and importance of notions of innateness.

Apart from his political work (entirely absent here), Chomsky is best known for his syntactic theorising. Many of the essays here include perspicuous and puzzling examples of the kind he is famous for constructing; the contrast between *John was too clever to catch* and the equivalent *John was too clever to be caught*; between *John was clever to be caught* and the impossible *John was clever to catch*. It is striking that, in addition to these syntactic examples, much of the exemplification in these essays is lexical, with subtle arguments based on a range of deceptively simple items. The arguments are marshalled with the same forceful logic as previously, and the conclusions lead to the same world view he has been defending for forty years; but the arguments are fresh.

What is impressive about Chomsky's writing is not just its awesome breadth and remarkable scope, but that after half a century he still has the power to surprise: from the observation that human beings are not a natural kind to the importance of Japanese for the analysis of English;

from the rejection of his celebrated invention "deep structure" to the conjecture that language, despite its biological nature, may be close to perfection; from the tension between common sense and science to the implications of what we know about a brown house or a cup of tea. Everything combines to give a unique and compelling view of language and mind.

Acknowledgements

Chapter 1, "New horizons in the study of language" was given as a lecture at the University of Balearic Islands, Spain on 21 January 1997. Chapter 2, "Explaining language use" was first published in *Philosophical Topics* (1992, 20: 205–31) and is reprinted with permission of the editor of *Philosophical Topics*. Chapter 3, "Language and interpretation: philosophical reflections and empirical inquiry," was first published in 1992 in *Inference, Explanation, and Other Frustrations: Essays in the Philosophy of Science* (pp. 99–128); edited by John Earman, © The Regents of the University of California. This essay is reprinted with the permission of the University of California Press. Chapter 4, "Naturalism and dualism in the study of language and mind" is an edited version of a lecture given at the Agnes Cuming Lectures, University College, Dublin in April 1993 and was first published in the *International Journal of Philosophical Studies* (1994, 2: 181–200). It is reprinted with the permission of the *International Journal of Philosophical Studies*. Chapter 5, "Language as a natural object" is an edited version of the Jacobsen Lecture at University College, London on 23 May 1994, and the Homer Smith lecture at the New York University School of Medicine on 16 May 1994. A slightly modified version of this chapter was first published in 1995, along with Chapter 6 ("Language from an internalist perspective"), under the title "Language and nature" in *Mind* (104: 1–61). The modified version of this paper is reproduced with permission of Oxford University Press. Chapter 7, "Internalist explorations" will appear in a forthcoming volume of essays on Tyler Burge, edited by Professor Bjorn Ramberg, and is reprinted with permission of Professor Ramberg and MIT Press.

Introduction

During the past half-century, there has been intensive and often highly productive inquiry into human cognitive faculties, their nature and the ways they enter into action and interpretation. Commonly it adopts the thesis that "things mental, indeed minds, are emergent properties of brains," while recognizing that "those emergences are . . . produced by principles that control the interactions between lower level events – principles we do not yet understand" (Mountcastle 1998: 1). The word "yet" expresses the optimism that has, rightly or wrongly, been a persistent theme throughout the period.

The thesis revives eighteenth-century proposals that were put forth for quite compelling reasons: in particular, the conclusion that Newton appeared to have established, to his considerable dismay, that "a purely materialistic or mechanistic physics" is "impossible" (Koyré 1957: 210); and the implications of "Locke's suggestion" that God might have chosen to "superadd to matter *a faculty of thinking*" just as he "annexed effects to motion which we can in no way conceive motion able to produce" (Locke 1975: 541, Book IV, Chapter 3, Section 6). The precedents of the early modern period, and the thinking that lay behind them, merit closer attention than they have generally, in my opinion, received. It is also worth remembering that lack of understanding of "mind/brain interaction" is not the only respect in which progress has been limited since the origin of the modern scientific revolutions. While inquiry into higher mental faculties has achieved a great deal in some areas, the results do not reach the issues that were – sensibly in my view – taken to be at the heart of the problem. Some of these topics are touched on in the following chapters.

One domain in which there has been substantial progress is the study of language, particularly in the past 20 years. Here too, traditional questions remain at the horizon, if even there. My understanding of this work is that it (often implicitly) takes for granted some version of the thesis on mind/brain just quoted, and can reasonably be interpreted as part of psychology or, more broadly, human biology. Some have plausibly termed it "biolinguistics" (Jenkins 1999). Its topic is particular states of people, mostly their brains: call them "linguistic states." It seeks to unearth the nature and properties of such states, their development and variety, and their basis in innate biological endowment. That endowment appears to determine a "faculty of language" that is a distinctive component of higher mental faculties (as a system, that is, its elements may have all sorts of functions), a "species-property" that is shared among humans to close approximation, over a broad range. The faculty of language is a very recent evolutionary development and, as far as is known, is biologically isolated in crucial respects. Biolinguistic inquiry seeks unification with other approaches to the properties of the brain, in the hope that some day the slash "/" in the phrase "mind/brain" will gain more substantive content. It is concerned not only with the nature and development of linguistic states, but also with the ways they enter into the use of language. Included in principle, sometimes in fact, are the relations of these states to an external medium (production and perception), and their role in thinking and talking about the world and other human actions and interactions. In some domains, particularly with regard to problems of reference and meaning in natural language, the approach seems to me to suggest that considerable rethinking may be in order, for reasons discussed in the following chapters.

It has to be shown, of course, that this "naturalistic" approach is a proper way to investigate phenomena of language, and the use of language. A more ambitious thesis is that it is presupposed (at least tacitly, and sometimes in the face of explicit denial) by constructive work generally in these areas; and that something similar holds in the study of other cognitive faculties. It must also be shown that critiques are misguided, including those that are widespread and influential. I think all of this is rather plausible. The essays that follow, mostly based on talks over the past few years, attempt to provide some reasons for these conclusions, and to sketch some directions that seem to me appropriate and worth exploring.

1 New horizons in the study of language

The study of language is one of the oldest branches of systematic inquiry, tracing back to classical India and Greece, with a rich and fruitful history of achievement. From a different point of view, it is quite young. The major research enterprises of today took shape only about 40 years ago, when some of the leading ideas of the tradition were revived and reconstructed, opening the way to what has proven to be very productive inquiry.

That language should have exercised such fascination over the years is not surprising. The human faculty of language seems to be a true "species property," varying little among humans and without significant analogue elsewhere. Probably the closest analogues are found in insects, at an evolutionary distance of a billion years. There is no serious reason today to challenge the Cartesian view that the ability to use linguistic signs to express freely-formed thoughts marks "the true distinction between man and animal" or machine, whether by "machine" we mean the automata that captured the imagination of the seventeenth and eighteenth century, or those that are providing a stimulus to thought and imagination today.

Furthermore, the faculty of language enters crucially into every aspect of human life, thought, and interaction. It is largely responsible for the fact that alone in the biological world, humans have a history, cultural evolution and diversity of any complexity and richness, even biological success in the technical sense that their numbers are huge. A Martian scientist observing the strange doings on Earth could hardly fail to be struck by the emergence and significance of this apparently unique form of intellectual organization. It is even more natural that the topic, with its many mysteries, should have stimulated the curiosity of those who seek to understand their own nature and their place within the wider world.

Human language is based on an elementary property that also seems to be biologically isolated: the property of discrete infinity, which is exhibited in its purest form by the natural numbers 1, 2, 3, . . . Children do not learn this property; unless the mind already possesses the basic principles, no amount of evidence could provide them. Similarly, no child has to learn that there are three and four word sentences, but no three-and-a half word sentences, and that they go on forever; it is always possible to construct a more complex one, with a definite form and meaning. Such knowledge must come to us from "the original hand of nature," in David Hume's (1748/1975: 108, Section 85) phrase, as part of our biological endowment.

This property intrigued Galileo, who regarded the discovery of a means to communicate our "most secret thoughts to any other person with 24 little characters" (Galileo 1632/1661, end of first day) as the greatest of all human inventions. The invention succeeds because it reflects the discrete infinity of the language that these characters are used to represent. Shortly after, the authors of the Port Royal Grammar were struck by the "marvellous invention" of a means to construct from a few dozen sounds an infinity of expressions that enable us to reveal to others what we think and imagine and feel – from a contemporary standpoint, not an "invention" but no less "marvellous" as a product of biological evolution, about which virtually nothing is known, in this case.

The faculty of language can reasonably be regarded as a "language organ" in the sense in which scientists speak of the visual system, or immune system, or circulatory system, as organs of the body. Understood in this way, an organ is not something that can be removed from the body, leaving the rest intact. It is a subsystem of a more complex structure. We hope to understand the full complexity by investigating parts that have distinctive characteristics, and their interactions. Study of the faculty of language proceeds in the same way.

We assume further that the language organ is like others in that its basic character is an expression of the genes. How that happens remains a distant prospect for inquiry, but we can investigate the genetically-determined "initial state" of the language faculty in other ways. Evidently, each language is the result of the interplay of two factors: the initial state and the course of experience. We can think of the initial state as a "language acquisition device" that takes experience as "input" and gives the language as an "output" – an "output" that is internally represented in the mind/brain. The input and the output are both open to examination: we can study the course of experience and the properties of the languages that are acquired. What is learned in this way can tell us quite a lot about the initial state that mediates between them.

Furthermore, there is strong reason to believe that the initial state is common to the species: if my children had grown up in Tokyo, they would speak Japanese, like other children there. That means that evidence about Japanese bears directly on the assumptions concerning the initial state for English. In such ways, it is possible to establish strong empirical conditions that the theory of the initial state must satisfy, and also to pose several problems for the biology of language: How do the genes determine the initial state, and what are the brain mechanisms involved in the initial state and the later states it assumes? These are extremely hard problems, even for much simpler systems where direct experiment is possible, but some may be at the horizons of inquiry.

The approach I have been outlining is concerned with the faculty of language: its initial state, and the states it assumes. Suppose that Peter's language organ is in state L. We can think of L as Peter's "internalized language." When I speak of a language here, that is what I mean. So understood, a language is something like "the way we speak and understand," one traditional conception of language.

Adapting a traditional term to a new framework, we call the theory of Peter's language the "grammar" of his language. Peter's language determines an infinite array of expressions, each with its sound and meaning. In technical terms, Peter's language "generates" the expressions of his language. The theory of his language is therefore called a generative grammar. Each expression is a complex of properties, which provide "instructions" for Peter's performance systems: his articulatory apparatus, his modes of organizing his thoughts, and so on. With his language and the associated performance systems in place, Peter has a vast amount of knowledge about the sound and meaning of expressions, and a corresponding capacity to interpret what he hears, express his thoughts, and use his language in a variety of other ways.

Generative grammar arose in the context of what is often called "the cognitive revolution" of the 1950s, and was an important factor in its development. Whether or not the term "revolution" is appropriate, there was an important change of perspective: from the study of behavior and its products (such as texts), to the inner mechanisms that enter into thought and action. The cognitive perspective regards behavior and its products not as the object of inquiry, but as data that may provide evidence about the inner mechanisms of mind and the ways these mechanisms operate in executing actions and interpreting experience. The properties and patterns that were the focus of attention in structural linguistics find their place, but as phenomena to be explained along with innumerable others, in terms of the inner mechanisms that generate expressions. The approach is "mentalistic," but in what should be an uncontroversial sense. It is concerned with "mental aspects of the world," which stand alongside its mechanical, chemical, optical, and other aspects. It undertakes to study a real object in the natural world – the brain, its states, and its functions – and thus to move the study of the mind towards eventual integration with the biological sciences.

The "cognitive revolution" renewed and reshaped many of the insights, achievements, and quandaries of what we might call "the first cognitive revolution" of the seventeenth and eighteenth century, which was part of the scientific revolution that so radically modified our understanding of the world. It was recognized at the time that language involves "the infinite use of finite means," in Wilhelm von Humboldt's phrase; but the insight could be developed only in limited ways, because the basic ideas remained vague and obscure. By the middle of the twentieth century, advances in the formal sciences had provided appropriate concepts in a very sharp and clear form, making it possible to give a precise account of the computational principles that generate the expressions of a language, and thus to capture, at least partially, the idea of "infinite use of finite means." Other advances also opened the way to investigation of traditional questions with greater hope of success. The study of language change had registered major achievements. Anthropological linguistics provided a far richer understanding of the nature and variety of languages, also undermining many stereotypes. And certain topics, notably the study of sound systems, had been much advanced by the structural linguistics of the twentieth century.

The earliest attempts to carry out the program of generative grammar quickly revealed that even in the best studied languages, elementary properties had passed unrecognized, that the most comprehensive traditional grammars and dictionaries only skim the surface. The basic properties of languages are presupposed throughout, unrecognized and unexpressed. That is quite appropriate if the goal is to help people to learn a second language, to find the conventional meaning and pronunciation of words, or to have some general idea of how languages differ. But if our goal is to understand the language faculty and the states it can assume, we cannot tacitly presuppose "the intelligence of the reader." Rather, this is the object of inquiry.

The study of language acquisition leads to the same conclusion. A careful look at the interpretation of expressions reveals very quickly that from the earliest stages, the child knows vastly more than experience has provided. That is true even of simple words. At peak periods of language growth, a child is acquiring words at a rate of about one an hour, with extremely limited exposure under highly ambiguous conditions. The words are understood in delicate and intricate ways that are far beyond the reach of any dictionary, and are only beginning to be investigated. When we move beyond single words, the conclusion becomes even more dramatic. Language acquisition seems much like the growth of organs generally; it is something that happens to a child, not that the child does. And while the environment plainly matters, the general course of development and the basic features of what emerges are predetermined by the initial state. But the initial state is a common human possession. It must be, then, that in their essential properties and even down to fine detail, languages are cast to the same mold. The Martian scientist might reasonably conclude that there is a single human language, with differences only at the margins.

As languages were more carefully investigated from the point of view of generative grammar, it became clear that their diversity had been underestimated as radically as their complexity and the extent to which they are determined by the initial state of the faculty of language. At the same time, we know that the diversity and complexity can be no more than superficial appearance.

These were surprising conclusions, paradoxical but undeniable. They pose in a stark form what has become the central problem of the modern study of language: How can we show that all languages are variations on a single theme, while at the same time recording faithfully their intricate properties of sound and meaning, superficially diverse? A genuine theory of human language has to satisfy two conditions: "descriptive adequacy" and "explanatory adequacy." The grammar of a particular language satisfies the condition of descriptive adequacy insofar as it gives a full and accurate account of the properties of the language, of what the speaker of the language knows. To satisfy the condition of explanatory adequacy, a theory of language must show how each particular language can be derived from a uniform initial state under the "boundary conditions" set by experience. In this way, it provides an explanation of the properties of languages at a deeper level.

There is a serious tension between these two research tasks. The search for descriptive adequacy seems to lead to ever greater complexity and variety of rule systems, while the search for explanatory adequacy requires that language structure must be invariant, except at the margins. It is this tension that has largely set the guidelines for research. The natural way to resolve the tension is to challenge the traditional assumption, carried over to early generative grammar, that a language is a complex system of rules, each specific to particular languages and particular grammatical constructions: rules for forming relative clauses in Hindi, verb phrases in Swahili, passives in Japanese, and so on. Considerations of explanatory adequacy indicate that this cannot be correct.

The central problem was to find general properties of rule systems that can be attributed to the faculty of language itself, in the hope that the residue will prove to be more simple and uniform. About 15 years ago, these efforts crystallized in an approach to language that was a much more radical departure from the tradition than earlier generative grammar had been. This "Principles and Parameters" approach, as it has been called, rejected the concept of rule and grammatical construction entirely: there are no rules for forming relative clauses in Hindi, verb phrases in Swahili, passives in Japanese, and so on. The familiar grammatical constructions are taken to be taxonomic artifacts, useful for informal description perhaps but with no theoretical standing. They have something like the status of "terrestrial mammal" or "household pet." And the rules are decomposed into general principles of the faculty of language, which interact to yield the properties of expressions.

We can think of the initial state of the faculty of language as a fixed network connected to a switch box; the network is constituted of the principles of language, while the switches are the options to be determined by experience. When the switches are set one way, we have Swahili; when they are set another way, we have Japanese. Each possible human language is identified as a particular setting of the switches – a setting of parameters, in technical terminology. If the research program succeeds, we should be able literally to deduce Swahili from one choice of settings, Japanese from another, and so on through the languages that humans can acquire. The empirical conditions of language acquisition require that the switches can be set on the basis of the very limited information that is available to the child. Notice that small changes in switch settings can lead to great apparent variety in output, as the effects proliferate through the system. These are the general properties of language that any genuine theory must capture somehow.

This is, of course, a program, and it is far from a finished product. The conclusions tentatively reached are unlikely to stand in their present form; and, needless to say, one can have no certainty that the whole approach is on the right track. As a research program, however, it has been highly successful, leading to a real explosion of empirical inquiry into languages of a very broad typological range, to new questions that could never even have been formulated before, and to many intriguing answers. Questions of acquisition, processing, pathology, and others also took new forms, which have proven very productive as well. Furthermore, whatever its fate, the program suggests how the theory of language might satisfy the conflicting conditions of descriptive and explanatory adequacy. It gives at least an outline of a genuine theory of language, really for the first time.

Within this research program, the main task is to discover and clarify the principles and parameters and the manner of their interaction, and to extend the framework to include other aspects of language and its use. While a great deal remains obscure, there has been enough progress to at least consider, perhaps to pursue, some new and more far-reaching questions about the design of language. In particular, we can ask how good the design is. How close does language come to what some super-engineer would construct, given the conditions that the language faculty must satisfy?

The questions have to be sharpened, and there are ways to proceed. The faculty of language is embedded within the broader architecture of the mind/brain. It interacts with other systems, which impose conditions that language must satisfy if it is to be usable at all. We might think of these as "legibility conditions," in the sense that other systems must be able to "read" the expressions of the language and use them as "instructions" for thought and action. The sensorimotor systems, for example, have to be able to read the instructions having to do with sound, that is the "phonetic representations" generated by the language. The articulatory and perceptual apparatus have specific design that enables them to interpret certain phonetic properties, not others. These systems thus impose legibility conditions on the generative processes of the faculty of language, which must provide expressions with the proper phonetic form. The same is true of conceptual and other systems that make use of the resources of the faculty of language: they have their intrinsic properties, which require that the expressions generated by the language have certain kinds of "semantic representations," not others. We may therefore ask to what extent language is a "good solution" to the legibility conditions imposed by the external systems with which it interacts. Until quite recently this question could not seriously be posed, even formulated sensibly. Now it seems that it can, and there are even indications that the language faculty may be close to "perfect" in this sense; if true, this is a surprising conclusion.

What has come to be called "the Minimalist Program" is an effort to explore these questions. It is too soon to offer a firm judgment about the project. My own judgment is that the questions can now profitably be placed on the agenda, and that early results are promising. I would like to say a few words about the ideas and the prospects, and then to return to some problems that remain at the horizons.

The minimalist program requires that we subject conventional assumptions to careful scrutiny. The most venerable of these is that language has sound and meaning. In current terms, that translates in a natural way to the thesis that the faculty of language engages other systems of the mind/brain at two "interface levels," one related to sound, and the other to meaning. A particular expression generated by the language contains a phonetic representation that is legible to the sensorimotor systems, and a semantic representation that is legible to conceptual and other systems of thought and action.

One question is whether there are levels other than the interface levels: Are there levels "internal" to the language, in particular, the levels of deep and surface structure that have been postulated in modern work? (see, for example, Chomsky 1965; 1981a; 1986). The minimalist program seeks to show that everything that has been accounted for in terms of these levels has been misdescribed, and is as well or better understood in terms of legibility conditions at the interface: for those of you who know the technical literature, that means the projection principle, binding theory, Case theory, the chain condition, and so on.

We also try to show that the only computational operations are those that are unavoidable on the weakest assumptions about interface properties. One such assumption is that there are word-like units: the external systems have to be able to interpret such items as "Peter" and "tall." Another is that these items are organized into larger expressions, such as "Peter is tall." A third is that the items have properties of sound and meaning: the word "Peter" begins with closure of the lips and is used to refer to persons. The language therefore involves three kinds of elements:

- the properties of sound and meaning, called "features";
- the items that are assembled from these properties, called "lexical items"; and
- the complex expressions constructed from these "atomic" units.

It follows that the computational system that generates expressions has two basic operations: one assembles features into lexical items, the second forms larger syntactic objects out of those already constructed, beginning with lexical items.

We can think of the first operation as essentially a list of lexical items. In traditional terms, this list – called the lexicon – is the list of "exceptions," arbitrary associations of sound and meaning and particular choices among the inflectional properties made available by the faculty of language that determine how we indicate that nouns and verbs are plural or singular, that nouns have nominative or accusative case, and so on. These inflectional features turn out to play a central role in computation.

Optimal design would introduce no new features in the course of computation. There should be no indices or phrasal units and no bar levels (hence no phrase-structure rules or X-bar theory; see Chomsky

1995c). We also try to show that no structural relations are invoked other than those forced by legibility conditions or induced in some natural way by the computation itself. In the first category we have such properties as adjacency at the phonetic level, and argument-structure and quantifier-variable relations at the semantic level. In the second category, we have very local relations between features, and elementary relations between two syntactic objects joined together in the course of computation: the relation holding between one of these and the parts of the other is the relation of c-command; as Samuel Epstein (1999) has pointed out, this is a notion that plays a central role throughout language design and has been regarded as highly unnatural, though it falls into place in a natural way from this perspective. But we exclude government, binding relations internal to the derivation of expressions, and a variety of other relations and interactions.

As anyone familiar with recent work will be aware, there is ample empirical evidence to support the opposite conclusion throughout. Worse yet, a core assumption of the work within the Principles-and-Parameters framework, and its fairly impressive achievements, is that everything I have just proposed is false – that language is highly "imperfect" in these respects, as might well be expected. So it is no small task to show that such apparatus is eliminable as unwanted descriptive technology; or even better, that descriptive and explanatory force are extended if such "excess baggage" is shed. Nevertheless, I think that work of the past few years suggests that these conclusions, which seemed out of the question before that, are at least plausible, and quite possibly correct.

Languages plainly differ, and we want to know how. One respect is in choice of sounds, which vary within a certain range. Another is in the association of sound and meaning, which is essentially arbitrary. These are straightforward and need not detain us. More interesting is the fact that languages differ in inflectional systems: case systems, for example. We find that these are fairly rich in Latin, even more so in Sanskrit or Finnish, but minimal in English and invisible in Chinese. Or so it appears; considerations of explanatory adequacy suggest that here too appearance may be misleading, and in fact, recent work (Chomsky 1995c; 1998) indicates that these systems vary much less than appears to be the case from the surface forms. Chinese and English, for example, may have the same case system as Latin, but the phonetic realization is different. Furthermore, it seems that much of the variety of language can be reduced to properties of inflectional systems. If this is correct, then language variation is located in a narrow part of the lexicon.

Legibility conditions impose a three-way division among the features assembled into lexical items:

1. semantic features, interpreted at the semantic interface;
2. phonetic features, interpreted at the phonetic interface; and
3. features that are not interpreted at either interface.

In a perfectly designed language, each feature would be semantic or phonetic, not merely a device to create a position or to facilitate computation. If so, there are no uninterpretable formal features. That is too strong a requirement, it seems. Such prototypical formal features as structural case – Latin nominative and accusative, for example – have no interpretation at the semantic interface, and need not be expressed at the phonetic level. And there are other examples as well within inflectional systems.

In the syntactic computation, there seems to be a second and more dramatic imperfection in language design, at least an apparent one: the "displacement property" that is a pervasive aspect of language: phrases are interpreted as if they were in a different position in the expression, where similar items sometimes do appear and are interpreted in terms of natural local relations. Take the sentence "Clinton seems to have been elected." We understand the relation of "elect" and "Clinton" as we do when they are locally related in the sentence "It seems that they elected Clinton": "Clinton" is the direct object of "elect," in traditional terms, though "displaced" to the position of subject of "seems"; the subject and verb agree in inflectional features in this case, but have no semantic relation; the semantic relation of the subject is to the remote verb "elect."

We now have two "imperfections": uninterpretable features, and the displacement property. On the assumption of optimal design, we would expect them to be related, and that seems to be the case: uninterpretable features are the mechanism that implements the displacement property.

The displacement property is never built into the symbolic systems that are designed for special purposes, called "languages" or "formal languages" in a metaphoric usage: "the language of arithmetic," or "computer languages," or "the languages of science." These systems also have no inflectional systems, hence no uninterpreted features. Displacement and inflection are special properties of human language, among the many that are ignored when symbolic systems are designed for other purposes, which may disregard the legibility conditions imposed on human language by the architecture of the mind/brain.

The displacement property of human language is expressed in terms of grammatical transformations or by some other device, but it is always expressed somehow. Why language should have this property is an interesting question, which has been discussed since the 1960s without resolution. My suspicion is that part of the reason has to do with phenomena that have been described in terms of surface structure interpretation; many of these are familiar from traditional grammar: topic-comment, specificity, new and old information, the agentive force that we find even in displaced position, and so on. If that is correct, then the displacement property is, indeed, forced by legibility conditions: it is motivated by interpretive requirements that are externally imposed by our systems of thought, which have these special properties (so the study of language use indicates). These questions are currently being investigated in interesting ways, which I cannot go into here.

From the origins of generative grammar, the computational operations were assumed to be of two kinds:

- phrase-structure rules that form larger syntactic objects from lexical items, and
- transformational rules that express the displacement property.

Both have traditional roots, but it was quickly found that they differ substantially from what had been supposed, with unsuspected variety and complexity. The research program sought to show that the complexity and variety are only apparent, and that the two kinds of rules can be reduced to simpler form. A "perfect" solution to the problem of variety of phrase-structure rules would be to eliminate them entirely in favor of the irreducible operation that takes two objects already formed and attaches one to the other, forming a larger object with just the properties of the target of attachment: the operation we can call Merge. Recent work indicates that this goal may well be attainable.

The optimal computational procedure consists, then, of the operation Merge and operations to construct the displacement property: transformational operations or some counterpart. The second of the two parallel endeavors sought to reduce the transformational component to the simplest form; though unlike phrase-structure rules, it seems to be ineliminable. The end result was the thesis that for a core set of phenomena, there is just a single operation Move – basically, move anything anywhere, with no properties specific to languages or particular constructions. How it applies is determined by general principles interacting with the specific parameter choices – switch settings – that determine a particular language. The operation Merge takes two distinct objects X and Y and attaches Y to X. The operation Move takes a single object X and an object Y that is part of X, and merges Y to X.

The next problem is to show that it is, indeed, the case that uninterpretable features are the mechanism that implements the displacement property, so that the two basic imperfections of the computational system reduce to one. If it turns out that the displacement property is motivated by legibility conditions imposed by external systems of thought, as I just suggested, then the imperfections are eliminated completely and language design turns out to be optimal after all: uninterpreted features are required as a mechanism to satisfy a legibility condition imposed by the general architecture of the mind/brain.

The way this unification proceeds is quite simple, but to explain it coherently would go beyond the scope of these remarks. The basic intuitive idea is that uninterpretable features have to be erased to satisfy the interface condition, and erasure requires a local relation between the offending feature and a matching feature that can erase it. Typically these two features are remote from one another for reasons having to do with the way semantic interpretation proceeds. For example, in the sentence "Clinton seems to have been elected," semantic interpretation requires that "elect" and "Clinton" be locally related in the phrase "elect Clinton" for the construction to be properly interpreted, as if the sentence were actually "seems to have been elected Clinton." The main verb of the sentence, "seems," has inflectional features that are uninterpretable: it is singular/third person/masculine, properties that add nothing independent to the meaning of the sentence, since they are already expressed in the noun phrase that agrees with it, and are ineliminable there. These offending features of "seems" therefore have to be erased in a local relation, an explicit version of the traditional descriptive category of "agreement." To achieve this result, the matching features of the agreeing phrase "Clinton" are attracted by the offending features of the main verb "seems," which are then erased under local matching. But now the phrase "Clinton" is displaced.

Note that only the *features* of "Clinton" are attracted; the full phrase moves for reasons having to do with the sensorimotor system, which is unable to "pronounce" or "hear" isolated features separated from the phrase in which they belong. However, if for some reason the sensorimotor system is inactivated, then the features alone raise, and alongside of such sentences as "an unpopular candidate seems to have been elected," with overt displacement, we have sentences of the form "seems to have been elected an unpopular candidate"; here the remote phrase "an unpopular candidate" agrees with the verb "seems," which means that its features have been attracted to a local relation with "seem" while leaving the rest of the phrase behind. The fact that the sensorimotor system has been inactivated is called "covert movement," a phenomenon with quite interesting properties. In many languages – Spanish for example – there are such sentences. English has them too, though it is necessary for other reasons to introduce the semantically empty element "there," giving the sentence "there seems to have been elected an unpopular candidate"; and also, for quite interesting reasons, to carry out an inversion of order, so it comes out "there seems to have been an unpopular candidate elected." These properties follow from specific choices of parameters, which have effects through the languages generally and interact to give a complex array of phenomena which are only superficially distinct. In the case we are looking at, all reduce to the simple fact that uninterpretable formal features must be erased in a local relation with a matching feature, yielding the displacement property required for semantic interpretation at the interface.

There is a fair amount of hand-waving in this brief description. Filling in the blanks yields a rather interesting picture, with many ramifications in typologically different languages. But to go on would take us well beyond the scope of these remarks.

I'd like to finish with at least brief reference to other issues, having to do with the ways the internalist study of language relates to the external world. For simplicity, let's keep to simple words. Suppose that "book" is a word in Peter's lexicon. The word is a complex of properties, phonetic and semantic. The sensorimotor systems use the phonetic properties for articulation and perception, relating them to external events: motions of molecules, for example. Other systems of mind use the semantic properties of the word when Peter talks about the world and interprets what others say about it.

There is no far-reaching controversy about how to proceed on the sound side, but on the meaning side there are profound disagreements. Empirically-oriented studies seem to me to approach problems of meaning rather in the way they study sound, as in phonology and phonetics. They try to find the semantic properties of the word "book": that it is nominal not verbal, used to refer to an artifact not a substance like water or an abstraction like health, and so on. One might ask whether these properties are part of the meaning of the word "book" or of the concept associated with the word; on current understanding, there is no good way to distinguish these proposals, but perhaps some day an empirical issue will be unearthed. Either way, some features of the lexical item "book" that are internal to it determine modes of interpretation of the kind just mentioned.

Investigating language use, we find that words are interpreted in terms of such factors as material constitution, design, intended and characteristic use, institutional role, and so on. Things are identified and assigned to categories in terms of such properties – which I am taking to be semantic features – on a par with phonetic features that determine its sound. The use of language can attend in various ways to these semantic features. Suppose the library has two copies of Tolstoy's *War and Peace*, Peter takes out one, and John the other. Did Peter and John take out the same book, or different books? If we attend to the material factor of the lexical item, they took out different books; if we focus on its abstract component, they took out the same book. We can attend to both material and abstract factors simultaneously, as when we say that "the book that he is planning will weigh at least five pounds if he ever writes it," or "his book is in every store in the country." Similarly, we can paint the door white and walk through it, using the pronoun "it" to refer ambiguously to figure and ground. We can report that the bank was blown up after it raised the interest rate, or that it raised the rate to keep from being blown up. Here the pronoun "it," and the "empty category" that is the subject of "being blown up," simultaneously adopt both the material and institutional factors.

The facts about such matters are often clear, but not trivial. Thus referentially dependent elements, even the most narrowly constrained, observe some distinctions but ignore others, in ways that vary for different types of words in curious ways. Such properties can be investigated in many ways: language acquisition, generality among languages, invented forms, etc. What we discover is surprisingly intricate; and, not surprisingly, known in advance of any evidence, hence shared among languages. There is no *a priori* reason to expect that human language will have such properties; Martian could be different. The symbolic systems of science and mathematics surely are. No one knows to what extent the specific properties of human language are a consequence of general biochemical laws applying to objects with general features of the brain, another important problem at a still distant horizon.

An approach to semantic interpretation in similar terms was developed in interesting ways in seventeenth- and eighteenth-century philosophy, often adopting Hume's principle that the "identity which we ascribe" to things is "only a fictitious one" (Hume 1740: Section 27), established by the human understanding. Hume's conclusion is very plausible. The book on my desk does not have these strange properties by virtue of its internal constitution; rather, by virtue of the way people think, and the meanings of the terms in which these thoughts are expressed. The semantic properties of words are used to think and talk about the world in terms of the perspectives made available by the resources of the mind, rather in the way phonetic interpretation seems to proceed.

Contemporary philosophy of language follows a different course. It asks to what a word refers, giving various answers. But the question has no clear meaning. The example of "book" is typical. It makes little sense to ask to what *thing* the expression "Tolstoy's *War and Peace*" refers, when Peter and John take identical copies out of the library. The answer depends on how the semantic features are used when we think and talk, one way or another. In general, a word, even of the simplest kind, does not pick out an entity of the world, or of our "belief space." Conventional assumptions about these matters seem to me very dubious.

I mentioned that modern generative grammar has sought to address concerns that animated the tradition; in particular, the Cartesian idea that "the true distinction" (Descartes 1649/1927: 360) between humans and other creatures or machines is the ability to act in the manner they took to be most clearly illustrated in the ordinary use of language: without any finite limits, influenced but not determined by internal state, appropriate to situations but not caused by them, coherent and evoking thoughts that the hearer might have expressed, and so on. The goal of the work I have been discussing is to unearth some of the factors that enter into such normal practice. Only *some* of these, however.

Generative grammar seeks to discover the mechanisms that are used, thus contributing to the study of *how* they are used in the creative fashion of normal life. How they are used is the problem that intrigued the Cartesians, and it remains as mysterious to us as it was to them, even though far more is understood today about the mechanisms that are involved.

In this respect, the study of language is again much like that of other organs. Study of the visual and motor systems has uncovered mechanisms by which the brain interprets scattered stimuli as a cube and the arm reaches for a book on the table. But these branches of science do not raise the question of how people decide to look at a book on the table or to pick it up, and speculations about the use of the visual or motor systems, or others, amount to very little. It is these capacities, manifested most strikingly in language use, that are at the heart of traditional concerns: for Descartes in the early seventeenth century, they are "the noblest thing we can have" and all that "truly belongs" to us. Half a century before Descartes, the Spanish philosopher-physician Juan Huarte observed that this "generative faculty" of ordinary human understanding and action is foreign to "beasts and plants" (Huarte 1575/1698: 3; see also Chomsky 1966: 78f.) though it is a lower form of understanding that falls short of true exercise of the creative imagination. Even the lower form lies beyond our theoretical reach, apart from the study of mechanisms that enter into it.

In a number of areas, language included, a lot has been learned in recent years about these mechanisms. The problems that can now be faced are hard and challenging, but many mysteries still lie beyond the reach of the form of human inquiry we call "science", a conclusion that we should not find surprising if we consider humans to be part of the organic world, and perhaps one we should not find distressing either.

2 Explaining language use

In his John Locke lectures, Hilary Putnam argues "that certain human abilities – language speaking is the paradigm example – may not be theoretically explicable in isolation," apart from a full model of "human functional organization," which "may well be *unintelligible* to humans when stated in any detail." The problem is that "we are not, realistically, going to get a detailed explanatory model for the natural kind 'human being'," not because of "*mere* complexity" but because "we are partially opaque to ourselves, in the sense of *not* having the ability to understand one another as we understand hydrogen atoms." This is a "*constitutive* fact" about "human beings in the present period," though perhaps not in a few hundred years (Putnam 1978).

The "natural kinds" *human being* and *hydrogen atom* thus call for different kinds of inquiry, one leading to "detailed explanatory models," the other not, at least for now. The first category is scientific inquiry, in which we seek intelligible explanatory theories and look forward to eventual integration with the core natural sciences; call this mode of inquiry "naturalistic," focusing on the character of work and reasonable goals, in abstraction from actual achievement. Beyond its scope, there are issues of the scale of full "human functional organization," not a serious topic for (current) naturalistic inquiry but more like the study of everything, like attempts to answer such pseudo-questions as "how do things work?" or "why do they happen?" Many questions – including those of greatest human significance, one might argue – do not fall within naturalistic inquiry; we approach them in other ways. As Putnam stresses, the distinctions are not sharp, but they are useful nonetheless.

In a critical discussion of "sophisticated mentalism of the MIT variety" (specifically, Jerry Fodor's "language of thought"; Fodor 1975), Putnam adds some complementary observations on theoretical inquiry that would *not* help to explain language speaking. He considers the possibility that the brain sciences might discover that when we "think the word *cat*" (or a Thai speaker thinks the equivalent), a configuration C is formed in the brain. "This is fascinating if true," he concludes, perhaps a significant contribution to psychology and the brain sciences, "but what is its relevance to a discussion of the *meaning* of *cat*" (or of the Thai equivalent, or of C)? – the implication being that there is no relevance (Putnam 1988a).

We thus have two related theses. First, "language speaking" and other human abilities do not currently fall within naturalistic inquiry. Second, nothing could be learned about meaning (hence about a fundamental aspect of language speaking) from the study of configurations and processes of the brain (at least of the kind illustrated). The first conclusion seems to me understated and not quite properly formulated; the second, too strong. Let's consider them in turn.

The concept *human being* is part of our common-sense understanding, with properties of individuation, psychic persistence, and so on, reflecting particular human concerns, attitudes, and perspectives. The same is true of *language speaking*. Apart from improbable accident, such concepts will not fall within explanatory theories of the naturalistic variety; not just now, but ever. This is not because of cultural or even intrinsically human limitations (though these surely exist), but because of their nature. We may have a good deal to say about people, so conceived; even low-level accounts that provide weak explanation. But such accounts cannot be integrated into the natural sciences alongside of explanatory models for hydrogen atoms, cells, or other entities that we posit in seeking a coherent and intelligible explanatory model of the naturalistic variety. There is no reason to suppose that there is a "natural kind 'human being'"; at least if natural kinds are the kinds of nature, the categories discovered in naturalistic inquiry.

The question is not whether the concepts of common-sense understanding can themselves be studied in some branch of naturalistic inquiry; perhaps they can. Rather, it is whether in studying the natural world (for that matter, in studying these concepts, as part of the natural world), we view it from the standpoint provided by such concepts. Surely not. There may be scientific studies of some aspects of what people are and do, but they will not use the common-sense notions *human being* or *language speaking* – with their special role in human life and thought – in formulating their explanatory principles.

The same is true of common-sense concepts generally. Such notions as *desk* or *book* or *house*, let alone more "abstract" ones, are not appropriate for naturalistic inquiry. Whether something is properly described as a desk, rather than a table or a hard bed, depends on its designer's intentions and the ways we and others (intend to) use it, among other factors. Books are concrete objects. We can refer to them as such ("the book weighs five pounds"), or from an abstract perspective ("who wrote the book?"; "he wrote the book in his head, but then forgot about it"); or from both perspectives simultaneously ("the book he wrote weighed five pounds," "the book he is writing will weigh at least five pounds if it is ever published"). If I say "that deck of cards, which is missing a Queen, is too worn to use," that deck of cards is simultaneously taken to be a defective set and a strange sort of scattered "concrete object," surely not a mereological sum. The term *house* is used to refer to concrete objects, but from the standpoint of special human interests and goals and with curious properties. A house can be destroyed and rebuilt, like a city; London could be completely destroyed and rebuilt up the Thames in 1,000 years and still be London, under some circumstances. It is hard to imagine how these could be fit concepts for theoretical study of things, events, and processes in the natural world. Uncontroversially, the same is true of *matter, motion, energy, work, liquid*, and other common-sense notions that are abandoned as naturalistic inquiry proceeds; a physicist asking whether a pile of sand is a solid, liquid, or gas – or some other kind of substance – spends no time asking how the terms are used in ordinary discourse, and would not expect the answer to the latter question to have anything to do with natural kinds, if these are the kinds in nature (Jaeger and Nagel 1992).

It is only reasonable to expect that the same will be true of *belief, desire, meaning*, and *sound* of *words, intent*, etc., insofar as aspects of human thought and action can be addressed within naturalistic inquiry. To be an Intentional Realist, it would seem, is about as reasonable as being a Desk- or Sound-of-Language- or Cat- or Matter-Realist; not that there are no such things as desks, etc., but that in the domain where questions of realism arise in a serious way, in the context of the search for laws of nature, objects are not conceived from the peculiar perspectives provided by concepts of common-sense. It is widely held that "mentalistic talk and mental entities should eventually lose their place in our attempts to describe and explain the world" (Burge 1992). True enough, but it is hard to see the significance of the doctrine, since the same holds true, uncontroversially, for "physicalistic talk and phys-ical entities" (to whatever extent the "mental"–"physical" distinction is intelligible).

Even the most elementary notions, such as *nameable thing*, crucially involve such intricate notions as human agency. What we take as objects, how we refer to them and describe them, and the array of properties with which we invest them, depend on their place in a matrix of human actions, interests, and intent in respects that lie far outside the potential range of naturalistic inquiry. The terms of language may also indicate positions in belief systems, which enrich further the perspectives these terms afford for viewing the world, though in ways inappropriate to the ends of naturalistic inquiry. Some terms – particularly those lacking "internal relational structure" (notably, so-called "natural kind terms") – may do little more than that, as far as the natural-language lexicon is concerned. (See, among others, Moravcsik 1975; Chomsky 1975b; Moravcsik 1990; Bromberger 1992a.) By "internal relational structure" I mean the selectional properties of such words as "give" (which takes an agent subject, theme object, and goal indirect object), lacking for "cat," "liquid," etc. The concepts of natural language, and common-sense generally, are not even candidates for naturalistic theories.

Putnam extends his conclusions to Brentano's thesis that "intentionality won't be reduced and won't go away": "there is no scientifically describable property that all cases of any particular intentional phenomenon have in common" (say, thinking about cats) (Putnam 1988a). More generally, intentional phenomena relate to people and what they do as viewed from the standpoint of human interests and unreflective thought, and thus will not (so viewed) fall within naturalistic theory, which seeks to set such factors aside. Like falling bodies, or the heavens, or liquids, a "particular intentional phenomenon" may be associated with some amorphous region in a highly intricate and shifting space of human interests and concerns. But these are not appropriate concepts for naturalistic inquiry.

We may speculate that certain components of the mind (call them the "science-forming faculty," to dignify ignorance with a title) enter into naturalistic inquiry, much as the language faculty (about which we know a fair amount) enters into the acquisition and use of language. The products of the science-forming faculty are fragments of theoretical understanding, naturalistic theories of varying degrees of power and plausibility involving concepts constructed and assigned meaning in a considered and determinate fashion, as far as possible, with the intent of sharpening or otherwise modifying them as more comes to be understood. Other faculties of the mind yield the concepts of common-sense understanding, which enter into natural-language semantics and belief systems. These simply "grow in the mind," much in the way that the embryo grows into a person. How sharp the distinctions may be is an open question, but they appear to be real nevertheless.

Sometimes there is a resemblance between concepts that arise in these different ways; possibly naturalistic inquiry might construct some counterpart to the common-sense notion *human being*, as H_2O has a rough correspondence to *water* (though earth, air, and fire, on a par with water for the ancients, lack such counterparts). It is a commonplace that any similarities to common-sense notions are of no consequence for science. It is, for example, no requirement for biochemistry to determine at what point in the transition from simple gases to bacteria we find the "essence of life"; and if some such categorization were imposed, the correspondence to some common-sense notion would matter no more than for (topological) *neighborhood*, *energy*, or *fish*.

Similarly, it is no concern of the psychology-biology of organisms to deal with such technical notions of philosophical discourse as *perceptual content*, with its stipulated properties (sometimes dubiously attributed to "folk psychology," a construct that appears to derive in part from parochial cultural conventions and traditions of academic discourse). Nor must these inquiries assign a special status to veridical perception under "normal" conditions. Thus, in the study of determination of structure from motion, it is immaterial whether the external event is successive arrays of flashes on a tachistoscope that yield the visual experience of a cube rotating in space, or an actual rotating cube, or stimulation of the retina, or optic nerve, or visual cortex. In any case, "the computational investigation concerns the nature of the internal representations used by the visual system and the processes by which they are derived" (Ullman 1979: 3), as does the study of algorithms and mechanisms in this and other work along lines pioneered by David Marr (1982). It is also immaterial whether people might accept the nonveridical cases as "seeing a cube" (taking "seeing" to be having an experience, whether "as if" or veridical); or whether concerns of philosophical theories of intentional attribution are addressed. A "psychology" dealing with the latter concerns would doubtless not be individualistic, as Martin Davies (1991) argues, but it would also depart from naturalistic inquiry into the nature of organisms, and possibly from authentic folk psychology as well.[1] To take another standard example, on the (rather implausible) assumption that a naturalistic approach to, say, jealousy were feasible, it is hardly likely that it would distinguish between states involving real or imagined objects. If "cognitive science" is taken to be concerned with intentional attribution, it may turn out to be an interesting pursuit (as literature is), but it is not likely to provide explanatory theory or to be integrated into the natural sciences.

As understanding progresses and concepts are sharpened, the course of naturalistic inquiry tends towards theories in which terms are divested of distorting residues of common-sense understanding, and are assigned a relation to posited entities and a place in a matrix of principles: *real number*, *electron*, and so on. The divergence from natural language is two-fold: the constructed terms abstract from the intricate properties of natural-language expressions; they are assigned semantic properties that may well not hold for natural language, such as reference (we must beware of what Strawson once called "the myth of the logically proper name," in natural language, and related myths concerning indexicals and pronouns; P. Strawson 1952: 216). As this course is pursued, the divergence from natural language increases; and with it, the divergence between the ways we understand *hydrogen atom*, on the one hand, and *human being* (*desk, liquid, heavens, fall, chase, London, this*, etc.), on the other.

But even a strengthened version of Putnam's first thesis does not entitle us to move on to the second, more generally, to conclude that naturalistic theories of the brain are of no relevance to understanding what people do. Under certain conditions, people see tachistoscopic presentations as a rotating cube or light moving in a straight line. A study of the visual cortex might provide understanding of why this happens, or why perception proceeds as it does in ordinary circumstances. And comparable inquiries might have a good deal to say about "language speaking" and other human activities.

Take Putnam's case: the discovery that thinking of cats evokes C. Surely such a discovery might have some relevance to inquiry into what Peter means (or refers to, or thinks about) when he uses the term *cat*, hence to "a discussion of the meaning of *cat*." For example, there has been a debate – in which Putnam has taken part – about the referential properties of *cat* if cats were found to be robots controlled from Mars. Suppose that after Peter comes to believe this, his brain does, or does not, form C when he refers to cats (thinks about them, etc.). That might be relevant to the debate. Or, take a realistic case: recent studies of electrical activity of the brain (event-related potentials, ERPs) show distinctive responses to nondeviant and deviant expressions and, among the latter, to violations of:

1. word meaning expectancies;
2. phrase-structure rules;
3. the specificity-of-reference condition on extraction of operators; and
4. locality conditions on movement (Neville *et al.* 1991).

Such results surely might be relevant to the study of the use of language, in particular, the study of meaning.

We can proceed further. Patterns of electrical activity of the brain correlate with the five categories of structure noted: nondeviance, and four types of deviance. But the study of these categories is also a study of the brain, its states and properties, just as study of algorithms involved in seeing a straight line or in doing long division is a study of the brain. Like other complex systems, the brain can be studied at various levels: atoms, cells, cell assemblies, neural networks, computational–representational (C–R) systems, etc. The ERP study relates two such levels: electrical activity of the brain and C–R systems. The study of each level is naturalistic both in the character of the work and in that integration with the core natural sciences is a prospect that can be reasonably entertained. In the context of Putnam's discussion, discoveries about the brain at these levels of inquiry are on a par with a discovery about the (imagined) configuration C, when Peter thinks of cats.

In the case of language, the C–R theories have much stronger empirical support than anything available at other levels, and are far superior in explanatory power; they fall within the natural sciences to an extent that inquiry into "language speaking" at the other levels does not. In fact, the current significance of the ERP studies lies primarily in their correlations with the much richer and better-grounded C–R theories. Within the latter, the five categories have a place and, accordingly, a wide range of indirect empirical support; in isolation from C–R theories, the ERP observations are just curiosities, lacking a theoretical matrix. Similarly, the discovery that C correlates with use of *cat* would, as an isolated fact, be more of a discovery about C than about the meaning of *cat* – and for that reason alone would shed little light on the controversy about robots controlled from Mars. To take another case, the discovery of perceptual displacement of clicks to phrase boundaries is, for now, more of a discovery about the validity of the experiment than about phrase boundaries. The reason is that evidence of other sorts about phrase boundaries – sometimes called "linguistic" rather than "psychological" evidence (a highly misleading terminology) – is considerably more compelling and embedded in a much richer explanatory structure. If click experiments were found to be sufficiently reliable in identifying the entities postulated in C–R theories, and if their theoretical framework were deepened, one might rely on them in cases where "linguistic evidence" is indecisive; possibly more, as inquiry progresses. (On some misunderstandings of these matters see Chapter 3 of this volume; Chomsky 1991a; 1991b).

For the present, the best-grounded naturalistic theories of language and its use are C–R theories. We assume, essentially on faith, that there is some kind of description in terms of atoms and molecules, though without expecting operative principles and structures of language and thought to be discernible at these levels. With a larger leap of faith, we tend to assume that there is an account in neurological terms (rather than, say, glial or vascular terms, though a look at the brain reveals glial cells and blood as well as neurons.[2] It may well be that the relevant elements and principles of brain structure have yet to be discovered. Perhaps C–R theories will provide guidelines for the search for such mechanisms, much as nineteenth-century chemistry provided crucial empirical conditions for radical revision of fundamental physics. The common slogan that "the mental is the neurophysiological at a higher level" – where C–R theories are placed within "the mental" – has matters backwards. It should be rephrased as the speculation that the neurophysiological may turn out to be "the mental at a lower level" – that is, the speculation that neurophysiology might, some day, prove to have some bearing on the "mental phenomena" dealt with in C–R theories. As for the further claims of eliminative materialism, the doctrine remains a mystery until some account is given of the nature of "the material"; and given that account, some reason why one should take it seriously or care if successful theories lie beyond its stipulated bounds.

For the present, C–R approaches provide the best-grounded and richest naturalistic account of basic aspects of language use. Within these theories, there is a fundamental concept that bears resemblance to the common-sense notion "language": the *generative procedure* that forms *structural descriptions* (SDs), each a complex of phonetic, semantic, and structural properties. Call this procedure an *I-language*, a term chosen to indicate that this conception of language is internal, individual, and intensional (so that distinct I-languages might, in principle, generate the same set of SDs, though the highly restrictive innate properties of the language faculty may well leave this possibility unrealized). We may take the linguistic expressions of a given I-language to be the SDs generated by it. A linguistic expression, then, is a complex of phonetic, semantic, and other properties. To have an I-language is something like having a "way to speak and understand," which is one traditional picture of what a language is. There is reason to believe that the I-languages ("grammatical competence") are distinct from conceptual organization and "pragmatic competence," and that these systems can be selectively impaired and developmentally dissociated (see Yamada 1990; John Marshall 1990).

The I-language specifies the form and meaning of such lexical elements as *desk*, *work*, and *fall*, insofar as these are determined by the language faculty itself. Similarly, it should account for properties of more complex expressions: for example, the fact that "John rudely departed" may mean either that he departed in a rude manner or that it was rude of him to depart, and that, in either case, he departed (perhaps an event semantics should be postulated as a level of representation to deal with such facts; see Higginbotham 1985; 1989). And it should explain the fact that the understood subject of *expect* in example (1) depends on whether X is null or is *Bill*, with a variety of other semantic consequences:

(1)   John is too clever to expect anyone to talk to *X*.

And for the fact that, in my speech, *ladder* rhymes with *matter* but *madder* doesn't. In a wide range of such cases, nontrivial accounts are forthcoming. The study of C–R systems provides no little insight into how people articulate their thoughts and interpret what they hear, though of course it is as little – and as much – a study of these actions as the physiology and psychology of vision are studies of humans seeing objects.

A deeper inquiry into I-languages will seek to account for the fact that Peter has the I-language L_P while Juan has the I-language L_J – these statements being high-level abstractions, because in reality what Peter and Juan have in their heads is about as interesting for naturalistic inquiry as the course of a feather on a windy day. The basic explanation must lie in the properties of the language faculty of the brain. To a good approximation, the genetically-determined initial state of the language faculty is the same for Peter, Juan, and other humans. It permits only a restricted variety of I-languages to develop under the triggering and shaping effect of experience. In the light of current understanding, it is not implausible to speculate that the initial state determines the computational system of language uniquely, along with a highly structured range of lexical possibilities and some options among "grammatical elements" that lack substantive content. Beyond these possibilities, variation of I-languages may reduce to Saussurean arbitrariness (an association of concepts with abstract representations of sound) and parts of the sound system, relatively accessible and, hence, "learnable" (to use a term with misleading connotations). Small differences in an intricate system may, of course, yield large phenomenal differences, but a rational Martian scientist studying humans might not find the difference between English and Navajo very impressive.

The I-language is a (narrowly described) property of the brain, a relatively stable element of transitory states of the language faculty. Each linguistic expression (SD) generated by the I-language includes instructions for performance systems in which the I-language is embedded. It is only by virtue of its integration into such performance systems that this brain state qualifies as a language. Some other organism might, in principle, have the same I-language (brain state) as Peter, but embedded in performance systems that use it for locomotion. We are studying a real object, the language faculty of the brain, which has assumed the form of a full I-language and is integrated into performance systems that play a role in articulation, interpretation, expression of beliefs and desires, referring, telling stories, and so on. For such reasons, the topic is the study of human language.

The performance systems appear to fall into two general types: articulatory–perceptual, and conceptual–intentional.[3] If so, it is reasonable to suppose that a generated expression includes two *interface levels*, one providing information and instructions for the articulatory–perceptual systems, the other for the conceptual–intentional systems. One interface is generally assumed to be phonetic representation (Phonetic Form, PF). The nature of the other is more controversial; call it LF ("Logical Form").

The properties of these systems, or their existence, are matters of empirical fact. One should not be misled by unintended connotations of such terms as "logical form" and "representation," drawn from technical usage in different kinds of inquiry. Similarly, though there is a hint of the notions "deep grammar" and "surface grammar" of philosophical analysis, the concepts do not closely match. What is "surface" from the point of view of I-language is, if anything, PF, the interface with articulatory–perceptual systems. Everything else is "deep." The surface grammar of philosophical analysis has no particular status in the empirical study of language; it is something like phenomenal judgment, mediated by schooling, traditional authorities and conventions, cultural artifacts, and so on. Similar questions arise with regard to what is termed, much too casually, "folk psychology," as noted. One should regard such notions with caution: much may be concealed behind apparent phenomenal clarity.

The complex of I-language and performance systems enters into human action. It is an appropriate subject matter for naturalistic theories, which might carry us far towards understanding how and why people do what they do, though always falling short of a full account, just as a naturalistic theory of the body would fail to capture fully such human actions or achievements as seeing a tree or taking a walk.

Correspondingly, it would be misleading, or worse, to say that some part of the brain or an abstract model of it (for example, a neural net or programmed computer) sees a tree or figures out square roots. People in an ambiguous range of standard circumstances pronounce words, refer to cats, speak their thoughts, understand what others say, play chess, or whatever; their brains don't and computer programs don't – though study of brains, possibly with abstract modelling of some of their properties, might well provide insight into what people are doing in such cases. An algorithm constructed in a C–R theory might provide a correct account of what is happening in the brain when Peter sees a straight line or does long division or "understands Chinese,"[4] and might be fully integrated into a well-grounded theory at some other level of explanation (say, cells). But the algorithm, or a machine implementing it, would not be carrying out these actions, though we might decide to modify existing usage, as when we say that airplanes fly and submarines set sail (but do not swim). Nothing of substance is at stake. Similarly, while it may be that people carry out the action by virtue of the fact that their brains implement the algorithm, the same people would not be carrying out the action if they were mechanically implementing the instructions, in the manner of a machine (or of their brains). It may be that I see a straight line (do long division, understand English, etc.) by virtue of the fact that my brain implements a certain algorithm; but if I, the person, carry out the instructions mechanically, mapping some symbolic representation of the input to a representation of the output, neither I nor I-plus-algorithm-plus-external memory sees a straight line (etc.), again, for uninteresting reasons.[5]

It would also be a mistake, in considering the nature of performance systems, to move at once to a vacuous "study of everything." As a case in point, consider Donald Davidson's discussion of Peter as an "interpreter," trying to figure out what Tom has in mind when he speaks. Davidson observes that Peter may well use any information, background assumption, guesswork, or whatever, constructing a "passing theory" for the occasion. Consideration of an "interpreter" thus carries us to full models of human functional organization. Davidson concludes that there is no use for "the concept of a language" serving as a "portable interpreting machine set to grind out the meaning of an arbitrary utterance"; we are led to "abandon . . . not only the ordinary notion of a language, but we have erased the boundary between knowing a language and knowing our way around in the world generally." Since "there are no rules for arriving at passing theories," we "must give up the idea of a clearly defined shared structure which language-users acquire and then apply to cases" (Davidson 1986b: 446). "There is no such thing as a language," a recent study of Davidson's philosophy opens, with his approval (Davidson 1986b; Ramberg 1989).

The initial observation about "passing theories" is correct, but the conclusions do not follow. A reasonable response to the observation – if our goal is to understand what humans are and what they do – is to try to isolate coherent systems that are amenable to naturalistic inquiry and that interact to yield some aspects of the full complexity. If we follow this course, we are led to the conjecture that there is a generative procedure that "grinds out" linguistic expressions with their interface properties, and performance systems that access these instructions and are used for interpreting and expressing one's thoughts.

What about "the idea of a clearly defined shared structure which language-users acquire and then apply to cases"? Must we also postulate such "shared structures," in addition to I-language and performance systems? It is often argued that such notions as common "public language" or "public meanings" are required to explain the possibility of communication or of "a common treasure of thoughts," in Gottlob Frege's sense (Frege 1892/1965: 71). Thus, if Peter and Mary do not have a "shared language," with "shared meanings" and "shared reference," then how can Peter understand what Mary says? (Interestingly, no one draws the analogous conclusion about "public pronunciation.") One recent study holds that linguists can adopt an I-language perspective only "at the cost of denying that the basic function of natural languages is to mediate communication between its speakers," including the problem of "communication between *time slices of an idiolect*" (so-called "incremental learning"; Fodor and Lepore 1992).[6]

But these views are not well founded. Successful communication between Peter and Mary does not entail the existence of shared meanings or shared pronunciations in a public language (or a common treasure of thoughts or articulations of them), any more than physical resemblance between Peter and Mary entails the existence of a public form that they share. As for the idea that "the basic function of natural languages is to mediate communication," it is unclear what sense can be given to an absolute notion of "basic function" for any biological system; and if this problem can be overcome, we may ask why "communication" is the "basic function." Furthermore, the transition problem seems no more mysterious than the problem of how Peter can be the person he is, given the stages through which he has passed. Not only is the I-language perspective appropriate to the problems at hand, but it is not easy to imagine a coherent alternative.

It may be that when he listens to Mary speak, Peter proceeds by assuming that she is identical to him, modulo M, some array of modifications that he must work out. Sometimes the task is easy, sometimes hard, sometimes hopeless. To work out M, Peter will use any artifice available to him, though much of the process is doubtless automatic and unreflective.[7] Having settled on M, Peter will, similarly, use any artifice to construct a "passing theory" – even if M is null. Insofar as Peter succeeds in these tasks, he understands what Mary says as being what he means by his comparable expression. The only (virtually) "shared structure" among humans generally is the initial state of the language faculty. Beyond that we expect to find no more than approximations, as in the case of other natural objects that grow and develop.

Discussion of language and language use regularly introduces other kinds of shared structure: communities with their languages, common languages across a broader culture, etc. Such practices are standard in ordinary casual discourse as well. Thus, we say that Peter and Tom speak the same language, but Juan speaks a different one. Similarly, we say that Boston is near New York, but not near London, or that Peter and Tom look alike, but neither looks like John. Or, we might reject any of these assertions. There is no right or wrong choice in abstraction from interests that may vary in every imaginable way. There are also no natural categories, no idealizations. In these respects, speaking the same language is on a par with being-near or looking-like. A standard remark in an undergraduate linguistics course is Max Weinreich's quip that a language is a dialect with an army and a navy, but dialects are also nonlinguistic notions, which can be set up one way or another, depending on particular interests and concerns. Such factors as conquests, natural barriers (oceans, mountains), national TV, etc. may induce illusions on this matter, but no notion of "common language" has been formulated in any useful or coherent way, nor do the prospects seem hopeful. Any approach to the study of language or meaning that relies on such notions is highly suspect.

Suppose, for example, that "following a rule" is analyzed in terms of communities: Jones follows a rule if he conforms to the practice or norms of the community. If the "community" is homogeneous, reference to it contributes nothing (the notions *norm, practice, convention*, etc. raise further questions). If the "community" is heterogeneous – apart from the even greater unclarity of the notion of norms (practice, etc.) for this case – several problems arise. One is that the proposed analysis is descriptively inaccurate. Typically, we attribute rule-following in the case of notable *lack* of conformity to prescriptive practice or alleged norms. Thus we might say that Johnny, who is three, is following his own rule when he says *brang* instead of *brought*; or that his father Peter is following the "wrong rule" ("violating the rules") when he uses *disinterested* to mean *uninterested* (as most people do). But only a linguist would say that Johnny and Peter are observing Condition (B) of the Binding theory (Chomsky 1981a: 188), as does the "community" generally (in fact, the community of all language speakers, very likely). The more serious objection is that the notion of "community" or "common language" makes as much sense as the notion "nearby city" or "look alike," without further specification of interests, leaving the analysis vacuous.[8]

For familiar reasons, nothing in this suggests that there is any problem in informal usage, any more than in the ordinary use of such expressions as *Boston is near New York* or *John is almost home*. It is just that we do not expect such notions to enter into explanatory theoretical discourse. They may be appropriate for informal discussion of what people do, with tacit assumptions of the kind that underlie ordinary discourse in particular circumstances; or even for technical discourse, where the relevant qualifications are tacitly understood. They have no further place in naturalistic inquiry, or in any attempt to sharpen understanding.

Alleged social factors in language use often have a natural individualist–internalist interpretation. If Peter is improving his Italian or Gianni is learning his, they are (in quite different ways) becoming more like a wide range of people; both the modes of approximation and selection of models vary with our interests. We gain no insight into what they are doing by supposing that there is a fixed entity that they are approaching, even if some sense can be made of this mysterious notion. If Bert complains of arthritis in his ankle and thigh, and is told by a doctor that he is wrong about both, but in different ways, he may (or may not) choose to modify his usage to that of the doctor's. Apart from further detail, which may vary widely with changing contingencies and concerns, nothing seems missing from this account. Similarly, ordinary talk of whether a person has mastered a concept requires no notion of common language. To say that Bert has not mastered the concept *arthritis* or *flu* is simply to say that his usage is not exactly that of people we rely on to cure us – a normal situation. If my neighbor Bert tells me about his arthritis, my initial posit is that he is identical to me in this usage. I will introduce modifications to interpret him as circumstances require; reference to a presumed "public language" with an "actual content" for *arthritis* sheds no further light on what is happening between us, even if some clear sense can be given to the tacitly assumed notions. If I know nothing about elms and beeches beyond the fact that they are large deciduous trees, nothing beyond this information might be represented in my mental lexicon (possibly not even that, as noted earlier); the understood difference in referential properties may be a consequence of a condition holding of the lexicon generally: lack of indication of a semantic relation is taken to indicate that it does not hold.[9]

Questions remain – factual ones, I presume – as to just what kind of information is within the lexicon, as distinct from belief systems. Changes in usage, as in the preceding cases, may in fact be marginal changes of I-language, or changes in belief systems, here construed as (narrowly described) C–R systems of the mind, which enrich the perspectives and standpoints for thought, interpretation, language use and other actions (call them *I-belief systems*, some counterpart to beliefs that might be discovered in naturalistic inquiry). Work in lexical semantics provides a basis for empirical resolution in some cases (particularly in the verbal system, with its richer relational structure), keeping to the individualist–internalist framework.

Little is understood about the general architecture of the mind/brain outside of a few scattered areas, typically not those that have been the focus of the most general considerations of so-called "cognitive science." There has, for example, been much interesting discussion about a theory of belief and its possible place in accounting for thought and action. But substantive empirical work that might help in examining, refining, or testing these ideas is scarcely available. It seems reasonable at least to suppose that I-beliefs do not form a homogeneous set; the system has further structure that may provide materials for decisions about false belief and misidentification. Suppose that some I-beliefs are *identifying* beliefs and others not, or that they range along such a spectrum, where the latter (or the lesser) are more readily abandoned without affecting conditions for referring. Suppose, say, that Peter's information about Martin van Buren is exhausted by the belief that he was (1) the President of the United States and (2) the sixteenth President, (1) being more of an identifying belief than (2). If Peter learns that Lincoln was the sixteenth President he might drop the nonidentifying I-belief while using the term to refer. If he is credibly informed that all the history books are mistaken and van Buren wasn't a President at all, he is at a loss as to how to proceed. That seems a reasonable first step towards as much of an analysis as an internalist perspective can provide, and as much as seems factually at all clear. Further judgments can sometimes be made in particular circumstances, in varied and conflicting ways.[10]

It may be that a kind of public (or interpersonal) character to thought and meaning results from uniformity of initial endowment, which permits only I-languages that are alike in significant respects, thus providing some empirical reason to adopt some version of the Fregean doctrine that "it cannot well be denied that mankind possesses a common treasure of thoughts which is transmitted from generation to generation" (Frege 1892/1965: 71). And the special constructions of the science-forming faculty may also approach a public character (more to the point, for Frege's particular concerns). But for the systems that grow naturally in the mind, beyond the instantiation of initial endowment as I-language (perhaps also I-belief and related systems), the character of thought and meaning varies as interest and circumstance vary, with no clear way to establish further categories, even ideally. Appeals to a common origin of language or speculations about natural selection, which are found throughout the literature, seem completely beside the point.

Consider the shared initial state of the language faculty of the brain, and the limited range of I-languages that are attainable as it develops in early life. When we inquire into lexical properties, we find a rich texture of purely internalist semantics, with interesting general properties, and evidence for formal semantic relations (including analytic connections; see references on p. 22). Furthermore, a large part of this semantic structure appears to derive from our inner nature, determined by the initial state of our language faculty, hence unlearned and universal for I-languages. Much the same is true of phonetic and other properties. In short, I-language (including internalist semantics) seems much like other parts of the biological world.

We might well term all of this a form of syntax, that is, the study of the symbolic systems of C–R theories ("mental representation"). The same terminology remains appropriate if the theoretical apparatus is elaborated to include mental models, discourse representations, semantic values, possible worlds as commonly construed, and other theoretical constructions that still must be related in some manner to things in the world; or to the entities postulated by our science-forming faculty, or constructed by other faculties of the mind.

The internally-determined properties of linguistic expressions can be quite far-reaching, even in very simple cases. Consider again the word *house*, say, in the expression *John is painting the house brown*, a certain collection of structural, phonetic, and semantic properties. We say it is the same expression for Peter and Tom only in the sense in which we might say that their circulatory or visual systems are the same: they are similar enough for the purposes at hand. One structural property of the expression is that it consists of six words. Other structural properties differentiate it from *John is painting the brown house*, which has correspondingly different conditions of use. A phonetic property is that the last two words, *house* and *brown*, share the same vowel; they are in the formal relation of assonance, while *house* and *mouse* are in the formal relation of rhyme, two relations on linguistic expressions definable in terms of their phonological features.[11] A semantic property is that one of the two final words can be used to refer to certain kinds of things, and the other expresses a property of these. Here, too, there are formal relations expressible in terms of features of the items, for example, between *house* and *building*. Or, to take a more interesting property, if John is painting the house brown, then he is applying paint to its exterior surface, not its interior; a relation of entailment holds between the corresponding linguistic expressions.

Viewed formally, relations of entailment have much the same status as rhyme; they are formal relations among expressions, which can be characterized in terms of their linguistic features. Certain relations happen to be interesting ones, as distinct from many that are not, because of the ways I-languages are embedded in performance systems that use these instructions for various human activities.

Some properties of the expression are universal, others language-particular. It is a universal phonetic property that the vowel of *house* is shorter than the vowel of *brown*; it is a particular property that the vowel in my I-language is front rather than mid, as it is in some I-languages similar to mine. The fact that a brown house has a brown exterior, not interior, appears to be a language universal, holding of "container" words of a broad category, including ones we might invent: *box, airplane, igloo, lean-to*, etc. To paint a spherical cube brown is to give it a brown exterior. The fact that *house* is distinguished from *home* is a particular feature of the I-language. In English, I return to my home after work; in Hebrew, I return to the house.

When we move beyond lexical structure, conclusions about the richness of the initial state of the language faculty, and its apparently special structure, are reinforced. Consider such expressions as those in example (2):

(2) a   He thinks the young man is a genius.
   b   The young man thinks he is a genius.
   c   His mother thinks the young man is a genius.

In (2b) or (2c), the pronoun may be referentially dependent on *the young man*; in (2a) it cannot (though it might be used to refer to the young man in question, an irrelevant matter). The principles underlying these facts appear to be universal, at least in large measure;[12] again, they yield rich conditions on semantic interpretation, on intrinsic relations of meaning among expressions, including analytic connections. Furthermore, in this domain we have theoretical results of some depth, with surprising consequences. Thus, the same principles appear to yield the semantic properties of expressions of the form of example (1), on page 27.

Given the performance systems, the representation at the interface level PF imposes restrictive conditions on use (articulation and perception, in this case). The same is true of the LF representation, as illustrated in examples (1) and (2), or at the lexical level, in the special status of the exterior surface for container words. A closer look reveals further complexity. The exterior surface is distinguished in other ways within I-language semantics. If I see the house, I see its exterior surface; seeing the interior surface does not suffice. If I am inside an airplane, I see it only if I look out the window and see the surface of the wing, or if there is a mirror outside that reflects its exterior surface. But the house is not just its exterior surface, a geometrical entity. If Peter and Mary are equidistant from the surface – Peter inside and Mary outside – Peter is not near the house, but Mary might be, depending on the current conditions for nearness. The house can have chairs inside it or outside it, consistent with its being regarded as a surface. But while those outside may be near it, those inside are necessarily not. So the house involves its exterior surface and its interior. But the interior is abstractly conceived; it is the same house if I fill it with cheese or move the walls – though if I clean the house I may interact only with things in the interior space, and I am referring only to these when I say that the house is a mess or needs to be redecorated. The house is conceived as an exterior surface and an interior space (with complex properties). Of course, the house itself is a concrete object; it can be made of bricks or wood, and a wooden house does not just have a wooden exterior. A brown wooden house has a brown exterior (adopting the abstract perspective) and is made of wood (adopting the concrete perspective). If my house used to be in Philadelphia, but is now in Boston, then a physical object was moved. In contrast, if my home used to be in Philadelphia, but is now in Boston, then no physical object need have moved, though my home is also concrete – though in some manner also abstract, whether understood as the house in which I live, or the town, or country, or universe; a house is concrete in a very different sense. The *house – home* difference has numerous consequences: I can go home, but not go house; I can live in a brown house, but not a brown home; in many languages, the counterpart of *home* is adverbial, as partially in English too.

Even in this trivial example, we see that the internal conditions on meaning are rich, complex, and unsuspected; in fact, barely known. The most elaborate dictionaries do not dream of such subtleties; they provide no more than hints that enable the intended concept to be identified by those who already have it (at least, in essential respects). The I-variant of Frege's telescope operates in curious and intricate ways.

There seems at first glance to be something paradoxical in these descriptions. Thus, houses and homes are concrete but, from another point of view, are considered quite abstractly, though abstractly in very different ways; similarly, books, decks of cards, cities, etc. It is not that we have confused ideas – or inconsistent beliefs – about houses and homes, or boxes, airplanes, igloos, spherical cubes, etc. Rather, a lexical item provides us with a certain range of perspectives for viewing what we take to be the things in the world, or what we conceive in other ways; these items are like filters or lenses, providing ways of looking at things and thinking about the products of our minds. The terms themselves do not refer, at least if the term *refer* is used in its natural-language sense; but people can use them to refer to things, viewing them from particular points of view – which are remote from the standpoint of the natural sciences, as noted.

The same is true wherever we inquire into I-language. London is not a fiction, but considering it as London – that is, through the perspective of a city name, a particular type of linguistic expression – we accord it curious properties: as noted earlier, we allow that under some circumstances, it could be completely destroyed and rebuilt somewhere else, years or even millennia later, still being London, that same city. Charles Dickens described Washington as "the City of Magnificent Intentions," with "spacious avenues, that begin in nothing, and lead nowhere; streets, mile-long, that only want houses, roads, and inhabitants; public buildings that need but a public to be complete; and ornaments of great thoroughfares, which only lack great thoroughfares to ornament" – but still Washington. We can regard London with or without regard to its population: from one point of view, it is the same city if its people desert it; from another, we can say that London came to have a harsher feel to it through the Thatcher years, a comment on how people act and live. Referring to London, we can be talking about a location or area, people who sometimes live there, the air above it (but not too high), buildings, institutions, etc., in various combinations (as in *London is so unhappy, ugly, and polluted that it should be destroyed and rebuilt 100 miles away*, still being the same city). Such terms as *London* are used to talk about the actual world, but there neither are nor are believed to be things-in-the-world with the properties of the intricate modes of reference that a city name encapsulates. Two such collections of perspectives can fit differently into Peter's system of beliefs, as in Kripke's puzzle. (For extensive discussion from a somewhat similar point of view, see Bilgrami 1992.)

For purposes of naturalistic inquiry, we construct a picture of the world that is dissociated from these "common-sense" perspectives (never completely, of course; we cannot become something other than the creatures we are[13]). If we intermingle such different ways of thinking about the world, we may find ourselves attributing to people strange and even contradictory beliefs about objects that are to be regarded somehow apart from the means provided by the I-language and the I-belief systems that add further texture to interpretation. The situation will seem even more puzzling if we entertain the obscure idea that certain terms have a relation to things ("reference") fixed in a common public language, which perhaps even exists "independently of any particular speakers," who have a "partial, and partially erroneous, grasp of the language" (Dummett 1986); and that these "public-language terms" in the common language refer (in some sense to be explained) to such objects as London taken as a thing divorced from the properties provided by the city name (or some other mode of designation) in a particular I-language, and from the other factors that enter into Peter's referring to London. Problems will seem to deepen further if we abstract from the background of individual or shared beliefs that underlie normal language use. All such moves go beyond the bounds of a naturalistic approach, some of them, perhaps, beyond sensible discourse.

They also go beyond internalist limits, which is a different matter. A naturalistic approach does not impose internalist, individualist limits. Thus, if we study (some counterpart to) persons as phases in the history of ideally immortal germ cells, or as stages in the conversion of oxygen to carbon dioxide, we depart from such limits. But if we are interested in accounting for what people do, and why, insofar as that is possible through naturalistic inquiry, the argument for keeping to these limits seems persuasive.[14]

We began by considering the (hypothetical) discovery that Peter's brain produces the configuration C when he thinks about cats. We then moved to the more realistic example of ERPs, and the still more realistic case (from a scientific standpoint) of C–R systems; one may think of their elements as on a par with C, though now real, not hypothetical, we have reason to believe. The same would be true of a naturalistic approach that departs from these internalist limits, viewing Peter's brain as part of a larger system of interactions. The analogy would no longer be to the configuration C produced in Peter's brain when he thinks of cats, but to some physical configuration C′ involving C along with something else, perhaps something about cats. We are now in the domain of the hypothetical – I know of no serious candidate. But suppose that such an approach can be devised and proves to yield insight into questions of language use. If so, that might modify the ways we study language and psychology, but would not bridge the gap to an account of people and what they do.

We have to distinguish between a hypothetical externalist naturalism of the kind just sketched, and nonnaturalist externalism that attempts to treat human action (referring to or thinking about cats, etc.) in the context of communities, real or imagined things in the world, and so on. Such approaches are to be judged on their merits, as efforts to make some sense out of questions that lie beyond naturalistic inquiry – like questions about energy, falling stones, the heavens, etc. – in the ordinary sense of the terms. I have mentioned some reason for skepticism about recourse to communities and their practices, or public languages with public meanings. Consider further the other facet of externalism, an alleged relation between words and things.

Within internalist semantics, there are explanatory theories of considerable interest that are developed in terms of a relation R (read "refer") that is postulated to hold between linguistic expressions and something else, entities drawn from some stipulated domain D (perhaps semantic values).[15]

The relation R, for example, holds between the expressions *London* (*house*, etc.) and entities of D that are assumed to have some relation to what people refer to when they use the words *London* (*house*, etc.), though that presumed relation remains obscure. As noted, I think such theories should be regarded as a variety of syntax. The elements they postulate are on a par, in the respects relevant here, with phonological or phrase-structure representations, or the hypothetical brain configuration C; we might well include D and R within the SD (the linguistic expression), as part of an interface level.

Explanation of the phenomena of example (2) (on page 35) is commonly expressed in terms of the relation R. The same theories of binding and anaphora carry over without essential change if we replace *young* in example (2) by *average, typical*, or replace *the young man* by *John Doe*, stipulated to be the average man for the purposes of a particular discourse.[16] The same theories also carry over to anaphoric properties of the pronouns in examples (3) and (4):

(3)   a   It brings good health's rewards.
        b   Good health brings its rewards.
        c   Its rewards are what make good health worth striving for.

(4)   a   [There is a flaw in the argument], but it was quickly found.
        b   [The argument is flawed], but it was quickly found.

In terms of the relation R, stipulated to hold between *the average man, John Doe, good health, flaw*, and entities drawn from D, we can account for the differential behavior of the pronoun exactly as we would with *the young man, Peter, fly* ("there is a fly in the coffee"). The relations of anaphora differ in (4a and 4b), though there is no relevant difference in meaning between the bracketed clauses. And it might well turn out that these expressions, along with such others as "the argument has a flaw" (with the anaphoric options of (4a)), share still deeper structural properties, possibly even the same structural representation at the level relevant to the internal semantics of the phrases, a possibility that has been explored for some years (see Tremblay 1991).[17] The same is true in more exotic cases. It would seem perverse to seek a relation between entities in D and things in the world – real, imagined, or whatever – at least, one of any generality. One may imagine that the relation of elements of D to things in the world is more "transparent" than in the case of other syntactic representations, as the relation to sound waves is more "transparent" for phonetic than for phonological representation; but even if so, these studies do not pass beyond the syntax of mental representations. The relation R and the construct D must be justified on the same kinds of grounds that justify other technical syntactic notions; that is, those of phonology, or the typology of empty categories in syntax. An occasional resemblance between R and the term *refer* of ordinary language has no more significance than it would in the case of *momentum* or *undecidability*.

Specifically, we have no intuitions about R, any more than we do about *momentum* or *undecidability* in the technical sense, or about *c-command* or *autosegmental* in (other parts) of the C–R theories of syntax[18]; the terms have the meanings assigned to them. We have intuitive judgments about the notion used in such expressions as *Mary often refers to the young man as a friend (to the average man as John Doe, to good health as life's highest goal)*. But we have no such intuitions about the relation R holding between *Mary* (or *the average man, John Doe, good health, flaw*) and postulated elements of D. R and D are what we specify that they are, within a framework of theoretical explanation. We might compare R and D to P and PF, where P is a relation holding between an expression and its PF representation (between "took" and [tʰuk], perhaps), though in the latter case the concepts fit into a much better-grounded and richer theory of interface relations.

Suppose that postulation of R and D is justified by explanatory success within the C–R theory of I-language, alongside of P and PF, *c-command*, and *autosegmental*. That result lends no support to the belief that some R-like relation, call it R', holds between words and things, or things as they are imagined to be, or otherwise conceived. Postulation of such a relation would have to be justified on some grounds, as in the case of any other invented technical notion. And if we devise a relation R' holding between linguistic expressions and "things," somehow construed, we would have no intuitions about it – matters become only more obscure if we invoke unexplained notions of "community" or "public language," taken in some absolute sense. We do have intuitive judgments concerning linguistic expressions and the particular perspectives and points of view they provide for interpretation and thought. Furthermore, we might proceed to study how these expressions and perspectives enter into various human actions, such as referring. Beyond that, we enter the realm of technical discourse, deprived of intuitive judgment.

Take Putnam's influential Twin-Earth thought experiment (Putnam 1975). We can have no intuitions as to whether the term *water* has the same "reference" for Oscar and twin-Oscar: that is a matter of decision about the new technical term "reference" (some particular choice for R'). We have judgments about what Oscar and twin-Oscar might be referring to, judgments that seem to vary considerably as circumstances vary. Under some circumstances, Putnam's proposals about "same liquid," a (perhaps unknown) notion of the natural sciences, seem very plausible; under other circumstances, notions of sameness or similarity drawn from common-sense understanding seem more appropriate, yielding different judgments. It does not seem to me at all clear that there is anything general to say about these matters, or that any general or useful sense can be given to such technical notions as "wide content" (or any other notion fixing "reference") in any of the externalist interpretations.

If so, questions arise about the status of what Putnam, in his Locke lectures (Putnam 1988a: Chapter 2), calls the "social co-operation plus contribution of the environment theory of the *specification* of reference," a fuller and more adequate version of the "causal theory of reference" developed in his paper "The Meaning of 'Meaning'" (Putnam 1975) and Saul Kripke's *Naming and Necessity* (Kripke 1972), both now landmarks in the field.

"Social co-operation" has to do with "the division of linguistic labor": the role of experts in determining the reference of my terms *elm* and *beech*, for example. Putnam provides a convincing account for certain circumstances. Under some conditions, I would, indeed, agree that what I am referring to when I use the term *elm* is what is meant by an expert, perhaps an Italian gardener with whom I share only the Latin terms (though there is no meaningful sense in which we are part of the same "linguistic community" or speak a "common language"); under other conditions, probably not, but that is to be expected in an inquiry reaching as far as all of "human functional organization," virtually a study of everything. As mentioned earlier, it is not clear whether the question relates to I-language or I-belief, assuming the theoretical construction to be valid.

As for the "environment theory," it could contribute to specification of reference only if there were some coherent notion of "reference" (R') holding between linguistic expressions and things, which is far from obvious, though people do use these expressions (in various ways) to refer to things, adopting the perspectives that these expressions provide. There are circumstances in which the particular conclusions usually drawn seem appropriate, in which "same species," "same liquid," etc., help determine what I am referring to; and there are other circumstances in which they do not.[19]

It also seems unclear that metaphysical issues arise in this context. To take some of Kripke's examples, doubtless there is an intuitive difference between the judgment that Nixon would be *the same person* if he had not been elected President of the USA in 1968, while he would not be the same person if he were not a person at all (say, if he were a silicon-based person replica). But that follows from the fact that *Nixon* is a personal name, offering a way of referring to Nixon *as a person*; it has no metaphysical significance. If we abstract from the perspective provided by natural language, which appears to have no pure names in the logician's sense (the same is true of variables, at least if pronouns are considered variables, and of indexicals, if we consider their actual conditions of use in referring), then intuitions collapse: Nixon would be a different *entity*, I suppose, if his hair were combed differently. Similarly, the object in front of me is not essentially a desk or a table; that very object could be any number of different things, as interests, functions, intentions of the inventor, etc. vary. To cite some recent work, Joseph Almog's judgment that the mountain Nanga Parbat is a mountain *essentially* might be intelligible under some circumstances; however, contrary to what he assumes, his "coherent–abstraction test" seems to me to permit us, under other circumstances, to deprive Nanga Parbat of this property, leaving it as the same entity: say, if the sea level rises high enough for its top to become an island, in which case it is no more a mountain than Britain is; or if earth is piled around it up to its peak, but a millimeter away, in which case it is not a mountain but part of a plateau surrounded by a crevice, though it remains the very same entity (Almog 1991).

In summary, it is questionable that standard conclusions can survive a closer analysis of the technical notions "reference" (in some R'-like sense) or "specification of reference." There may well be justification for the notion R internal to C–R theories (basically a syntactic notion, despite appearances). But there seems to be little reason to suppose that an analogous notion R' can be given a coherent and useful formulation as a relation holding between expressions and some kind of things, divorced from particular conditions and circumstances of referring. If that is so, there will also be no reasonable inquiry into a notion of "sense" or "content" that "fixes reference" (R'), at least for natural language, though there is a promising (syntactic) inquiry into conditions for language use (including referring).

As discussed earlier, naturalistic inquiry may lead to the creation of language-like accretions to the I-language; for these, an R'-like notion may be appropriate, as terms are divested of the I-language properties that provide interpretive perspectives and semantic relations, are dissociated from I-belief, and are assigned properties lacking in natural language. These constructed systems may use resources of the I-language (pronunciation, morphology, sentence structure, etc.), or may transcend them (introducing mathematical formalisms, for example). The I-language is a product of the language faculty, abstracted from other components of the mind; this is an idealization of course, hence to be justified or rejected on the basis of its role in an explanatory framework. The picture could be extended, plausibly it seems, by distinguishing the system of common-sense belief from products of the science-forming faculty. The latter are neither I-languages nor I-belief systems, and for these it may well be appropriate to stipulate a relation R'.

Some of the motivation for externalist approaches derives from the concern to make sense of the history of science. Thus, Putnam argues that we should take the early Niels Bohr to have been referring to electrons in the quantum-theoretic sense, or we would have to "dismiss all of his 1900 beliefs as totally wrong," (Putnam 1988a) perhaps on a par with someone's beliefs about angels, a conclusion that is plainly absurd. The same is true of pre-Dalton chemists speaking of atoms. And perhaps, on the same grounds, we would say that chemists pre-Avogadro were referring to what we call atoms and molecules, though for them the terms were interchangeable, apparently.

The discussion assumes that such terms as *electron* belong to the same system as *house, water,* and pronominal anaphora, so that conclusions about *electron* carry over to notions in the latter category. That assumption seems to be implicit in Putnam's proposal that "To determine the intrinsic complexity of a task is to ask, *How hard is it in the hardest case?*," the "hardest case" for "same reference" or "same meaning" being posed by such concepts as *momentum* or *electron* in physics. But the assumption is dubious. The study of language should seek a more differentiated picture than that, and what is true of the technical constructions of the science-forming faculty might not hold for the natural-language lexicon. Suppose we grant the point nevertheless. Agreeing further that an interest in intelligibility in scientific discourse across time is a fair enough concern, still it cannot serve as the basis for a general theory of meaning; it is, after all, only one concern among many, and not a central one for the study of human psychology. Furthermore, there are internalist paraphrases. Thus we might say that in Bohr's earlier usage, he expressed beliefs that were literally false, because there was nothing of the sort he had in mind in referring to electrons; but his picture of the world and articulation of it was structurally similar enough to later conceptions so that we can distinguish his beliefs about electrons from beliefs about angels. What is more, that seems a reasonable way to proceed.

To take a far simpler example from the study of language, consider a debate some 30 years ago over the nature of phonological units. Structural phonologists postulated segments (phonemes) and phonetic features, with a certain collection of properties. Generative phonologists argued that no such entities exist, and that the actual elements have somewhat different properties. Suppose that one of these approaches looks correct (say, the latter). Were structural phonologists therefore referring all along to segments and features in the sense of generative phonology? Surely not. They flatly denied that, and were right to do so. Were they talking gibberish? Again, surely not. Structuralist phonology is intelligible; without any assumption that there are entities of the kind it postulated, much of the theory can be reinterpreted within generative phonology, with results essentially carried over. There is no principled way to determine how this is done, or to determine the "similarity of belief" between the two schools of thought or what thoughts and beliefs they shared. Sometimes it is useful to note resemblances and reformulate ideas, sometimes not. The same is true of the earlier and later Bohr. Nothing more definite is required to maintain the integrity of the scientific enterprise or a respectable notion of progress towards the truth about the world, insofar as it falls within human cognitive capacity.

It is worth noting that an analysis in these terms, eschewing externalist assumptions on fixation of reference, is consistent with the intuitions of respected figures. The discussion of the meaning of *electron*, *water*, etc. projects backwards in time, but we can project forward as well. Consider the question whether machines can think (understand, plan, solve problems, etc). By standard externalist arguments, the question should be settled by the truth about thought: what is the essence of Peter's thinking about his children, or solving a quadratic equation, or playing chess, or interpreting a sentence, or deciding whether to wear a raincoat? But that is not the way it seemed to Ludwig Wittgenstein and Alan Turing, to take two notable examples. For Wittgenstein, the question whether machines think cannot seriously be posed: "We can only say of a human being and what is like one that it thinks" (Wittgenstein 1958: 113), maybe dolls and spirits; that is the way the tool is used. Turing, in his classic 1950 paper, wrote that the question whether machines can think

may be too meaningless to deserve discussion. Nevertheless I believe that at the end of the century the use of words and general educated opinion will have altered so much that one will be able to speak of machines thinking without expecting to be contradicted. (Turing 1950: 442)

Wittgenstein and Turing do not adopt the standard externalist account. For Wittgenstein, the questions are just silly: the tools are used as they are; and if the usage changes, the language has changed, the language being nothing more than the way we use the tools. Turing too speaks of the language of "general educated opinion" changing, as interests and concerns change. In our terms, there will be a shift from the I-languages that Wittgenstein describes to new ones, in which the old word *think* will be eliminated in favor of a new word that applies to machines as well as people. To ask in 1950 whether machines think is as meaningful as the question whether airplanes and people (say, high jumpers) really fly; in English airplanes do and high jumpers don't (except metaphorically), in Hebrew neither do, in Japanese both do. Such facts tell us nothing about the (meaningless) question posed, but only about marginal and rather arbitrary variations of I-language. The question of what *atom* meant pre-Dalton, or *electron* for Bohr in 1900, seems comparable, in relevant respects, to the question of what *think* meant for Wittgenstein and Turing; not entirely comparable, because *think*, *atom*, and *electron* should probably not be regarded as belonging to a homogeneous I-language. In all these cases, the internalist perspective seems adequate, not only to the intuitions of Wittgenstein and Turing, but to an account of what is transpiring; or what might happen as circumstances and interests vary.

Perhaps one might argue that recent semantic theories supersede the intuitions of Wittgenstein and Turing because of their explanatory success. That does not, however, seem a promising idea; explanatory success will hardly bear that burden. In general, we have little reason now to believe that more than a Wittgensteinian assembly of particulars lies beyond the domain of internalist inquiry, which is, however, far richer and informative than Wittgenstein, John Austin (1962), and others supposed.

Naturalistic inquiry will always fall short of intentionality. At least in these terms, "intentionality won't be reduced and won't go away," as Putnam puts it, and "language speaking" will remain not "theoretically explicable" (Putnam 1998a: 1). The study of C–R systems, including "internalist semantics," appears to be, for now, the most promising form of naturalistic inquiry, with a reasonably successful research program; understanding of performance systems is more rudimentary, but within the range of inquiry, in some respects at least. These approaches raise problems of the kind familiar throughout the natural sciences, but none that seem qualitatively different. Pursuing them, we can hope to learn a good deal about the devices that are used to articulate thoughts, interpret, and so on. They leave untouched many other questions, but it remains to be shown that these are real questions, not pseudo-questions that indicate topics of inquiry that one might hope to explore – but little more than that.

3   Language and interpretation: philosophical reflections and empirical inquiry

In the philosophical literature of the past 40 years, there have been several influential currents that seem to me problematic in important, even essential respects. I have in mind, in the first place, approaches that take as their point of departure certain conceptions of how language is studied, or should be studied, by the empirical scientist – or the "field linguist," to use the terms of Quine's familiar paradigm. One can include here Quine, Donald Davidson, and others who have moved towards a form of pragmatism and "naturalized epistemology," incorporating questions thought to be of philosophical significance within their conception of empirical science, but also others who adopt a different starting point: Michael Dummett, and many of those influenced by Wittgenstein and ordinary language philosophy, for example.

To illustrate the flavor of these ideas, take some comments of Richard Rorty in Lepore (1986) on Davidson. He writes that "Davidson is surely right that Quine 'saved philosophy of language as a serious subject' by getting rid of the analytic–synthetic distinction. Quine's best argument for doing so was that the distinction is of no use to the field linguist" (Rorty 1986: 339).

As for the "field linguist," all that he "has to go on is his observation of the way in which linguistic is aligned with non-linguistic behavior in the course of the native's interaction with his environment, an interaction which [the linguist] takes to be guided by rules of action . . . ," specifically, the "regulative principle" that "most of the native's rules are the same as ours, which is to say that most of them are true" (p. 340; "rules" here apparently referring to beliefs). We need not be concerned about "a conceptual scheme, a way of viewing things, a perspective (or . . . a language, or a cultural tradition), [because] the field linguist does not need them, [so] therefore philosophy does not need them either" (p. 344). Quine and Davidson agree that "a theory of meaning for a language is what comes out of empirical research into linguistic behavior," when this is properly pursued, in accord with the doctrines of "holism and behaviorism" (p. 352).

This line of thought, Rorty continues, leads to a form of pragmatism that he espouses and attributes to James and Dewey, including crucially the denial of any relations of "'being made true' which hold between beliefs and the world." Rather, "We understand all there is to know about the relation of beliefs to the world when we understand their causal relations with the world" (p. 335).

Putting aside the conclusions that Rorty reaches,[1] consider his assumptions. If the best argument for dispensing with the analytic–synthetic distinction is that it is of no use to the field linguist, then virtually everyone who actually works in descriptive semantics, or ever has, must be seriously in error, since such work is shot through with assumptions about connections of meaning, which will (in particular) induce examples of the analytic-synthetic distinction. One would be hard put to find studies of language that do not assign structures and describe the meaning of *kill*, *so*, etc., in such a way that there is a qualitative distinction – determined by the language itself – between the sentences "John killed Bill, so Bill is dead," and "John killed Bill, so John is dead." Or, to take another case, it would be difficult to find a study of referential dependence in natural language that does not conclude that the language itself determines that the relation holds between *Mary* and *herself* in (1), but not when the same expression is embedded in the context "I wonder who –," yielding (2).

(1)   Mary expects to feed herself.

(2)   I wonder who Mary expects to feed herself.

Such syntactic–semantic properties will induce cases of the analytic–synthetic distinction; thus they will yield a distinction between "Mary expects to feed herself, so Mary expects to feed *Mary*" (analytic, with the three occurrences of *Mary* taken to be coreferential), and "I wonder who Mary expects to feed herself, so I wonder who Mary expects to feed *Mary*" (not analytic, under the same interpretation). But what Quine is alleged to have demonstrated goes beyond the matter of analyticity, reaching the conclusion that there are no semantic connections that can be attributed to the language faculty itself as distinct from our general systems of belief; elsewhere, Rorty takes this to be one of the two fundamental discoveries that undermine a traditional world picture.

As is well known, Quine and others have offered their own account of these distinctions. I return to these proposals, and how they might be evaluated in accordance with the canons of inquiry of the natural sciences, but merely note here that reference to "the field linguist" can surely not be understood as reference to those who actually do linguistic work. Rather, it has a normative character, referring to the way such work ought to be done, keeping to the conditions of "holism and behaviorism" legislated by the philosopher, but not followed in practice by the errant scientist. While it might turn out on investigation that this stance is justifiable, those with an appreciation of the history of the discipline might be pardoned some initial skepticism.

To select another example to illustrate the flavor of these discussions, consider Dummett's argument in the same volume (Dummett 1986) that the "fundamental sense" in which we must understand the concept of language is the sense in which Dutch and German are different languages (he gives a different example, but the point is the same), each of them a particular social practice "in which people engage," a practice that "is learned from others and is constituted by rules which it is part of social custom to follow" (p. 473). Thus Dutch and German exist in this "fundamental sense," "independently of any particular speakers"; every individual speaker "has" such a language, but typically has only a "partial, and partially erroneous, grasp of the language." The intended import of Dummett's proposal is far-reaching. He is telling us what notion of "language" is essential for philosophical purposes, for the theory of meaning in particular; and also, as he makes clear, it is this concept of language that is in his view required for explaining the use of language, specifically, for understanding "what long-range theory someone brings to a first linguistic encounter with another." It is, therefore, a proposal that bears on the empirical study of language, of people, of what they know and what they do. Perhaps he means to allow that linguists may follow some different course for their special concerns, but clearly these proposals bear on the proper practice in empirical inquiry into language and its use.

Here the paradoxical flavor is of a somewhat different order. It lies in the conflict between Dummett's proposal and the commonplace assumption in empirical practice that there is no useful general sense in which we can characterize "language" so that Dutch and German are two distinct "languages," which people know only "partially" and "erroneously." This is so whether we are studying language structure, psycholinguistics, language change, typology, problems of communication, or whatever. People who live near the Dutch border can communicate quite well with those living on the German side, but they speak different languages in accordance with the sense of the term that Dummett argues is "fundamental"; and those on the German side of the border, with their "partial knowledge" of the "language German", may understand nothing spoken by people living in some other region, who "have" a different "partial knowledge" of the "language German" in Dummett's sense. It is for such reasons as these that no such concept plays any role in empirical inquiry into language or psychology. Such terms as "English" and "Japanese" are used for general expository discourse, but with the understanding that their common-sense usage, which Dummett rather uncritically adopts, is to be abandoned when we turn to actual study of language, behavior, and communication.[2] If Dummett's concept is indeed fundamental for empirical inquiry and for philosophical purposes, then either philosophy, or the empirical study of language and behavior, or both, are in deep trouble, for reasons that should be familiar. The concept of language that Dummett takes to be essential involves complex and obscure sociopolitical, historical, cultural, and normative-teleological elements. Such elements may be of some interest for the sociology of identification within various social and political communities and the study of authority structure, but they plainly lie far beyond any useful inquiry into the nature of language or the psychology of users of language.

To take one example, consider the study of language acquisition. In ordinary usage, we say that a child of five and a foreign adult are on their way towards acquiring English, but we have no way to designate whatever it is that they "have." The child, in the normal course of events, will come to "have" English (at least partially and erroneously), though the foreigner probably will not. But if all adults were suddenly to die and children were somehow to survive, then whatever it is they are speaking would be a human language, though one that does not now exist. Ordinary usage provides no useful way to describe any of this, since it involves too many disparate and obscure concerns and interests, which is one reason why the concept of language that Dummett adopts is useless for actual inquiry. This matter is of some importance when we consider the reliance on notions of "misuse of language," "community norms," "social practice," and "rule following" that are often adopted as if they are sufficiently clear; they are not.[3]

In this connection, it is perhaps worthwhile to recall some further truisms; in rational inquiry, in the natural sciences or elsewhere, there is no such subject as "the study of everything." Thus it is no part of physics to determine exactly how a particular body moves under the influence of every particle or force in the universe, with possible human intervention, etc. This is not a topic. Rather, in rational inquiry we idealize to selected domains in such a way (we hope) as to permit us to discover crucial features of the world. Data and observations, in the sciences, have an instrumental character. They are of no particular interest in themselves, but only insofar as they constitute evidence that permits one to determine fundamental features of the real world, within a course of inquiry that is invariably undertaken under sharp idealizations, often implicit and simply common understanding, but always present. The study of "language" in Dummett's sense verges on "the study of everything," and is therefore not a useful topic of inquiry, though one might hope, perhaps, to build up to a study of aspects of such questions in terms of what comes to be understood about particular components of this hopeless amalgam.

The conception of language as a "social practice" that Dummett and others propose raises further questions, as becomes clear when it is applied to concrete examples. Consider again examples (1) and (2) on page 47. In example (1), *feed herself* is taken to be predicated of Mary, but in example (2) it is predicated of some (female) person distinct from Mary; thus from example (2) it follows that I wonder which female person Mary expects to feed that very person, but not that I wonder which person Mary expects to feed Mary herself. The example raises many pertinent questions, among them, how we know these facts. The answer seems to be that the initial state of the shared language faculty incorporates certain principles concerning referential dependence (Binding Theory); and when certain options left undetermined in the initial state are fixed by elementary experience, then we have no more choice as to how to interpret examples (1) and (2) than we have about whether to perceive something as a red triangle or as a person. Social custom appears to have nothing to do with the matter in such cases, though in all of them, early experience helps set certain details of the invariant, biologically-determined mechanisms of the mind/ brain. The same seems to be true rather generally. Taken literally at least, the proposals of Dummett and others concerning "social practice" appear to be false, as a matter of empirical fact. At the very least, some argument would be required to show why they should be considered seriously.

If language is construed as a social practice in the manner of these discussions, then it is tempting to understand knowledge of language as the learned ability to engage in such practices, as Dummett suggests or – more generally – as an ability that can be exercised by speaking, understanding, reading, talking to oneself, etc.: "to know a language just is to have the ability to do these and similar things" (Kenny 1984: 138).[4] The temptation is reinforced by a common construal of knowledge more generally as a kind of ability. This view contrasts with the conception of a language as a generative procedure that assigns structural descriptions to linguistic expressions, knowledge of language being the internal representation of such a procedure in the brain (in the mind, as we may say when speaking about the brain at a certain level of abstraction). From this point of view, ability to use one's language (to put one's knowledge to use) is sharply distinguished from having such knowledge. The latter conception has two primary virtues:

1. It seems to be the right way to approach the study of human knowledge – knowledge of language in particular – within the general framework of the natural sciences, and it has proven a highly productive approach.
2. It is very much in accord with normal pre-analytic usage, a secondary but not entirely insignificant matter.

In contrast, the approach in terms of practical ability has proven entirely unproductive and can be sustained only by understanding "ability" in a way that departs radically from ordinary usage.

To see why this is so, suppose that Jones, a speaker of some variety of what we call "English" in informal usage, improves his ability to speak his language by taking a public-speaking course, or loses this ability because of an injury or disease (then recovers that ability, say, with a drug). Note that a speaker of "Japanese", under the same circumstances, would recover *Japanese*, not English, with the same drug, and plainly recovery in such cases differs radically from acquisition; a child could not acquire English or Japanese without any evidence. In all such cases, something remains constant, some property K, while ability to speak, understand, etc. varies. In ordinary usage, we say that K is knowledge of language; thus Jones's knowledge remained constant while his ability to put his knowledge to use improved, declined, recovered, etc. The account in terms of internal representation of a generative procedure accords with informal usage in this case. Note further that other evidence (say, from autopsy, were enough known about the brain sciences) might lead us to conclude that Smith, who never recovered English, not having taken the drug, nevertheless retained his knowledge of English intact after having completely lost his ability to speak and understand. (For more extensive discussion of these matters, and of possible alternative accounts, see Chomsky 1980; 1986.)

If knowledge is ability, then the property K must be a kind of ability, though plainly not ability in the quite useful normal sense of the word, since ability varied while K remained constant. We must therefore contrive a new technical sense of the term "ability," call it *K-ability*. Then K-ability remained constant while ability varied.[5] K-ability is completely divorced from ability, and has the properties of the old concept of knowledge; it might as well be called "knowledge," doctrinal matters aside.

It is rather ironic that these moves should be presented as in the spirit of the later Wittgenstein, who constantly argued against the practice of constructing artificial concepts, divorced from ordinary usage, in defense of certain philosophical doctrines. In fact, the Wittgensteinian construal of knowledge as a species of ability seems to be a paradigm example of the practice that Wittgenstein held to be a fundamental source of philosophical error.

Notice that similar considerations show that *knowing-how* – for example, knowing how to ride a bicycle – cannot be analyzed in terms of abilities, dispositions, etc.; rather, there appears to be an irreducible cognitive element. Notice finally that an account of knowledge in terms of ability, taken in anything like its normal sense, has proven utterly unproductive. One might try accounting for the simple examples (1) and (2) in terms of Jones's abilities, for example. No such endeavor has ever been undertaken, and a close look at the problems makes it reasonably clear why it would have no hope of success.

The paradoxical flavor of ideas in the range I have been sampling becomes clearer when we look more closely at some of the specific injunctions. Take again Rorty's observation, taken as obvious without discussion, that "all the linguist has to go on is his observation of the way in which linguistic is aligned with non-linguistic behavior in the course of the native's interaction with the environment" (Rorty 1986: 339), apart from the "regulative principle" that the native informant is generally speaking truly. This conception, he notes, is drawn from Quine and Davidson. Thus in Quine's familiar paradigm of "radical translation" (Quine 1960; 1987), "field linguists" observing Jones must support their hypotheses *entirely* in terms of observation of Jones's behavior (or that of members of the "Jungle community," taken to be homogeneous; if it is not homogeneous, none of the arguments will go through, and if it is homogeneous, we may dismiss the community in favor of Jones without loss for these purposes, as I will do). I should note that in referring to Quine, textual questions arise, since – in response to queries and criticism – he has given many different versions of his paradigm, and these are not consistent (see Chomsky 1975: 187f., 198ff.). However, it is the one just cited, which Davidson and Rorty adopt, that is necessary if we are to be able to draw from Quine's paradigm any of the conclusions that are held to be important.

Before proceeding, let us note again that these prescriptions are radically different from the actual practice of the "field linguist." They are also completely foreign to the standard methods of the natural sciences. In the philosophical literature, the issues are generally discussed with regard to the theory of meaning and, in particular, with regard to aspects of the theory of meaning about which little is known (not, say, in connection with such matters as referential dependence, about which a good deal is understood). This is dubious practice, because it means that controls on speculation by empirical knowledge and theoretical understanding are very slight. But if the doctrine has any validity, it should hold with regard to all of our attributions of linguistic competence, and Quine, at least, has been clear that this is so. Thus he explicitly argues that the same considerations hold when his "field linguist" alleges that in the sentence "John contemplated the problem" there are two phrases: the noun phrase *John* and the verb phrase *contemplated the problem*, not, say, the two phrases *John contemplated* and *the problem* or *John contemp* and *lated the problem*. According to Quine, at least when he is keeping to the assumptions required for his well-known conclusions to follow, this attribution of some property (knowledge, or whatever we choose to call it) to the informant Jones must be based exclusively on evidence about *Jones's behavior*; in fact, evidence used in accord with highly restrictive canons that he outlines. The same would also be true in the study of sound structure, relations of anaphors and antecedents, or whatever.[6]

It is worth noting that no linguist, or empirical scientist generally, would ever agree to be bound by such strictures. A comparable assumption in biology would be that in testing hypotheses about embryological development of humans, we cannot consider evidence obtained from the study of E. coli, or fruit flies, or apes, or physics. To mention one crucial case, in actual practice, every linguist approaches the study of a particular language on the basis of assumptions drawn from the study of other languages. Thus any linguist operating by the norms of the sciences would readily use evidence derived from the study of Japanese to help ground assumptions about Jones's knowledge of English. The logic is straightforward, and quite correct. There is overwhelming empirical evidence that people are not genetically "tuned" to acquire one rather than another language; rather, the "initial state" of their language faculty may be assumed to be uniform to a very good approximation. Presented with an array of evidence, the child acquires a specific language, making use of the resources of the initial state that determine a substantial part of the knowledge (competence) acquired; the initial state can be regarded as a fixed biologically-determined function that maps evidence available into acquired knowledge, uniformly for all languages.[7] Study of Japanese may, of course, provide us with evidence, perhaps compelling evidence, about the initial state, namely, by means of a comparison between what comes to be known and what is presented, the two being mediated by the resources of the initial state. If speakers of Japanese employ some formal property of language structure (say, *c-command*) in interpreting referential dependence, and the evidence available to the

Japanese child does not somehow "compel" or is not even conducive to this uniform result, we are entitled to attribute to the initial state a version of Binding Theory, incorporating this property and relevant principles involving it, and thus to explain the facts observed. But the initial state is shared by the English speaker Jones, and hypotheses about his initial state will of course have consequences as to the proper description of the cognitive state he attains. The conclusions derived from Japanese concerning Jones's knowledge of English might be far-reaching. Thus evidence about referential dependence in Japanese might prove relevant for determining the position of phrase boundaries in English.[8]

All of this is just standard scientific practice, never questioned – or even discussed, because it is so uncontroversial – in the natural sciences. However, Quine and those influenced by his paradigm are enjoining the "field linguist" to depart radically from the procedures of the sciences, limiting themselves to a small part of the relevant evidence, selected in accordance with behaviorist dogma; and also to reject the standard procedures used in theory construction in the sciences. The point is not academic: the normal practice of descriptive linguists crucially exploits these assumptions, which again should be the merest truisms.

We may put the point differently. The linguist and the child face radically different tasks. The child, endowed with certain innate capacities, acquires knowledge of a language – automatically, and with little if any choice in the matter. The linguist is trying to find out what knowledge the child acquires, and what innate properties of the mind/brain are responsible for this process of growth of knowledge (trying to find out what the child knows in advance of experience, to use a locution that seems to be quite appropriate). The linguist will quite properly use conclusions about innate properties, however derived, for the description of the knowledge attained, in particular, for the study of meaning, this domain having the same status as any other.

In fact, Quine's injunctions, consistently applied, would be still more extreme than this example indicates. Thus evidence from language pathology, or genetic variation, or neural structure, or biochemistry, or in fact evidence from any source, would be regarded by any scientist as potentially relevant in principle to determining the nature of the initial state or the state of knowledge attained, since these are simply elements of the natural biological world. Quine too insists on this point with regard to study of the natural world, apart from the study of humans above the neck when undertaken by "linguists," in his sense of this term. If it could be shown that some facts about the neural structure of the brain provide a natural realization of rule systems of one kind (say, with the breakdown of "John contemplated the problem" into the two phrases *John* and *contemplated the problem*), but not other kinds, then this line of argument would be acceptable in the sciences to help settle the question of what is the correct description of Jones's knowledge – the cognitive state attained by Jones (the question of the choice of constituent structure in the case in question). The same is true with regard to the theory of meaning, or any empirical inquiry. But all of these paths, familiar in the natural sciences, are excluded by fiat under the Quinean conditions on the work of the "linguist" in accord with the paradigm that is widely adopted in the philosophical literature.

Quine has qualified these doctrines in interesting ways. A closer look at these qualifications reveals more clearly the arbitrary character of the stipulations imposed and the persistent misunderstanding of the empirical issues. As an example of arbitrary stipulation, consider Quine's discussion of the evidence that might lead us to assign one or another constituent structure to the sentences of Jones's English (Quine 1986). If this evidence derives from psycholinguistic experiments on perceived displacement of clicks,[9] then it counts; if the evidence derives from conditions on referential dependence in Japanese or on the formation of causative constructions in numerous languages, then it does not count – though this is evidence interpreted in the normal manner of the natural sciences, along the lines discussed a moment ago. Perhaps Quine might be interpreted as holding that evidence of the former type (so-called "psychological evidence") is in fact more powerful and persuasive than the so-called "linguistic evidence"; if so, this would simply be another error, since the opposite is the case, for the present at least. In fact, Quine appears to hold that the evidence differs in its epistemological character, a notion that is completely untenable. Evidence does not come labelled "for confirming theories" ("psychological evidence") or "for purposes of 'simplicity and general translatability'" ("linguistic evidence"). It is just evidence, good or bad, compelling or noncompelling, given the theoretical frameworks in which it can be interpreted for the purposes of sharpening or confirming hypotheses.

As an example of misunderstanding of empirical issues, consider Quine's discussion of the so-called "coordinate structure constraint," a descriptive generalization that covers, for example, the radical difference in status between the interrogative expressions derived by questioning "Mary" in the sentences "John saw Bill and Mary" and "John saw Bill with Mary": that is, the difference between "who did John see Bill and?," "who did John see Bill with?" Quine concludes that the "striking uniformity" exhibited in this constraint is not "a hint of a trait of all language," but "a hint of genetic kinship of the languages that seem most readily grammatized in these terms."[10] This conclusion, however, is based on a serious misunderstanding of the empirical issues at stake. The problem is to explain how each child knows the relevant difference between "who did John see Bill and?" and "who did John see Bill with?" It cannot be that the child relies on evidence from the history of language, and the child typically has no relevant experience to determine (by "induction," or whatever) that the simple rule "Front-*wh*-phrase" is somehow blocked in the expression "John saw Bill and who" but not in "John saw Bill with who" (in colloquial English). Children do not, for example, produce "who did John see Bill and?," then to be informed by their parents that this is not the way it is done; and languages have not "drifted" to incorporate this "simplification" of the rule of question-formation over many millennia.[11] The problem, in short, is one of poverty of stimulus, and speculations about genetic kinship of languages have nothing whatsoever to do with it, in this and innumerable other similar cases.[12]

A similar refusal to permit the study of language to be pursued in the manner of the natural sciences is illustrated in other connections. Consider Davidson's article "A Nice Derangement of Epitaphs" in the volume cited earlier (Lepore 1986). Davidson considers the thesis that the goal of the descriptive study of meaning is to construct "an explicit theory" that "is a model of the interpreter's linguistic competence," a "recursive theory of a certain sort," and that we can "describe what an interpreter can do" only by appeal to such a theory. He then proceeds: "It does not add anything to this thesis to say that if the theory does correctly describe the competence of an interpreter, some mechanisms in the interpreter must correspond to the theory" (Davidson 1986b: 438). Similar points have been made by Dummett and others.[13]

For anyone approaching these problems from the standpoint of the natural sciences, the final comment quoted is utterly wrongheaded. If it had any validity, the analogous comment would apply in the study of visual perception, or chemistry. As elsewhere, it adds a great deal to the thesis to say that "some mechanisms in the interpreter . . . correspond to the theory." That is, natural scientists who construct a theory that "describes what an interpreter can do" will proceed to attribute to the subject certain fixed and explicit mechanisms that would have the properties assumed in this descriptive account, not others. The attribution might be at an abstract level, in terms of mentally-represented rule systems, or in terms of other abstract entities such as neural nets, or in terms of cellular structure, or whatever; all of this is standard natural science. Having proceeded to attribute specific structure and mechanisms to the person's mind/brain – often at some remove from unknown "more elementary" physical mechanisms – the natural scientist is then in a position to test the theory in terms of a wide array of evidence, for example, evidence drawn from other languages in the manner just illustrated, or evidence from pathology or the brain sciences or biochemistry. Davidson's injunction blocks these efforts to employ the methods of rational inquiry in the sciences to determine whether the postulated account of the interpreter is indeed true, and to modify it if (as is likely) it is not.

The same problem arises when Quine, David Lewis (1983), Dummett, and many others object that some philosophical problem arises when linguists attribute to a speaker–hearer a specific internalized rule-system, and then seek to determine whether this theory of the person is true by the standard methods of the sciences. Perhaps this is even pure "folly," as Quine has argued (1972: 447), to be overcome by proper reflection on methodology. The perceived problem is that for a fixed array of observed behavior, or a fixed infinite set of utterances selected on some obscure basis and taken by the philosopher to be "the language," it is of course possible to construct infinitely many different theories that are consistent with this evidence ("grammars," as they are sometimes called); it is therefore held to be an unwarranted move to postulate that one of them is "true" and others "false" – unless, Quine sometimes holds, there is "psychological evidence" – with its mysterious properties that "linguistic evidence" lacks – to support one or another hypothesis. The argument is often buttressed by an analogy to the study of formal languages, which are completely irrelevant and highly misleading in this connection. If valid, the argument would hold throughout the sciences; in fact, it is nothing more than a form of skepticism that no one takes seriously in the study of the natural world for reasons that were clear by the seventeenth century, as Richard Popkin observes (Popkin 1979).[14] The natural scientist will attribute to the subject a specific system, not some other one (a "grammar," to use a misleading term), and will then proceed to determine whether this assumption is correct by seeking evidence of as wide a variety as possible, including crucially evidence from other languages, along the lines just discussed. Of course, there will always remain empirical indeterminacy, since this is empirical science, not mathematics, but that is all there is to say about the matter. A considerable literature exists arguing the contrary, but it is based on fundamental fallacies of reasoning.[15] Among these fallacies are the mistaken assumptions just discussed: that evidence about Jones's competence can only be drawn from Jones's behavior (interpreted in terms of the regulative principle about truth), and that it adds nothing to a description of Jones's behavior to attribute to Jones a specific internal mechanism, perhaps a particular system of rules or some form of neural organization that realizes them.

The point can be illustrated, again, with the matter of phrase-structure boundaries. Suppose we have two kinds of evidence for the placement of the major boundary after the subject in "John – contemplated the problem," evidence from referential dependence in Japanese ("linguistic evidence") and evidence from perceptual displacement of clicks ("psychological evidence"). The first kind of evidence is subject to the familiar sort of indeterminacy. So is the second. Suppose that under experimental conditions established to yield the right results (typically, after many attempts that go wrong), clicks will be perceptually displaced to the subject–predicate boundary, not the verb–object boundary. These results can be interpreted as supporting the conclusion that the structure is [NP – V NP], not [NP V – NP] or [NP – V – NP]. But it is easy to apply Quine's argument to show that there is "no fact of the matter" in this case (Quine 1960: 303; see Chomsky 1980: 15). Plainly, there are many other interpretations of the experimental results. Perhaps clicks are perceptually displaced to the middle of a constituent, not its boundary; or perhaps the subject is responding by identifying the phrase-structure boundary directly below the major one. All other relevant experiments could be reinterpreted along similar lines, as can certainly be done in principle – though it is not so simple in practice, in the case of the "psychological" or "linguistic" evidence. The issues are the same throughout; or rather, there are no issues relevant here, since they hold of empirical inquiry generally.

When conclusions are drawn about phrase boundaries or other aspects of language on the basis of "linguistic evidence," Quine is reluctant to accept them "without further light on the nature of the supposed equipment,"[16] but when the same conclusions are based on "psychological evidence," these qualms do not arise. This epistemological dualism makes no sense whatsoever; it is a long step backwards from traditional metaphysical dualism, which was a rational reaction, on assumptions now known to be faulty,[17] to perceived empirical problems. The qualms, such as they are, are in principle the same, whatever the evidence on which conclusions are based, and are simply features of empirical inquiry. As for the "supposed equipment," it raises no problems of principle that differ from those characteristic of all theory construction in the empirical sciences.

Yet another paradox arises within this framework. Linguists, it is argued, are not permitted to attribute one particular language system rather than others to the individual or idealized community that they are studying;[18] they are not permitted to explore what is true of the brain, described at the level at which we construct rule systems and the like. But something is true of the brain; there is something about my brain that is more or less like yours and crucially different from the brain of a speaker of Swahili. Therefore someone should be permitted to study these aspects of the real world, but not linguists, who are restricted to inquiry into Jones's behavior and may not proceed to attribute specific mechanisms to Jones's mind/brain and to use evidence from other languages (or from any domain, in principle) to verify the accuracy of their conclusions about these mechanisms. Accepting these terminological strictures about what the linguist must do, the rational step is to abandon linguistics (including the study of meaning in accord with the conditions stipulated in the Quinean paradigm). Having abandoned these pointless pursuits, we may now turn to this other subject, where we are permitted to attribute specific mechanisms to Jones's mind/brain and to investigate these hypotheses by the methods of the sciences, using whatever evidence is at hand: in fact, the actual practice of linguists that is condemned in this curious, though extremely influential tradition in modern philosophy, which, in a final irony, prides itself on its "naturalism" and adherence to the methods of the sciences.

In his most recent efforts to justify the strictures he imposes, Quine (1987) offers the following argument. For the linguist, he argues, "the behaviorist approach is mandatory." The reason is that in acquiring language, "we depend strictly on overt behavior in observable situations ... There is nothing in linguistic meaning, then, beyond what is to be gleaned from overt behavior in observable circumstances" (Quine 1987: 5), and the same holds true, by parity of argument, for the study of pronunciation, phrase structure, or whatever aspect of language we choose. Furthermore, as he makes explicit once again, the relevant behavior for the linguist is that of the natives to whom he or she is imputing knowledge of language: "If translators disagree on the translation of a Jungle sentence but no behavior on the part of the Jungle people [tacitly assumed to be homogeneous] could bear on the disagreement, then there is simply no fact of the matter," (Quine 1990: 38) and the linguist who holds that there are facts to be discovered, and that some theories (grammars) are correct and others not, is guilty of serious methodological error or pure "folly" (recall that the "translator" stands for the language learner as well[19] and that the same argument holds for pronunciation, phrase structure, etc.).

Consider now the following analogous argument. In reaching its final physical structure in the passage from embryo to mature state, the organism depends strictly on nutrition provided from outside (including oxygen, etc.). There is nothing in the physical structure of the mature organism, then, beyond what is to be gleaned from the nutritional inputs. The student of human development and its outcome, then, must limit attention to these inputs; for the biologist, "the nutritionist approach is mandatory." The argument is the same as Quine's, and we see at once why it is untenable. True, the embryo "depends" on the nutritional environment just as the language learner "depends" on overt behavior. But what does the term "depends" include? Here we turn to the structure of the organism, which we may think of abstractly as a mapping M of external inputs into mature state. In the absence of such structure, observed behavior will lead to no knowledge of language and nutrition will lead to no growth. Quine of course recognizes this. Thus Quine's field linguist, pursuing the path of the language learner, "tentatively associates a native's utterance with the observed concurrent situation," and is permitted to make use of other hypotheses that allegedly correspond to capacities with which the language learner is endowed. If clarified, these hypotheses would constitute a theory of the innate structure of the organism and the mapping M.

As is agreed on all sides, without innate structure there is no effect of the external environment in language (or other) growth; in particular, without innate structure Jones could not have developed in a specific way from embryo to person, and his language faculty could not have assumed the state of mature competence that underlies and accounts for Jones's behavior. The child is endowed with this innate structure and therefore grows to maturity along a course that is largely inner-directed; the task of the scientist is to discover what the innate endowment is and what is the nature of the state attained. Currently, the best theory is that the initial state of the language faculty incorporates certain general principles of language structure, including phonetic and semantic principles, and that the mature state of competence is a generative procedure that assigns structural descriptions to expressions and interacts with the motor and perceptual system and other cognitive systems of the mind/brain to yield semantic and phonetic interpretations of utterances. A vast range of empirical evidence is relevant in principle to determining just how this proposal should be spelled out in detail. Again, all of this is normal science, yielding theories that are true or false[20] regarding Jones's competence and his initial state, part of the human biological endowment. Perhaps this approach should be abandoned in terms of some other conception, now unavailable; however, to establish this conclusion it does not suffice to demand that the linguist abandon the methods of the sciences.

As in his earlier formulations of these ideas, Quine's specific stipulations about the innate structure (hence the mapping M) are completely arbitrary and, apart from their historical antecedents, here irrelevant. There is no reason to accept them in the case of language, just as comparable dogmatism about "dependence" would be rejected out of hand in the study of other aspects of the growth of organisms. Furthermore, there is compelling evidence that they are false, insofar as they are explicit. As in the study of physical development generally, the rational investigator will dismiss these dogmatic assumptions about the nature of "dependence" (that is about innate structure) along with other doctrines such as those just sketched, and will use whatever evidence can be found concerning the structure of the organism, the mapping M, and the nature of the states attained in particular cases. The conclusions that Quine, Davidson, Rorty and many others draw remain unargued. Nothing can be resurrected from the Quinean picture with regard to these matters, so far as I can see, though some of his conclusions – in particular, with regard to "meaning holism" – may well turn out to be correct, at least in large part.

Let us return now to the "analytic-synthetic" distinction, and the Davidsonian argument (Davidson 1986a: 313) that by "getting rid of it," Quine "saved philosophy of language as a serious subject." Recall that what is at issue here is not simply this distinction, but the question of language-determined semantic connections generally. As I mentioned, we cannot appeal to Rorty's argument, attributed to Quine, that the "field linguist" finds the distinction "of no use." In practice, semantic structure is regularly attributed to lexical items in descriptive work and theoretical studies on the semantics of natural language, and from these and other structural properties, semantic connections of various kinds are derivable, including analytic connections. There are good reasons for these standard assumptions about lexical structure. Acquisition of lexical items poses what is sometimes called "Plato's problem" in a very sharp form. As anyone who has tried to construct a dictionary or to work in descriptive semantics is aware, it is a very difficult matter to describe the meaning of a word, and such meanings have great intricacy and involve the most remarkable assumptions, even in the case of very simple concepts, such as what counts as a nameable thing. At peak periods of language acquisition, children are acquiring ("learning") many words a day, perhaps a dozen or more, meaning that they are acquiring words on very few exposures, even just one. This would appear to indicate that the concepts are already available, with much or all of their intricacy and structure predetermined, and that the child's task is to assign labels to concepts, as might be done with limited evidence given sufficiently rich innate structure. And these conceptual structures appear to yield semantic connections of a kind that will, in particular, induce an analytic-synthetic distinction, as a matter of empirical fact.

To the extent that anything is understood about lexical items and their nature, it seems that they are based on conceptual structures of a specific and closely integrated type. It has been argued plausibly that concepts of a locational nature – including goal and source of action, object moved, etc. – enter widely into lexical structure, often in quite abstract ways. In addition, notions like actor, recipient of action, instrument, event, intention, causation and others are pervasive elements of lexical structure, with their specific properties and interrelations. Consider, say, the words *chase* or *persuade*. They clearly involve a reference to human intention. To chase Jones is not only to follow him, but to follow him with the intent of staying on his path, perhaps to catch him. To persuade Smith to do something is to cause him to decide or intend to do it; if he never decides or intends to do it, we have not succeeded in persuading him. Furthermore, he must decide or intend by his own volition, not under duress; if we say that the police persuaded Smith to confess by torture, we are using the term ironically. Since these facts are known essentially without evidence, it must be that the child approaches language with an intuitive understanding of concepts involving intending, causation, goal of action, event, and so on; furthermore, it must be that the child places the words that are heard in a nexus that is permitted by the principles of universal grammar, which provide the framework for thought and language, and are common to human languages as systems that enter into various aspects of human life. These elements also appear to enter into an integrated "conceptual scheme," a component of the initial state of the language faculty that is fleshed out in specific ways, with predetermined scope and limits, in the course of language growth, one aspect of cognitive development. There may be revision and restructuring of such conceptual schemes, (see Carey 1985), but care must be taken to separate out the various factors that enter into the course of development, including, quite possibly, genetically-determined maturation that yields effects perceived only in late stages of cognitive growth.

Notice again that we appear to have connections of meaning in such cases as these; we have a rather clear distinction between truths of meaning and truths of fact. Thus, if John persuaded Bill to go to college, then Bill at some point decided or intended to go to college and did so without duress; otherwise, John did not persuade Bill to go to college. Similarly if John killed Bill, then Bill is dead (though John may or may not be, depending on the facts). These are truths of meaning, not of fact. The *a priori* framework of human thought, within which language is acquired, provides necessary connections among concepts, reflected in connections of meaning among words and, more broadly, among expressions involving these words, as in the example of referential dependence mentioned earlier. Syntactic relations provide a rich array of further examples. For example, there seems to be a clear distinction between the sentence "everyone who lives upstairs lives upstairs" and "everyone who lives upstairs is happy." Quine appears to believe that this distinction is more problematic and obscure than his distinction between "grammatical" and "ungrammatical," which he regards as somehow crucial for the linguist's investigations.[21] The opposite is the case. In fact, an absolute distinction between "grammatical" and "ungrammatical" appears to have little if any significance. It can be established one way or another or, perhaps better, not at all, since it is doubtful that the concept, in Quine's sense, plays any role in the theory of language. The reasons were discussed in the earliest work in generative grammar; this work is, in fact, the only work in which an effort was made to develop such a concept in some manner that might be relevant to linguistic theory, but in terms that were long ago understood to be inappropriate.[22]

It appears, then, that one of the central conclusions of modern philosophy is rather dubious: namely, the contention – often held to have been established by work of Quine and others – that one can make no principled distinction between questions of fact and questions of meaning, that it is a matter of more or less deeply held belief. This conclusion has been supported by reflection on an artificially narrow class of examples; among them concepts that have little or no relational structure. In the case of such sentences as "cats are animals," for example, it is not easy to find evidence to decide whether the sentence is true as a matter of meaning or fact, or whether there is an answer to the question in this case, and there has been much inconclusive controversy about the matter. When we turn to concepts with an inherent relational structure such as *persuade* or *chase*, or to more complex syntactic constructions such as those exhibiting referential dependence or causative and relative constructions, then it seems that semantic connections are readily discerned. Contrary to what Rorty and others assert, this is the common assumption of empirical work in the study of linguistic meaning, and, furthermore, it seems to be a reasonable assumption.

The status of a statement as a truth of meaning or of empirical fact can only be established by empirical inquiry, and considerations of many sorts may well be relevant; for example, inquiry into language acquisition and variation among languages. The question of the existence of analytic truths and semantic connections more generally is an empirical one, to be settled by inquiry that goes well beyond the range of evidence ordinarily brought to bear in the literature on these topics. Suppose that two people differ in their intuitive judgments as to whether I can persuade John to go to college without his deciding or intending to do so (see Harman 1980). We are by no means at an impasse. Rather, we can construct conflicting theories and proceed to test them. One who holds that the connection between *persuade* and *decide* or *intend* is conceptual will proceed to elaborate the structure of the concepts, their primitive elements, the principles by which they are integrated and related to other cognitive systems, and so on; and will seek to show that other properties of language and other aspects of the acquisition and use of language can be explained in terms of the very same assumptions about the innate structure of the language faculty, in the same language and others, and that the same concepts play a role in other aspects of thought and understanding. One who holds that the connection is one of deeply held belief, not connection of meaning, has the task of developing a general theory of belief fixation that will yield the right conclusions in these and numerous other cases. Suppose one holds, with Paul Churchland for example, that the connection is based on the "semantic importance" of sentences relating *persuade* and *decide* or *intend* (that is, that these sentences play a prominent role in inference, or serve to introduce the term *persuade* to the child's vocabulary, and thus are more important than others for communication (Paul Churchland 1979: 51f.)). One then faces the task of showing that these empirical claims are in fact true. The first tack – in terms of innate conceptual structure – seems far more promising to me, and is the only approach that has any results or even proposals to its credit; it is, however, a matter of empirical inquiry, not pronouncements on the basis of virtually no evidence. Specifically, arguments against the first (conceptual) approach in terms of indeterminacy, unclarity, open issues, etc. establish nothing unless it is shown that alternative approaches in terms of some (now unavailable) theories of belief fixation or semantic importance are not subject to these problems.

The whole matter requires extensive rethinking, and much of what has been generally assumed for the past several decades about these questions appears to be dubious at best. There is, it seems rather clear, a rich conceptual structure determined by the initial state of the language faculty (perhaps drawing from the resources of other genetically-determined faculties of mind), waiting to be awakened by experience. All of this is much in accord with traditional rationalist conceptions and even, in some respects, the so-called "empiricist" thought of James Harris, David Hume, and others.

Many have found such conclusions completely unacceptable, even absurd; the idea that there is something like an array of innate concepts and that these are to a large degree merely "labeled" in language acquisition – as the empirical evidence suggests – certainly departs radically from many common assumptions. Some, for example Hilary Putnam, have argued that it is entirely implausible to suppose that we have "an innate stock of notions" including *carburetor* and *bureaucrat* (Putnam 1988a: 15). If he were correct about this, it would not be particularly to the point, since the problem arises in a most serious way in connection with simple words such as *table, person, chase, persuade, kill*, etc. However, his argument for the examples that he cites is not compelling. It is that to have given us this innate stock of notions, "evolution would have had to be able to anticipate all the contingencies of future physical and cultural environments. Obviously it didn't and couldn't do this" (p. 15).

Notice that the argument is invalid from the start. To suppose that, in the course of evolution, humans come to have an innate stock of notions including *carburetor* and *bureaucrat* does not entail that evolution was able to anticipate *every* future physical and cultural contingency – only these contingencies. That aside, notice that a very similar argument had long been accepted in immunology: namely, the number of antigens is so immense, including even artifically synthesized substances that had never existed in the world, that it was considered absurd to suppose that evolution had provided "an innate stock of antibodies"; rather, formation of antibodies must be a kind of "learning process" in which the antigens played an "instructive role." But this assumption might well be false. Niels Kaj Jerne won the Nobel Prize for his work challenging this idea, and upholding his own conception that an animal "cannot be stimulated to make specific antibodies, unless it has already made antibodies of this specificity before the antigen arrives" (Jerne 1985: 1059), so that antibody formation is a selective process in which the antigen plays a selective and amplifying role.[23] Whether or not Jerne is correct, he certainly could be, and the same could be true in the case of word meanings, the argument being quite analogous.

Furthermore, there is good reason to suppose that the argument is at least in substantial measure correct even for such words as *carburetor* and *bureaucrat*, which, in fact, pose the familiar problem of poverty of stimulus if we attend carefully to the enormous gap between what we know and the evidence on the basis of which we know it. The same is often true of technical terms of science and mathematics, and it surely appears to be the case for the terms of ordinary discourse. However surprising the conclusion may be that nature has provided us with an innate stock of concepts, and that the child's task is to discover their labels, the empirical facts appear to leave open few other possibilities. Other possibilities (say, in terms of "generalized learning mechanisms") have yet to be coherently formulated, and if some day they are, it may well be that the apparent issue will dissolve.

In fact, it is not clear what thesis is being proposed by Putnam and others who reject what they call "the innateness hypothesis"; I should add that though I am alleged to be one of the exponents of this hypothesis, perhaps even the arch-criminal, I have never defended it and have no idea what it is supposed to be. Whatever the truth may be about antibody formation, it is based on the innate resources of the body and its immune system, and the task of the scientist is to find out what these resources are. Exactly the same is true of concept formation and language acquisition. For this reason, people who are supposed to be defenders of "the innateness hypothesis" do not defend the hypothesis or even use the phrase, because there is no such general hypothesis; rather, only specific hypotheses about the innate resources of the mind, in particular, its language faculty. General arguments against some un-formulated "innateness hypothesis" have no bearing on actual hypotheses about innateness, in the case of growth of language and conceptual systems or other forms of physical growth.

Putnam offers a counter-argument to the one just sketched on analogy to the immune system. He points out that concepts "often arise from *theories*," and the number of possible theories (or perhaps even "theory *types*") is so immense, even for "short" theories, as to make "the idea that evolution exhausted all the possibilities in advance wildly implausible" (Putnam 1988a: 128). The argument is correct, but again irrelevant. In the first place, we are considering what humans are capable of acquiring, and there is no reason to believe that "all theories" can be learned or constructed by humans, nor is it even clear what sense this thesis has.[24] Furthermore, Putnam's original argument was supposed to bear on the specific words *carburetor* and *bureaucrat*, and no cardinality argument is relevant to these cases, or to any substantive empirical hypothesis about innate structure. In other words, his argument that "evolution couldn't have done that" simply does not hold in the cases for which it is offered. The argument that evolution couldn't have done "everything" – even what is beyond human capacity – might hold if one could make some sense of it; such an argument would not, however, be relevant here, even if it could be given in a coherent form.

In the same connection, Putnam argues that the thesis of "meaning holism," with the Quinean principle that "revision can strike anywhere," contributes to undermining certain conclusions concerning the innate structure of conceptual systems and language generally. But this line of argument is questionable. Suppose that the thesis of "meaning holism" is correct in the sense that, as Putnam puts it, there are no "'psychologically real' entities which have enough of the properties we preanalytically assign to 'meanings' to warrant an identification," and reference is fully determined only on holistic grounds. Nevertheless, it does not follow that semantic connections cannot be completely fixed and stable as a matter of biological endowment. Thus certain relations may remain stable as other considerations lead to various choices about fixing of reference. Furthermore, empirical considerations of the kind discussed earlier bear on the question of whether it is indeed true that "revision can strike anywhere." The point cannot be established for natural language by reference to the practice of the natural sciences from which Putnam draws many of his examples; these arguments, assuming them to be correct, do not suffice to show the absence of intrinsic semantic and conceptual structure based on fixed properties of the human mind. The thesis of "holism" may be correct in some measure or form, but the questions of semantic connections in natural language remain to be settled by empirical study, and – for the present at least – the evidence appears to support their existence – rather strongly, it seems to me.

Let us pursue further Davidson's argument in his paper "A Nice Derangement of Epitaphs," (1986b) in which he purports to show that the study of actual communication undermines a "commonly accepted account of linguistic competence and communication" and shows that "there is no such thing as a language, not if a language is anything like what many philosophers and linguists have supposed. There is therefore no such thing to be learned, mastered, or born with" (Davidson 1986b: 446). This conception of language, which Davidson believes to be refuted, is founded on three basic assumptions concerning what he calls "first language" or "prior theory," a "complex system or theory" shared more or less by speaker and hearer (p. 436). The assumptions are:

1. that the prior theory is "systematic" in the sense that the *interpreter* who has this theory is able to interpret utterances on the basis of properties of their parts and the structure of the utterance;
2. that this method of interpretation is shared; and
3. that the component elements of the system are governed by learned conventions or regularities.

The third of these assumptions is untenable for other reasons, but instead of delaying on this matter, let us present it in the form required for Davidson's argument: the component elements of the system are available, as he puts it, "in advance of occasions of interpretation"; it is a fixed element in communication situations, for interpreters at a fixed state of language knowledge.

To refute this conception, Davidson observes that in ordinary communication situations the interpreter makes use of all sorts of conjectures and assumptions about what the speaker may have in mind, relying on properties of the situation, the speaker's presumed intentions, and so on. The interpreter thus "adjusts his theory," modifying the "prior theory" to a "passing theory" that is "geared to the occasion." But this "passing theory cannot in general correspond to an interpreter's linguistic competence." This "passing theory is not a theory of what anyone (except perhaps a philosopher) would call an actual natural language" (Davidson 1986b: 443), Davidson continues, and "'Mastery' of such a language would be useless, since knowing a passing theory is only knowing how to interpret a particular utterance on a particular occasion" (p. 443). Furthermore, communication can proceed quite well when the prior theory is not shared by speaker and hearer, and the prior theory too is not what "we would normally call a language" since it is a psychological particular, specific to the speaker-hearer with features that are not shared through the "community." The interpreter has some kind of "strategy," a "mysterious process by which a speaker or hearer uses what he [or she] knows in advance plus present data to produce a passing theory," and for communication, what two people need "is the ability to converge on passing theories from utterance to utterance." Given these facts, there is no longer any use for "the concept of a language," for "shared grammar or rules," for a "portable interpreting machine set to grind out the meaning of an arbitrary utterance"; rather, we need something more evanescent, mysterious and "holistic," "the ability to converge on a passing theory from time to time" (p. 445). We thus are led to "abandon . . . not only the ordinary notion of a language, but we have erased the boundary between knowing a language and knowing our way around in the world generally . . . In linguistic communication nothing corresponds to a linguistic competence" (pp. 445–6) based on the three principles just mentioned, because "there are no rules for arriving at passing theories." At the conclusion of the discussion, however, Davidson asserts that a passing theory is derived somehow "from a private vocabulary and grammar," that is, from a "prior theory" meeting the first and perhaps a version of the third condition, but possibly not shared in the "community"; there is then a "prior theory" and there are surely certain methods, not others, "for arriving at passing theories," whether or not one wants to call these methods "rules" (p. 446).

The various parts of the argument are largely correct, but they do not seem to show very much. In particular, no reason has been offered to doubt that there is a "prior theory" in the usual sense of the study of language and knowledge of language; that is, a specific generative procedure incorporated in a specific mature state of the language faculty. Of course, this "prior theory" will be quite different from what is called "a language" in ordinary usage, but this is because no such concept plays a role in empirical inquiry into language and mind, as already noted.

In the face of Davidson's arguments, we may continue to suppose that there is, to very good first approximation, a fixed and invariant language faculty which maps presented evidence onto a system of rules and principles (or whatever turns out to be correct with regard to the cognitive state attained) that assign interpretations to utterances. Call this acquired system a "generative procedure." To know a language is to have an internal representation of this generative procedure, which we will express at various levels of abstraction from "more elementary" mechanisms and will seek to relate to such mechanisms, in the normal manner of the natural sciences.[25] Proceeding in accord with normal practice, we may also seek to construct a "parser" – a device, also attributed to the mind/brain – which incorporates the generative procedure attained along with other specified structures and properties,[26] and maps presented utterances into structural descriptions that are interpreted by other components of mind. So far, we are dealing with feasible questions of empirical inquiry.

There is also a further problem, which we can formulate in vague terms but which cannot be studied in practice: namely, to construct an "interpreter" which includes the parser as a component along with all other capacities of the mind – whatever they may be – and accepts nonlinguistic as well as linguistic inputs. This interpreter, presented with an utterance and a situation, assigns some interpretation to what is being said by a person in this situation. The study of communication in the actual world of experience is the study of the interpreter, but this is not a topic for empirical inquiry, for the usual reasons: there is no such topic as the study of everything. Similarly, science does not investigate other phenomena of the world as presented to us in everyday experience. The interpreter – as Davidson correctly observes – includes everything that people are capable of doing, which is why it is not an object of empirical inquiry, and why nothing sensible can be said about it. We might hope to learn something about various elements of the interpreter, proceeding by the normal methods of the sciences, beginning with the "private vocabulary and grammar" that constitute the language attained, proceeding to the parser, then perhaps – to the extent feasible – turning to other elements of the mind and of situations that enter into normal human life. However, if we begin with the demand for a theory of everything, we will find nothing; it is unnecessary to construct elaborate arguments to establish this point.[27] The situation is no different in the far more advanced sciences. The proper conclusion is not that we must abandon concepts of language that can be productively studied, but that the topic of successful communication in the actual world of experience is far too complex and obscure to merit attention in empirical inquiry, except as a guide to intuitions as we pursue research designed to lead to some understanding of the real world, communication included. These observations have no bearing on whether or not there is a "prior theory," that is, an internalized generative procedure, in the normal sense of empirical practice.

Davidson's "passing theory" is not a useful notion; about this, he is surely correct. The interpreter will construct all sorts of "passing theories" (though, crucially, not *any* sort), changing moment to moment, because the interpreter as Davidson conceives it includes everything available to human intelligence; it makes no sense, however, to call its transient states "theories" or to consider them a subject of direct inquiry. Crucially, nothing in Davidson's argument bears on the assumption that the "prior theory" (though not understood quite in his terms) remains a fixed and invariant element of the "interpreter" (as of the narrower idealized parser), and that it enters into the functioning of the interpreter.

In this discussion, Davidson focuses attention on malapropisms and so-called "misuse of language" more generally. Here some care is necessary. Let's again take Jones, a speaker of a variety of what we informally call "English." Jones has mastered a generative procedure that associates with utterances structural descriptions, including semantic properties, and has other capacities of mind that allow him to produce and interpret linguistic expressions making use of these structural descriptions. Let us call this generative procedure his "I-language," where *I* is to suggest "internalized" (in the mind/brain) and "intensional" (in that the procedure is a function enumerating structural descriptions, considered in intension with a particular description).[28] Here we are referring to specific postulated mechanisms of the mind/brain, considered abstractly.

Jones may speak in a way that is not in accord with his I-language, or may offer judgments inconsistent with his I-language; judgments about ourselves, like others, can be mistaken, and much more than I-language is involved in behavior. This is an uninteresting case of misuse of language; call it the "individual sense."

Suppose that Jones, like most of us, normally says such things as "hopefully, we'll be able to solve that problem," or uses the word "disinterested" to mean uninterested. Various authority figures tell us that this is "wrong," a "mistake," or not in accord with the "rules of English." Jones is "misusing his language," namely English, a language of which he has only a partial and perhaps distorted knowledge, as in Dummett's "fundamental sense" of language. Even if 95 per cent of the population – or for that matter everyone but William Safire and a few others – were to behave in the manner of Jones, these cases would still constitute "misuse of language." Or Jones may try to adapt to the practice of some community for some reason, or perhaps for no reason at all, and may fail to do so, in which case people observing Jones may speak informally of a misuse of the language of this community. These concepts of "misuse of language," which we may call "the community sense," may be of interest for the study of the sociology of group identification, authority structure, and the like, but they have little bearing on the study of language, so far as we know. We understand this perfectly well in the case of pronunciation. Thus to say that one variety of English is "right" and another "wrong" makes as much sense as saying that Spanish is right and English wrong; and the same is true – though for some reason the point seems more obscure – with regard to other aspects of language.

Another possible sense of the concept "misuse of language" derives from Hilary Putnam's notion of "the division of linguistic labor." Thus in the lexicon represented in my mind/brain, the entry for "elm" and "beech," or "mass" and "kinetic energy," may include an indication that the reference for these terms is to be determined by experts to whom I defer. Then I might apply the terms inaccurately, in the sense that the reference is not in accord with the determinations of these experts. In this case, I might be said to be "misusing my own language."[29] Let us call this the "expert sense" of misuse of language. Again, nothing of great moment appears to follow, surely nothing relating to the approach to language within the framework of individual psychology sketched earlier, and typically followed in practice.[30] Notice that no useful concept of "language" or "community" emerges from these considerations. Thus my expert for "elm" and "beech" may be an Italian gardener who speaks not a word of English, and who corrects my usage through reference to the technical Latin names that we share; and my expert for "mass" and "kinetic energy" may be a monolingual German physicist. But we would not conclude that German and Italian are included in English, or that all of us form a "community" in any useful sense of the term.

Is there any other concept of "misuse of language"? I am aware of none. If so, the concept plays no important role in the study of language, meaning, communication, or whatever. To take some examples of the kind that Tyler Burge has discussed, suppose that Jones uses the term "arthritis" to refer to a pain in the thigh. Suppose this is the usage of his village, but not the usage of the outside community. Jones is not misusing his language in the individual sense; his usage is true to his I-language. In his village, he is not misusing his language in the community sense, but outside its borders, he is. Depending on how "arthritis" is represented in Jones's mental lexicon, he may or may not be misusing his language in the "expert sense." How should we attribute beliefs about arthritis to Jones? Here intuitions differ, and it may be that evidence is too slim, for the moment, to settle the point satisfactorily. Putting aside the "expert sense," suppose we use the term "I-belief" to refer to the concept that is like belief, except that Jones has the same belief within his village and in the wider community, namely, the belief that we would express, in our I-language, by saying that he has some kind of body pain.[31] This may or may not be the same as the concept of belief in our ordinary language, but it is the concept that seems to be required for the study of what is misleadingly called "the causation of behavior" – misleadingly, because it is unclear that behavior is "caused" in any useful sense of the term. Clearly, there is no reason to suppose that the concepts of general psychology will be those of ordinary usage, just as the concepts of physics, or of the subbranch of psychology called "linguistics," typically are not. Nor is it at all obvious to me that there is a reasonable branch of science (or to be more accurate, human science, meaning the kind of scientific inquiry that humans, with their particular cognitive capacities, are capable of under-taking) that deals with questions of this nature.

It has not, I think, been established that there is anything more to say about the matter. In particular, reference to "misuse of language," to "norms," to "communities," and so on seems to me to require much more care than is often taken. These concepts are obscure, and it is not clear that they are of any use for inquiry into language and human behavior. Any argument that relies on these notions merits careful scrutiny, and I doubt that familiar arguments can withstand it. Communities are formed in all sorts of overlapping ways, and the study of communities and their norms quickly degenerates into the study of everything. The fact remains that Jones speaks and understands the way he does on the basis of the I-language he has acquired in the course of language growth; and if Jones does or does not follow what we choose, for some transient purpose, to call "community norms" or "social prac-tice," it is on the basis of this internalized I-language (along with much else). Boris, a monolingual speaker of some variety of Russian, has a different I-language, and follows different "norms." I can understand

Jones, within limits, because my I-language is not too different from his, and because he and I more or less share other unknown properties that enter into the full interpreter; this is not a topic of empirical inquiry as it stands, in its unanalyzed complexity. That seems to me the way we should approach these questions.

In these terms, we can develop a concept of "knowledge of language" that is appropriate for the inquiry into language and mind; namely, mastery and internal representation of a specific I-language. The linguist's grammar is a theory of the I-language, and universal grammar is the theory of the initial state of the language faculty. Jones's I-language is one particular mature state – or output, regarding the language faculty as a function that maps evidence into I-language. What about the concept language? We might simply understand languages as I-languages, thus taking a language to be something like "a way of speaking," the "finite means" that provide for "infinite use" in the terms of Wilhelm von Humboldt's characterization of language (1836: 122, paragraph 13; 1988: 91; see also Chomsky 1964: 17), also an effort to capture his concept of language as a "process of generation" rather than a set of "generated objects." We thus take language to be, in effect, a "notion of structure" that guides the speaker in forming "free expressions," in Otto Jespersen's terms (1924: 19; see also Chomsky 1977). For empirical inquiry, I think that is an appropriate decision, though obviously not for ordinary discourse. Alternatively we might want to construct a concept of language divorced from cognitive states, perhaps along lines suggested by James Higginbotham (1989). Taking knowledge of language to be a cognitive state, we might construe the "language" as an abstract object, the "object of knowledge," an abstract system of rules and principles (or whatever turns out to be correct) that is an image of the generative procedure, the I-language, represented in the mind and ultimately in the brain in now-unknown "more elementary" mechanisms. Since the language in this sense is completely determined by the I-language, though abstracted from it, it is not entirely clear that this further step is motivated; perhaps it is, however.

In these terms, it seems to me that the questions about language and its use that can be subjected to empirical inquiry can readily be formulated, and as far as we now know, best addressed. There may well be many other questions that are not subject to empirical inquiry in the manner of the sciences – and perhaps never will be – if humans are themselves part of the natural world, and thus have specific biological capacities with their scope and limits, like every other organism. We must be careful not to succumb to illusions about evolution and its adaptive miracles. There is nothing in the theory of evolution that suggests that we should be able to answer questions that we can pose, even in principle, even if they have answers, or that we should be able to pose the right questions. To the extent that we can, we have empirical science, a kind of chance convergence of properties of the mind and properties of the extra-mental world. There is nothing surprising about this; we take for granted that something similar is true of rats and bees, and should not be surprised to learn that humans are biological organisms, not angels. Within the limits of human science, however, it seems to me that the best guess as of the present is that the framework I have just briefly outlined is a proper one for inquiry into the empirical questions about language and mind; and within it, there are some notable successes and many intriguing prospects.

4   Naturalism and dualism in the study of language and mind

The terms of the title can be understood in various ways, along with the frameworks in which they are embedded. I would like to outline interpretations that I think are useful and proper, and to suggest a more general thesis, which would require much more comprehensive argument: that there is no coherent alternative to proceeding in this way for the range of issues addressed, and that other endeavors in roughly the same realm are clarified and facilitated if understood as extensions of the approach outlined.

Deflating the terms

Putting "language" aside for the moment, let's begin by taking the other terms of the title in ways that are innocent of far-reaching implications, specifically, divorced from any metaphysical connotations. Take the term "mind" or, as a preliminary, "mental." Consider how we use such terms as "chemical," "optical," or "electrical." Certain phenomena, events, processes, and states are called "chemical" (etc.), but no metaphysical divide is suggested by that usage. These are just various aspects of the world that we select as a focus of attention for the purposes of inquiry and exposition. I will understand the term "mental" in much the same way, with something like its traditional coverage, but without metaphysical import and with no suggestion that it would make any sense to try to identify the true criterion or mark of the mental. By "mind," I mean the mental aspects of the world, with no concern for defining the notion more closely and no expectation that we will find some interesting kind of unity or boundaries, any more than elsewhere; no one cares to sharpen the boundaries of "the chemical."

Furthermore, I keep here to the human mind (visual system, reasoning, language, etc.). There is no quest for a unified science of locomotion, ranging from amoeba to eagle to science-fiction spaceship; or of communication, ranging from cell to poetic discourse to imagined extraterrestrials. Rather, biologists study how dolphins swim and ants communicate, beginning with an "internalist" and "individualist" account (in contemporary jargon). In so doing, they have little interest in how the terms "dolphin," "communicate," etc. are used in the informal discourse in which the questions are initially posed. Rather, they develop concepts appropriate to their purpose of explanation and understanding. Ordinary discourse and common-sense thought are in no way denigrated by the procedure; rather they are liberated from inappropriate and destructive demands. The same is true of other scientific inquiry with broader concerns (for example the study of ant communities).[1]

We may carry over these observations – truisms, I think – to the study of human language and the human mind. Since the brain, or elements of it, are critically involved in linguistic and other mental phenomena, we may use the term "mind" – loosely but adequately – in speaking of the brain, viewed from a particular perspective developed in the course of inquiry into certain aspects of human nature and its manifestations. There are empirical assumptions here – that the brain, not the foot, is the relevant bodily organ, that humans are alike enough in language capacity so that human language can be regarded as a natural object, and so on. But these need not detain us.

Let us also understand the term "naturalism" without metaphysical connotations: a "naturalistic approach" to the mind investigates mental aspects of the world as we do any others, seeking to construct intelligible explanatory theories, with the hope of eventual integration with the "core" natural sciences. Such "methodological naturalism" can be counterposed to what might be called "methodological dualism," the view that we must abandon scientific rationality when we study humans "above the neck" (metaphorically speaking), becoming mystics in this unique domain, imposing arbitrary stipulations and *a priori* demands of a sort that would never be contemplated in the sciences, or in other ways departing from normal canons of inquiry.

There are interesting questions as to how naturalistic inquiry should proceed, but they can be put aside here, unless some reason is offered to show that they have a unique relevance to this particular inquiry. That has not been done, to my knowledge. Specifically, skeptical arguments can be dismissed in this context. We may simply adopt the standard outlook of modern science, in essence, the anti-foundationalism of the seventeenth century reaction to the Cartesian skeptical crisis, as Richard Popkin describes it: "the recognition that absolutely certain grounds could not be given for our knowledge, and yet that we possess standards for evaluating the reliability and applicability of what we have found out about the world," thus "accepting and increasing the knowledge itself" while recognizing that "the secrets of nature, of things-in-themselves, are forever hidden from us" (Popkin 1979: 139ff.). It may well be of interest to proceed beyond but, if so, the place to look for answers is where they are likely to be found: in the hard sciences, where richness and depth of understanding provides some hope of gaining insight into the questions. To raise them with regard to inquiries barely attempting to gain a foothold is pointless, scarcely more than a form of harassment of emerging disciplines.

Naturalism, so understood, should be uncontroversial, though its reach remains to be determined; and the dualistic alternative should be highly controversial. I think that the opposite has been true, a curious feature of recent intellectual history. Explanatory theories of mind have been proposed, notably in the study of language. They have been seriously challenged, not for violating the canons of methodological naturalism (which they seem to observe, reasonably well), but on other grounds: "philosophical grounds," which are alleged to show that they are dubious, perhaps outrageous, irrespective of success by the normal criteria of science; or perhaps that they are successful, but do not deal with "the mind" and "the mental." I will suggest that such critiques are commonly a form of methodological dualism, and that advocacy (or tacit acceptance) of that stance has been a leading theme of much of the most interesting work in recent philosophy of mind and language.

Plainly, a naturalistic approach does not exclude other ways of trying to comprehend the world. Someone committed to it can consistently believe (I do) that we learn much more of human interest about how people think and feel and act by reading novels or studying history or the activities of ordinary life than from all of naturalistic psychology, and perhaps always will; similarly, the arts may offer appreciation of the heavens to which astrophysics does not aspire. We are speaking here of theoretical understanding, a particular mode of comprehension. In this domain, any departure from this approach carries a burden of justification. Perhaps one can be given, but I know of none.

Language in naturalistic inquiry

To help frame the discussion, let's consider for a moment where methodological naturalism leads us in the study of mind, language in particular. I think to something like the following, on current understanding.

The brain has a component – call it "the language faculty" – that is dedicated to language and its use. For each individual, the language faculty has an initial state, determined by biological endowment. Serious pathology apart, such states are so similar across the species that we can reasonably abstract to *the* initial state of the language faculty, a common human possession. The environment triggers and to a limited extent shapes an internally-directed process of growth, which stabilizes (pretty much) at about puberty. A serious study will attempt to determine what "pure" states of the language faculty would be under ideal conditions, abstracting from a host of distortions and interferences in the complex circumstances of ordinary life, thus hoping to identify the real nature of the language faculty and its manifestations; at least, so the canons of methodological naturalism dictate. This point of view, adopted without comment in naturalistic inquiry generally, is often considered contentious or worse in the domain of language and mind, an illustration of the dualism that I suggested is prevalent and pernicious.

A state attained by the language faculty characterizes an infinite class of linguistic expressions, each a certain array of phonetic, structural, and semantic properties. My state specifies the properties of the last sentence; yours is similar enough so that your mind can (sometimes) find an appropriate analogue to what I say, in which case you have means for determining my intentions (the perceived expression being only part of your evidence, and communication being a "more or less" affair). The state attained is a computational (generative) system. We may call that state a language or, to avoid pointless terminological controversy, an *I-language*, "I" chosen to suggest that the conception is internal, individual, and intensional (in the technical sense; that is, the characterization of a function in intension). For Jones to have the (I-)language, L, is for his language faculty to be in state L. Particular signals are manifestations of linguistic expressions (spoken, written, signed, whatever); speech acts are manifestations of linguistic expressions in a broader sense. The expressions can be understood as "instructions" to other systems of the mind/brain that "follow them" in the use of language.

On the (very weak) empirical assumptions of these remarks, the notion I-language is straightforward; that the brain is a complex system with states and properties is not controversial. It remains to spell out this conception of "state of the brain" and to discover its properties. Other notions of "language" require some further justification – which, I believe, is not easy to give.

The class of expressions generated by the (I-)language L should not be confused with a category of well-formed sentences, a notion that has no known place in the theory of language, though informal exposition has sometimes obscured the point, leading to much confusion and wasted effort. Thus, so-called "deviant" expressions may be characterized by Jones's language L with quite definite properties; it could turn out that it assigns a specific interpretation to every possible signal, the latter notion determined by properties of the initial state.

It may be that the computational system itself is (virtually) invariant, fixed by innate biological endowment, variation among languages and language types being limited to certain options in the lexicon; quite restricted options. Slight changes in an intricate system may yield what appear to be dramatic phenomenal differences; thus, languages may appear to differ radically from one another, though they differ only in rather marginal ways, it appears. Something like that is what any rational scientist observing humans would expect; otherwise, there would be little hope of accounting for the specificity, richness, and intricacy of the state attained on the basis of very limited information from the environment. Comparable assumptions are taken for granted without discussion in the study of growth and development generally. A naturalistic approach makes no distinction in the unique case of mental processes.

As far as is known, even the most rudimentary properties of the initial and attained states are not found among other organisms or, indeed, in the biological world, apart from its points of contact with inorganic matter. Nor are there more than very weak relations to anything discovered in the brain sciences. So we face the problems of unification that are common in the history of science, and do not know how – or if – they will be resolved.

I'll put aside here any further account of the results of naturalistic inquiry, returning to the questions of naturalism and dualism more generally.

Varieties of naturalism

Methodological naturalism is not to be confused with other varieties. To clarify what I do and don't mean, consider a useful recent exposition of the concept of naturalism by Baldwin (1993: 171). He opens by noting that "A prominent theme of current philosophy is that of the 'naturalisation' of philosophy. Daniel Dennett has written that 'One of the happiest trends in philosophy in the last twenty years has been its Naturalisation'" (p. 171). That the trend is prominent is doubtless true; that it is happy seems to me open to question. In any event, it is distinct from the form of naturalism I am advocating here.

Baldwin finds "two different types of naturalism at work in current philosophy," what he calls *metaphysical* and *epistemic*. The former is what "Dennett has in mind when he celebrates the 'naturalisation' of philosophy": the thought that, as Dennett puts it, "philosophical accounts of our minds, our knowledge, our language must in the end be continuous with, and harmonious with, the natural sciences" (p. 172) – unlike, say, Fregean Platonism, which is not continuous with hypotheses "advanced by the natural sciences," so it is alleged.

Contemporary epistemic naturalism derives from Willard Quine's "epistemology naturalized," which stipulated that the study of knowledge and belief must be incorporated within a narrow branch of behaviorist psychology of no known scientific interest, a strange move in itself, which has evoked surprisingly little challenge. A broader version, Baldwin observes, considers "natural relations" between external situations and mental states without arbitrary strictures. The broader version can be viewed as an outgrowth of the rational psychology of the seventeenth century, which held, as Lord Herbert put it, that there are "principles or notions implanted in the mind" that "we bring to objects from ourselves . . . [as] . . . a direct gift of Nature, a precept of natural instinct" – "common notions" and "intellectual truths" that are "imprinted on the soul by the dictates of Nature itself," which, though "stimulated by objects," are not "conveyed" by them (Herbert 1624/1937: 133). Baldwin cites Thomas Reid as the source of a kind of "naturalised epistemology," expressing a similar point of view but "freed from Hume's [or any earlier] commitment to the theory of ideas" (Baldwin 1993: 181); that is, freed from earlier attempts to spell out what Reid calls the "original and natural judgments" that "nature hath given to the human understanding" as "part of our constitution" and that make up "*the common-sense of mankind*" (Reid 1785: 600–1). Since nothing replaces the outline of a theory that is abandoned, it is hard to see how this "naturalization" progresses beyond earlier versions. On the contrary, the work of the Cartesians and Cambridge Platonists is considerably more advanced in many respects, in my opinion. Later, Charles Sanders Peirce (1957: 253) proposed that human thought is guided by a principle of "abduction" that "puts a limit upon admissible hypotheses" and that is innate in us, providing the human mind with "a natural adaptation to imagining correct theories of some kind" (p. 238) a result of natural selection, he suggested (with little plausibility). There are many further ramifications, including recent "evolutionary epistemology." (For some discussion, see Chomsky 1966: Chapter 4; 1968/72; 1975: Chapter 1.)

The enterprise of epistemic naturalism is uncontentious, apart from the term, which is misleading in a peculiarly modern way. The epistemic naturalism of the seventeenth and eighteenth century was science, an attempt to construct an empirical theory of mind; Hume, for one, compared his enterprise with Isaac Newton's. Epistemic naturalism, in contrast, is presented as a "philosophical position," something apparently different. We plainly cannot read back into earlier periods a distinction between science and philosophy that developed later. We would not use the term "visual naturalism" to refer to the empirical study of the growth and functioning of the visual system (also a topic of earlier rational psychology), implying that there was some coherent alternative for the same realm of problems. The term "epistemic naturalism" seems to me misleading in much the same way, not to speak of the special versions deriving from Quine's "epistemology naturalized."

For a methodological naturalist, traditional epistemic naturalism is normal science (see Chapter 3 of this volume, pp. 52–3), however we evaluate particular implementations. Inquiry into the initial state of the language faculty, for example, is an attempt to discover the "principles or notions implanted in the mind" that are a "direct gift" of nature, that is, our biological endowment. As elsewhere, the inquiry is initiated by common-sense formulations. Take the informal locution "Jones knows (speaks, understands, has) English." The observation focuses attention on a state of the world, including a state of Jones's brain, a cognitive state, that underlies Jones's knowledge of many particular things: his knowing how to interpret linguistic signals, or that certain expressions mean what they do, and so on. We would like to know how Jones's brain reached this cognitive state. Inquiry into the matter leads to empirical hypotheses about biological endowment, interactions with the environment, the nature of the states attained, and their interactions with other systems of the mind (articulatory, perceptual, conceptual, intentional, etc.). Resulting theories of the growth of language are sometimes called theories of a "Language Acquisition Device" (LAD), which effects a transition from the initial state of the language faculty to later states, mapping experience to state attained; the theory of the initial state is sometimes called "Universal Grammar" (UG), adapting a traditional notion to a somewhat different context. (I ignore below the distinctions between the theory of LAD and UG.) In my terms, this is study of the mind; others disagree, for reasons to which I will return.

Metaphysical naturalism seems far more problematic than traditional epistemic naturalism. One question, which Baldwin raises, is "what the 'natural' sciences are." A possible answer is: whatever is achieved in pursuing naturalistic inquiry. But that doesn't seem to be what is intended; let us put the question to the side for a moment. A related problem is to explain what are "philosophical accounts of our minds, our knowledge, our language," and how they differ from "scientific accounts," particularly if they are "continuous with the natural sciences" (Baldwin 1993: 172). Does the doctrine mean that a theory of mind should be "continuous" and "harmonious" with today's physics? That is surely unacceptable; tomorrow's physics may well not meet that condition. With some Peircean ideal of what science will be "in the limit"? Not very helpful, even if meaningful. Perhaps tomorrow's physics will incorporate some version of today's accounts (whether termed "philosophical" or not), even if the latter are not continuous with today's physics.

If so, it will be nothing new in the history of the sciences. One persistent goal is to unify various theories about the world, but the process has taken many a different course. Large-scale reduction is not the usual pattern; one should not be misled by such dramatic examples as the reduction of much of biology to biochemistry in the middle of the twentieth century. Repeatedly, the more "fundamental" science has had to be revised, sometimes radically, for unification to proceed. Suppose that a nineteenth century philosopher had insisted that "chemical accounts of molecules, interactions, properties of elements, states of matter, etc. must in the end be continuous with, and harmonious with, the natural sciences," meaning physics as then understood. They were not, because the physics of the day was inadequate. By the 1930s, physics had radically changed, and the accounts (themselves modified) were "continuous" and "harmonious" with the new quantum physics. Suppose that a seventeenth-century scientist were to have imposed the same demand on celestial mechanics, referring to the prevailing "mechanical philosophy" and rejecting Newton's mystical theory (as Leibniz and Huygens did), because it was incompatible with "the laws of mechanics." (See Dijksterhuis 1986: 479f.) Though understandable, the reaction would have been (and was) surely wrong: fundamental physics had to be radically changed for unification to proceed.

We have no idea where that process will lead, or even how far human intelligence can reach in attaining such understanding of the natural world; we are, after all, biological organisms, not angels. The latter observation, again uncontentious, suggests another way to answer the question of "what the 'natural' sciences are." Among the aspects of the mind are those that enter into naturalistic inquiry; call them "the science-forming faculty" (SFF). Equipped with SFF, people confront "problem situations," consisting of certain cognitive states (of belief, understanding, or misunderstanding), questions that are posed, and so on (essentially, what Sylvain Bromberger calls a "p-predicament"; see his essays collected in Bromberger 1992b). Often SFF yields only a blank stare. Sometimes it provides ideas about how the questions might be answered or reformulated, or the cognitive state modified, ideas that can then be evaluated in ways that SFF offers (empirical test, consistency with other parts of science, criteria of intelligibility and elegance, etc.). Like other biological systems, SFF has its potential scope and limits; we may distinguish between *problems* that in principle fall within its range, and *mysteries* that do not. The distinction is relative to humans; rats and Martians have different problems and mysteries and, in the case of rats, we even know a fair amount about them. The distinction also need not be sharp, though we certainly expect it to exist, for any organism and any cognitive faculty. The successful natural sciences, then, fall within the intersection of the scope of SFF and the nature of the world; they treat the (scattered and limited) aspects of the world that we can grasp and comprehend by naturalistic inquiry, in principle. The intersection is a chance product of human nature. Contrary to speculations since Peirce, there is nothing in the theory of evolution, or any other intelligible source, that suggests that it should include answers to serious questions we raise, or even that we should be able to formulate questions properly in areas of puzzlement.

Specifically, it is unknown whether aspects of the theory of mind – say, questions about consciousness – are problems or mysteries for humans, though in principle we could discover the answer, even discover that they are mysteries; there is no contradiction in the belief that SFF might permit us to learn something about its limits. (See Chomsky, 1968 ch. 3; 1975, ch. 4. On the possible limits, and the relevance to philosophical inquiry, see particularly McGinn 1991; 1993.)

The question "what the 'natural' sciences are," then, might be answered narrowly, by asking what they have achieved; or more generally, by inquiry into a particular faculty of (the human) mind, with its specific properties. Something else, however, seems to be wanted; what it is remains unclear.

It is instructive to look more closely at the origins of modern science. In brief, progress into the seventeenth century laid the basis for the "mechanical philosophy," eliminating fantasies about forms of objects floating through the air and implanting themselves in brains, and mystical forces and powers, "occult qualities" of sympathy, antipathy, and so on, which allowed such absurdities as action at a distance through a vacuum. The Cartesians observed that certain phenomena of nature (notably, the normal use of language) did not seem to fall within the mechanical philosophy, postulating a new principle to account for them. Given their metaphysics, they postulated a second substance (*res cogitans*, mind), for other reasons as well. Implementation aside, the move was not unreasonable, in fact, not unlike Newton's reasoning when he discovered the inadequacies of the mechanical philosophy. Postulation of something that lies beyond the mechanical philosophy gives rise to two tasks: to develop the theory and to solve the unification problem; in the Cartesian case, the "mind–body problem." All of this is normal science; wrong, but that is also the norm.

Just as the mechanical philosophy appeared to be triumphant, it was demolished by Newton, who reintroduced a kind of "occult" cause and quality, much to the dismay of leading scientists of the day, and of Newton himself. The Cartesian theory of mind (such as it was) was unaffected by his discoveries, but the theory of body was demonstrated to be untenable. To put it differently, Newton eliminated the problem of "the ghost in the machine" by exorcising the machine; the ghost was unaffected. He also left us with the conclusion that common-sense intuition – the "folk physics" that was the basis for the mechanical philosophy – cannot be expected to survive the transition to rational inquiry into the nature of things. The mind–body problem disappeared, and can be resurrected, if at all, only by producing a new notion of body (material, physical, etc.) to replace the one that was abandoned; hardly a reasonable enterprise, it would seem. Lacking that, the phrase "material" ("physical," etc.) world simply offers a loose way of referring to what we more or less understand and hope to unify in some way.

The natural conclusion, drawn shortly after by La Mettrie and later Joseph Priestley, is that human thought and action are properties of organized matter, like "powers of attraction and repulsion," electrical charge, and so on. (La Mettrie 1747; see also Cohen 1941; Yolton 1983; Wellman 1992.) Adopting that view, we seek to determine the properties of these things in the world and to account for mental phenomena in terms of them, to show how they arise in the individual and species, and to relate these conclusions to whatever else is known about organized matter (the new version of the unification problem). On the last problem, there is no progress to speak of. Nor has there been real progress in accounting for the properties of normal use of language, and other phenomena, that led the Cartesians to postulate a second substance (though the limits of mechanism are no longer an issue). These may well turn out to be mysteries-for-humans. There has been progress in understanding the mechanisms of mind from the more abstract point of view of UG, LAD, the states attained, and their inter-actions with other cognitive systems; and in the study of some of these (for example, conceptual development). On naturalistic assumptions, these are parts of the natural sciences – good or bad, right or wrong.

The natural sciences attempt to understand the world in its chemical, electrical, mental, etc. aspects. Does the world include mysterious Newtonian forces affecting bodies separated by empty space, or electrical and magnetic fields that, though mathematical objects, are "*real* physical 'stuff'" because of the way they "push each other along through empty space" (Penrose 1989: 185–6). Or curved space that "seemed to take all definite structure away from anything we can call solidity," or perhaps, "at a very deep bottom" nothing but bits of information (Wheeler 1994: 294f.). Does it include Herbert's common notions and principles as part of "natural instinct," Humean ideas, thoughts and concepts, computational principles and states, and so on? Naturalistic inquiry seeks answers to these questions, as self-critically as it can, escaping arbitrary assumptions when these can be detected, though aware that biological constraints on human thought cannot be overcome, while cultural ones may not be easy to unravel.

Let us return to the allegation that a theory of mind, TM, that introduces such notions as "grasping Fregean senses" is not harmonious with or continuous with hypotheses "advanced by the natural sciences." If one means the natural sciences of today, excluding TM, then the observation is correct though uninteresting. The right questions have to do with the status of TM on naturalistic grounds, and the unification problem (if TM has some plausibility). If the allegation means that the unification problem lies beyond human capacity, that could be right, but would not bear on the scientific status of TM. We need not consider speculations about the "true" science, perhaps beyond human intellectual reach. What else does metaphysical naturalism demand? That is not clear.

Shall we understand metaphysical naturalism to be the demand for unity of nature? If so, it could be taken as a guiding idea, but not as a dogma. "Ninety percent of the matter of the universe," physicists tell us, "is what is now called dark matter – dark because we don't see it; dark because we don't know what it is," indeed "we do not have the slightest idea of what 90 percent of the world is made of." (Weisskopf 1989). Suppose dark matter turns out to be crucially different from the 10 per cent of the world about which there are some ideas. The possibility cannot be discounted in principle; stranger things have been accepted in modern science. Nor can it be excluded in the case of theories of mind. Though there is no reason to entertain the hypothesis, some version of Cartesianism (with a far richer concept of body) could in principle turn out to be true, consistent with a naturalist stance.

Materialism and its critics

Metaphysical naturalism will be a coherent position if its advocates tell us what counts as "physical" or "material." Until that is done, we cannot comprehend the doctrine, let alone such derivative notions as "eliminative materialism" and the like. In practice, versions of the latter seem to be little more than pronouncements as to where the answers lie and, as such, are of no special interest.

Critics of these doctrines seem to me to be faced with the same problem: what are they criticizing? One of the most prominent is Thomas Nagel, who gives a lucid account of prevailing views and his critique of them, directed specifically to the questions that concern me here (Nagel 1993). I think the issues are wrongly put, though in an interesting way, and the conclusions suspect for this and other reasons, including those on LAD and the theory of mind, with which he concludes.

Nagel states that "the mind–body problem was posed in its modern form only in the seventeenth century, with the emergence of the scientific conception of the physical world on which we are now all brought up" (1993: 97) (the Newtonian conception). But that has the story reversed. The mind–body problem made sense in terms of the mechanical philosophy that Newton undermined, and has not been coherently posed since. If so, discussion cannot proceed in Nagel's terms without some new account of the nature of body (material, physical, etc.) and mind.

This perspective on the issues and their origins leads to a misleading account of current contributions as well. Thus Nagel outlines John Searle's "radical thesis" that "consciousness is a physical property of the brain" that is "irreducible to any *other* physical property, a position which, if properly clarified (which Nagel considers unlikely), "would be a major addition to the possible answers to the mind–body problem" (1993: 103). This thesis is the "metaphysical heart" of Searle's proposal: in his own words, "consciousness is a higher-level or emergent property of the brain"; it is "as much of the natural biological order as . . . photosynthesis, digestion, or mitosis."

Valid or not, the thesis is not radical; rather, it is – and was – the natural reaction to Newton's demolition of the mechanical philosophy, hence of the mind–body problem, at least in its Cartesian form. As noted, the view that thought and action (including consciousness) are properties of organized matter, no more reducible to others than electromagnetic properties are reducible to mechanics, was put forth by eighteenth century scientists – not, however, as a possible answer to the mind–body problem, which had (and has) no coherent formulation. As for the metaphysical import of the thesis, it is on a par with the import of the relation between classical mechanics and electromagnetic theory.

Nagel assumes a prior understanding of mind and body, mental and physical, and gives some indication of what he means. Expressing a standard view, he takes "the essence of mind" to be consciousness: "all mental phenomena are either actually or potentially conscious" (1993: 97). Whether intended as a terminological or substantive proposal, that formulation requires an explanation of the notion "potentially conscious"; Nagel adopts Searle's (1992) proposal on the matter, but it seems to face serious difficulties.

Suppose we take consciousness to be the mark of the mental. What about body? That Nagel identifies with what is "capable of description by physical science" (excluding consciousness, whether by fiat or discovery is not clear). Thus he understands materialism (which he says is accepted by most contemporary philosophers) to be the belief "that everything there is and everything that happens in the world must be capable of description by physical science" – a view that he takes to be coherent, but false. Adopting it, one attempts "some sort of reduction of the mental to the physical – where the physical, by definition, is that which can be described in nonmental terms" (that is, terms that do not involve "potential consciousness"). "What is needed to complete the materialist world picture is some scheme of the form, 'mental phenomena – thoughts, feelings, sensations, desires, perceptions, etc. – are nothing but . . . ,' where the blank is to be filled in by a description that is either explicitly physical or uses only terms that can apply to what is entirely physical," or perhaps gives "assertability conditions" on "externally observable grounds." "The various attempts to carry out this apparently impossible task," Nagel continues, "and the arguments to show that they have failed, make up the history of the philosophy of mind during the past fifty years." Left unresolved, and presumably unresolvable, is the mind–body problem, which is the problem of "finding a place in the world for our minds themselves, with their perceptual experiences, thoughts, desires, scientific theory-construction, and much else that is not described by physics."

The belief that the questions are coherent and significant is widely shared. Thus, in an instructive review of a century of the philosophy of mind, Tyler Burge discusses the emergence of "naturalism" ("materialism," "physicalism") in the 1960s as "one of the few orthodoxies in American philosophy" (1992: 32). This is the view that there are no mental states (properties, etc.) "over and above ordinary physical entities, entities identifiable in the physical sciences or entities that common-sense would regard as physical." He describes "eliminationism," one major strand of the effort "to make philosophy scientific," as "the view that mentalistic talk and mental entities would eventually lose their place in our attempts to describe and explain the world" (Burge 1992: 33), perhaps wrong, but surely an important thesis. That is, however, less than obvious.

Consider Nagel's notions "capable of description by physical science" and "described by physics." What do they mean? He offers the example of liquidity, with its "transparent" relation to the behavior of molecules. The relation can't be all that transparent. A century ago molecules were regarded by leading physicists as convenient fictions, and states of matter, as later learned, were not "capable of description" by then-existing physics. True, a branch of science not then unified with physics could provide much illumination in terms of its own theoretical constructs, as of much else; but the same is true today of some of the domain of the mental (in my sense). Why are these accounts less "physical" than chemistry was a century ago? Or less physical than Newton's occult forces, and on to today's arcane and counterintuitive theoretical posits? Perhaps the naturalistic accounts of mental phenomena will some day be unified with physics, which may again have to be revised, in which case the relations will also become "transparent."

As for the thesis of eliminativism in Burge's (again standard) formulation, we may ask why it is of any significance. Replace "mental" by "physical" in the thesis. Uncontroversially, "physicalistic talk and physical entities" have long ago "lost their place in our attempts to describe and explain the world," if by "physicalistic" and "physical" we mean the notions that enter into our common discourse and thinking. Why should we expect anything different of "mentalistic talk and mental entities"? Suppose I say, "the rock dropped from the skies, rolled down the hill, and hit the ground." The statement cannot be translated into the theories that have been developed to describe and explain the world, nor is there any interesting weaker relation; the terms belong to different intellectual universes. But no one takes this to constitute a body–body problem. Nor do the natural sciences aspire to distinguish this description from the statement that the rock fell down a crevice, which could be the same event viewed from a different perspective (with the hill not distinguished from surrounding terrain). Methodological naturalists do not expect to find counterparts to such informal statements as these within the explanatory theories they self-consciously devise; nor of "John took his umbrella because he thought it was going to rain," or "John is in pain," or "John speaks English" – though they hope, in all cases, that naturalistic inquiry might yield understanding and insight in the domains opened to inquiry by discourse reflecting common-sense perspectives.

Similar questions arise quite broadly. Take Donald Davidson's "anomalism of the mental," the view that, while there are causal relations between mental and physical events, there are no psychophysical laws that connect them in an appropriate explanatory scheme. As Davidson puts it, one should not compare truisms about what people generally will do under certain conditions "with a law that says how fast a body will fall in a vacuum," because "in the latter case, but not the former, we can tell in advance whether the condition holds, and we know what allowance to make if it doesn't," (Davidson 1980: 233) a position on the mind–body problem that Burge describes as "profound but controversial" though inadequately clarified. (For a sympathetic discussion, see Evnine 1991.) The argument does not seem entirely compelling. For the same reason we should also not compare truisms about balls rolling down hills or a storm brewing in the West with the law of falling bodies, but we are not concerned about the lack of "physico-physical laws" connecting ordinary discourse about events in the world and explanatory theories of nature. It is argued that "folk psychology" is different from, say, "folk mechanics" or "folk chemistry" because of its *a priori* character and intimate relation to notions of rationality, reasons, intentions, first-person perspective, and so on. The domains are surely different, but it is unclear that they differ in "anomalism" in the sense of the discussion. Insofar as scientific inquiry might undermine one's conviction that the Sun is setting or that objects are impenetrable (while leaving such convictions in place in other parts of life), it seems that it might in principle have similar effects on one's convictions about the nature of beliefs (say, with regard to the role of rationality). Much of what people believe about beliefs is *a posteriori* (consider the debates about holism and innateness) and we have *a priori* beliefs about balls rolling down hills and storms brewing. Folk mechanics (etc.) seems no more susceptible than folk psychology to the formulation of bridge laws. As Davidson argues, mental event tokens are not tokens of physical event types (under informal description). The same is true of physical event tokens and physical objects, as common-sense construes them; only by fantastic accident will human language have natural kind terms, if natural kinds are the kinds of nature.[2]

To change terminology slightly, let us speak of "events mentalistically described" ("m-events") and "events physicalistically described" ("p-events"), referring to accounts in ordinary language, reserving the terms *mental, chemical, optical,* etc. for events postulated by naturalistic inquiry in the mental, chemical, optical, etc. domains – all of these being "physical events," a redundant term for events; same for objects, and so on. Then we expect to find causal relations between m-events and physical events, but no laws connecting them within explanatory science; the same is true of p-events. Beliefs, desires, perceptions, rocks rolling towards the ground, storms brewing, etc. are not subject to scientific laws, nor are there bridge laws connecting them to the sciences. Uncontroversially, science does not try to capture the content of ordinary discourse, let alone more creative acts of imagination. Paraphrasing

Nagel, we cannot "find a place in the world" of physics for physical phenomena, as we describe them in physicalistic talk (p-phenomena), so it is not surprising that the same is true of m-phenomena as captured in mentalistic talk.

Perhaps one should stress again that the reach of naturalistic inquiry may be quite limited, not approaching questions of serious human concern, however far-reaching its intellectual interest may prove to be. That is surely the present condition, and might so remain. Eliminativism, Nagel comments caustically, dismisses the "primitive theory" that was "the province of such simple folk as Flaubert, Proust, and Henry James." Eliminativism does not seem to me a coherent position, but naturalism will hardly seek to annex this province, any more than it incorporates such trivial matters as rocks rolling down hills and storms brewing; on the contrary, it frees the explorer from irrelevant demands (see note 1).

Note that the truth of normal physicalistic talk and the status of the entities it postulates are not in question here. These are different topics. Nor is any question raised about the study of common-sense concepts as a branch of naturalistic inquiry (ethnoscience). It is interesting to learn how notions of language appear in the culture of the Navajo, (for an enlightening account, see Witherspoon 1977) or on the streets of New York, or even in the more self-consciously contrived culture of academic philosophy. The same is true of notions of physical objects and interaction, space, life and its origins, and so on. But such endeavors have to be taken seriously; they are not casual pursuits, and are not to be confused with naturalistic inquiry into the nature of what folk science addresses in its own ways, using possibly different faculties of mind. Ethnoscience is a branch of science that studies humans, seeking to understand their modes of interpretation of the world, the diversity of these systems, and their origins. Separate branches of science study the nature of what humans are sorting out and interpreting in their peculiar ways, whether the phenomena are optical, electrical, mechanical, or mental. Meanwhile, we continue to employ our concepts, sometimes choosing reflectively to refine and modify them, in trying to deal with the problems of ordinary life. These are distinct pursuits.

Ethnoscience asks how people interpret and evaluate what they find around them. It is concerned with accounts of objects striving to reach their natural place and of the motion of the heavenly bodies against the fixed stars; of the basic substances earth, air, fire, and water and how they combine to yield the phenomena of nature; of vital forces that guide biological development and differentiation; of beliefs, desires, fears, and other elements that enter into accounts of purposive action; and so on. It is not a trivial empirical claim that in some cultural tradition people interpret motion in terms of contact; or, along Davidsonian lines, that they attribute beliefs and desires in terms of criteria of rationality and normativity with a holistic perspective, in their efforts to evaluate actions. These are strong claims, requiring evidence. It might turn out that beliefs and desires are attributed to creatures (perhaps humans) on entirely different grounds, perhaps as a reflection of instinctive modes of interpretation determined by innate endowment (common-sense), and that such attributions are systematically made even when the agents observed are considered to be acting in utterly irrational ways, or driven by instinct in contexts in which the question of rationality does not arise.

Whatever the ethnoscientist may discover about the nature of an "intentional stance" in Daniel Dennett's sense, two further directions for scientific inquiry open up. One is about people: what are the origins of their modes of understanding; specifically, what role does innate endowment play in developing a cosmology, or judging that another person is reaching for a book or reading one, or hurrying to catch the bus. A second direction considers the topics that people are attempting to understand in the instinctively grounded and culturally shaped ways of the folk sciences. What is the truth about cosmology, the formation of continents, the diversity of insects, planning one's actions, and so on. The answers, insofar as they are accessible to human intelligence, will be framed in terms appropriate to the problems at hand, with little concern for the intellectual apparatus of the folk sciences, and no expectation that constructs and principles that are developed will receive direct expression in terms of more "fundamental" branches of science, even if the unification problem has been solved. The end result may be to explain why folk-scientific interpretations more or less work, whether they are concerned with planets and flowers, or with a master chess player or a child building a tower with blocks (see Burge 1992; for some comments on attribution of mental states, in this context, see Chomsky 1969).

Returning to the critique of materialism – say, along Nagel's lines – it seems to face several problems. The presupposed concepts "physical" or "material" have no clear sense; nor will "mental," unless some sense can be given to the notion of *potential* consciousness and, even then, it is unclear what the interest of this particular category would be, as distinct from many others. It is not the business of the sciences to express the content of ordinary discourse about anything, physical or mental. There seems to be no coherent doctrine of materialism and metaphysical naturalism, no issue of eliminativism, no mind–body problem.

Problems mount when we look at how specific empirical questions are addressed. Nagel considers one: the proposal that there is a "Language Acquisition Device [LAD], which allows a child to learn the grammar of a language on the basis of the samples of speech it encounters" (1993: 109). He considers this a reputable part of science, right or wrong. But it is incorrect, he argues, to describe LAD as a "psychological mechanism," as I do: it should be seen as "simply a physical mechanism – for it is incapable of giving rise to subjective conscious thought whose content consists of those rules themselves" (p. 109). Putting aside this conception of "the essence of mind" and the accuracy of the description of LAD (which I would not quite give this way), note that Nagel's assertion appears to be an empirical one about the "capability" of some physical system. Again, we have the crucial matter of "potential consciousness," now presented as an empirical hypothesis. We return to that.

What would be the reaction to a theory of LAD (of UG) by an avowed "eliminative materialist," say Quine, whom Burge identifies as the originator of the doctrine? Quine puts forth the "naturalistic thesis" that "The world is as natural science says it is, insofar as natural science is right" (Quine 1992: 9); but that is not informative until we are told what "natural science" is. I suggested several possible answers, but Quine seems to have something else in mind. He takes natural science to be "theories of quarks and the like." What is "like enough" to be part of science? Neurons are evidently allowed, along with certain psychological processes: thus language, Quine asserts, "is linked to our neural input by neural mechanisms of association or conditioning." The empirical evidence is overwhelming that association and conditioning have little to do with language acquisition or use, but that seems not to matter; one wonders why. Whatever the answer, we find examples of what Quine favors (quarks, neural inputs, conditioning) and disfavors (the devices of LAD, that is, the operative mechanisms, so far as is known). But we are offered no reasons for the decisions, or more than a few examples to suggest their scope.

The "naturalistic thesis" proposed reveals the same arbitrariness in other domains. Thus Quine reiterates here the view he has often expounded that "reification of bodies comes in stages in one's acquisition of language," the "last stage" being recognition of identity over time. If that is an empirical hypothesis, one wants to know how it can be put forth with such confidence. It is surely not obvious, or even particularly plausible. We need not keep to anecdotal evidence; infant studies of past years provide considerable reason to believe that such "reification" appears in the first few months of life, long before any manifestation of language. (For general review, see Spelke 1990; on more recent work, see Baillargeon 1993; see also note 3 of this chapter.)

Since the theories of LAD to which Nagel refers dismiss the dogmas about association and conditioning, and postulate mechanisms that are not (at least currently, maybe never) expressible in terms of quarks or neurons, they presumably do not fall within science, in Quine's sense. This is much like chemistry a century ago, or celestial mechanics at the time of Newton, by similar reasoning. Perhaps the empirical investigation of "reification" also fails Quine's criteria, for the same reason.[3] We seem to be faced with an extreme example of methodological dualism, over and above the obscure character of the notions "materialism" and "eliminativism."

Access to consciousness

Let us turn now to the characterization of the mental in terms of access to consciousness, yielding the mind–body distinction, many hold. Adopting this characterization, Nagel concludes that LAD (and the state attained, an I-language, henceforth language) is only a physical mechanism, not a psychological mechanism, "for it is incapable of giving rise to subjective conscious thought whose content consists of those rules themselves" (1993: 109). Suppose that one option of variation among languages has to do with left–right orientation, English being syntactically "left-headed" ("see – the book," "in – the room," etc.) and Japanese "right-headed" (the mirror image, throughout). However, Johnny is not aware, and cannot tell us, that he is setting the "head parameter" as left–right on the basis of the evidence "see the book," etc., though perhaps that is exactly what is happening. Similarly, Mary has no conscious awareness that she is using principle (C) of binding theory when she interprets example (1) differently from example (2), excluding the option of referential dependence of *he* on *Bill* in example (1) but allowing it in example (2). Thus she does not interpret example (1) as (1′) but may interpret example (2) as (2′) (*he* = *Bill* in both cases):

(1)   He thinks Bill is a nice guy.

(2)   The woman he married thinks Bill is a nice guy.

(1′)   Bill thinks he is a nice guy.

(2′)   The woman Bill married thinks he is a nice guy.

Furthermore, this lack of awareness reaches to "potential consciousness," a notion yet to be clarified. Perhaps it means that no creature with Mary's language faculty, with these "physical mechanisms," can have the consciousness Mary lacks, an important empirical truth. Consequently, the theories of LAD and of the language do not cross the body–mind divide; they are not about the mind, about psychological mechanisms.

To take an example from a different domain, Mary is not consciously aware that she is using a *rigidity principle* that interprets visual presentations as a rigid object in motion when she sees what she takes to be a cube rotating in space. And three-month-old Johnny cannot tell us, and may not be aware, of the beliefs about object constancy ("reification") and trajectory that lead him to expect an object to appear in a particular form, time span, and place after passing behind a barrier (see Spelke 1990; Baillargeon 1993). Accordingly we cannot speak of the states and properties attributed to Mary and Johnny as psychological mechanisms of vision – at least, if potential consciousness is also lacking in these cases.

A similar idea is presented by Michael Dummett, though with different terminology. He regards the theories of LAD and the language attained as "psychological hypotheses," though neither offers a "philosophical explanation," because they do not tell us "the form in which [the body of knowledge] is delivered"; conscious awareness would, however, carry us past that divide (Dummett 1991: 97). Presumably the same would hold with regard to object constancy and the like. Here the distinction is not mind–body, but science–philosophy. For the sciences, the theories (accuracy aside) tell us everything relevant about the form in which the body of knowledge is delivered; however for the theory of meaning, (and, presumably, language and thought generally, and perhaps vision, reification, etc.), some additional kind of explanation is required, a "philosophical explanation," that goes beyond science.

In both cases, we have a crucial distinction – perhaps a metaphysical distinction – based on access to consciousness.

Nagel's account follows Searle's in the book he is reviewing (see Burge 1992). We can trace the argument in its contemporary form back to Quine's influential distinction between "fitting" and "guiding." Quine objects to a traditional doctrine (reinterpreted within contemporary linguistics) that speakers are "guided" by a perhaps unconscious "notion of structure" in forming and interpreting newly created "free expressions" (Jespersen 1924: 19). This is an "enigmatic doctrine," Quine holds, perhaps pure "folly" (Quine 1972: 447). We may speak of guiding only when rules are consciously applied to "cause" behavior; otherwise we may only say that behavior "fits" or "obeys" some system of rules, just as a planet obeys the law of falling bodies, and we must not attribute "psychological reality" to some particular conception of the nature of the organism that "obeys" the rules.

Once again, Quine adopts an extreme form of dualism. In the case of falling bodies, we are permitted – indeed, enjoined – to attribute "physical reality" to a particular conception of their nature and to the postulated principles. Plainly, we cannot account for the state attained by the language faculty and the ways it enters into behavior simply on the assumption that the brain has mass and obeys the law of falling bodies. More structure is needed. A naturalistic approach would proceed exactly as in the case of planets and ants; in this case, seeking a theory of initial and attained state, the relation between them, and the relation of the attained state to performance and judgments, attributing "reality" to whatever is postulated in the best theory we can devise. The level of understanding is far less in the vastly more intricate case of complex organisms, but that is not pertinent here.

A doctrinal divide is held to separate the cases: what is required in one case (falling bodies) is barred in the other (humans "above the neck"). Again, consciousness makes the difference, along with "causation of behavior," a notion with its own nontrivial problems. We have little reason to believe that normal behavior *is* caused, at least in any known sense of that term, nor would a methodological naturalist dogmatically assume otherwise.

Quine's reasoning would seem to apply in the same way to the visual example. Johnny and Mary are not "guided" by principles of rigidity, object constancy, and so on. Their behavior only "fits" these principles, as Mars satisfies the law of falling bodies. A theory of states of the brain that incorporates such principles to account for Mary's and Johnny's behavior, however well it might meet naturalistic standards, is methodologically defective; at best enigmatic, at worst folly. (As mentioned, Quine's view on this matter is difficult to determine. See note 3.)

These ideas appear in many other variants. They are not easy to assess. Thus, no plausible reason is given for the strictures, no indication that they are more than terminological demands of no particular interest. The most developed version is the one that Nagel adopts from Searle. Let us briefly look at that.

The unexplained dualism of Quine's distinction does not seem to have elicited much concern, but many see the consequences of the specific formulation as counterintuitive. Take the phenomenon of blindsight: Alice, who has sustained cerebral damage, distinguishes reliably between visual presentations (say, a drawing of a house on fire and of one that is not), but insists that they are identical, lacking any awareness of what enters into her differential behavior. In Quine's terms, we cannot speak of guiding here, only fitting (so it seems; see Quine

1992: 9; note 3). In other versions, we cannot attribute to Alice "mental representations," though we could for John, who is aware of and reports the difference, as Alice did before her injury. In Alice's case we have only "physical mechanisms," in John's "psychological mechanisms"; or, in a different usage, for Alice we have only a "psychological hypothesis," not a "philosophical explanation," as we do for John. None of these seem attractive consequences.

Searle hopes to avoid them by introducing the notion of access to consciousness *in principle* – what Nagel, in his review, calls the *potential* for consciousness.[4] Searle's "Connection Principle" (CP) requires accessibility in principle for attribution of mental states and processes. In the case of blindsight, Searle holds that Alice has access in principle to the representation, or the rule, or whatever. Blindsight is a case of mere "blockage," not "inaccessibility in principle," so we may speak of mental processes in Alice's case, as in John's. The conclusion will have substance when the term "in principle" is explained.

Suppose that Jane is identical to Alice (in relevant respects, a qualification henceforth omitted), except for her history: her neural condition was not the result of post-natal injury but of an injury at conception, which led to the condition. Presumably she too has "access in principle"; CP still holds (otherwise, the whole exercise was pointless; the time of the injury can hardly be relevant). Suppose that this injury at conception affected the genes in such a way as to yield blindsight; again, presumably, CP holds or the results are no less counterintuitive. Proceeding, suppose that Susan is identical to Jane except that the genetic change was due to a mutation, so that she is identical to Jane in genetic constitution, though she did not suffer blindsight through injury, as Alice and Jane did. Again, CP must hold, or the exercise was pointless. Susan, then, suffers only "blockage." Suppose that Susan's genetic property is transmitted, leading finally to a new subspecies. We now have the John-species and the Susan-species, exactly alike in their perceptual mechanisms. Members of the Susan-species are unaware of and cannot report the mental representations and rules that guide them. But the two subspecies are otherwise indistinguishable; and there is even some cross-species identity of visual mechanisms, as in the case of Alice and Jane after injury. Since CP holds of Susan, it presumably holds of the Susan-species; otherwise, again, we have completely pointless terminological stipulations.

Let's now take the language case. Suppose we discover that our evolutionary history matches that of the Susan-species. That is, our forebears were actually a John-species, fully aware of how they set the head parameter, determined referential dependence, and so on, and able to describe it all clearly to Martian scientists observing them. But a mutation took place (or perhaps an injury causing a genetic change, as in the case of Jane) and propagated, leading to us, a Susan-species, deprived of this ability. Suppose we even discover that we just haven't tested the right informants yet. The two subspecies are intermingled, and behave exactly alike; short of inquiring into awareness, none of us, and no scientist, can find any difference among the members. CP held for the earlier John-species, and for its remnants among us; hence for us as well, unless we choose to make terminological decisions which, as before, reveal the whole endeavor to be pointless.

But this is, completely the wrong result. The whole point of the exercise was to show that the naturalistic inquiry into language and mind does not yield "psychological reality," or "psychological mechanisms," or "philosophical explanations," or "mental representations," or "guiding" by rules. Crucially, the CP must determine that we have no access to the mechanisms and their operation *in principle*. We do not suffer mere "blockage"; rather, the mechanisms of our brain are "incapable of giving rise to subjective conscious thought whose content consists of those rules themselves" (Nagel 1993: 109), because all this lies beyond *potential* consciousness.

To save the story, it seems that we must insist that the John-species cannot exist in the case of language (though it can, and does, in the case of blindsight, namely humans): it is impossible for there to exist an organism exactly like us except that it is fully conscious of the content of the rules that it is following as it learns (and uses) a language. That, at last, looks like an empirical hypothesis, not a terminological stipulation. On what basis do we assert it? Or if the claim is not empirical but conceptual, what are the grounds for it? And whether we accept it or not – whether as an empirical or conceptual thesis – what possible interest does it have? How does it differ from some pronouncement about "the essence of the chemical" (electrical, optical, etc.)?

Similar questions arise in the case of object perception discussed earlier, and difficulties can be elaborated, leading to still further paradox. None of these questions arise in naturalistic inquiry, which has no place for such notions as "access in principle" or "potentially conscious" or CP, no notion of "philosophical explanation" beyond explanation, no privileged categories of evidence (like awareness, or "psychological" versus "linguistic" evidence), no mind–body distinction, no methodological (or other) dualism.

The effort to maintain these dualisms is reminiscent of attempts to salvage the idea that knowledge is a kind of ability, in the face of the fact that ability can improve or decline – or even be completely lost

– while knowledge remains unchanged, as illustrated, for example, by loss of ability to speak (swim, etc.) after injury and recovery without relevant input as effects of the injury recede. The natural conclusion is that knowledge (how . . . , that . . . , or whatever) has a crucial cognitive element, and ability to use knowledge is not to be confused with knowledge. To avoid the conclusion, a new technical concept with the properties of knowledge is constructed – called "ability" – but distinct from the ordinary concept, a move that is particularly odd when undertaken in alleged defense of a Wittgensteinian point of view. (See note 4 for references and discussion.)

Further varieties of dualism

Much of the discussion of rule-following in the literature takes as a model arithmetical or traffic rules, or those given in grammar books, or others with a normative character. A crucial feature of rule-following, then, is that error must be possible in the sense of violation of the norm. Whatever the interest of this discussion, it is not to the point here. Rules of language – for example, the principles of UG, or those that guide Mary's judgments about examples (1) and (2) above (see p. 93) – are not normative in this sense. Mary's judgments and other behavior can be "in error," for any number of reasons; for example, inattention or parsing difficulty (as in "garden path" sentences, or expressions that overwhelm perceptual capacities). Mary can also decide to violate her rules, perhaps for quite good reasons, say for literary effect. Judgments and behavior may also be inconsistent with norms in many ways: norms stipulated in various authoritarian structures, common practice in communities of the endlessly varying sort that individuals may be associated with, by choice or external pressure, and so on. Numerous questions arise of fact, policy, etc., but there seem to be none of principle, apart from questions that reduce to skeptical arguments of no special interest in this connection. (For further discussion, see Chomsky 1986.)

Should we speak of "following rules" in the case of Mary's linguistic judgments and behavior? The question is not very interesting, for reasons already mentioned; no one expects common discourse to survive the transition to explanatory theory. However, for the record, to speak of Mary as following rules in this case would be closer to common usage than the standard philosophical convention that requires a link to consciousness. In fact, it keeps fairly close to common usage except in one respect. We typically use the term "rule-following" in the case of *deviation* from community norms, not observance of them, as in the technical usage of philosophical discourse. Thus if Johnny says "I brang my lunch home," normal usage would be that he is following the rule for "sing," etc. – mistakenly, in that authority figures or some other standards call for "brought." Similarly if he uses "puppy" to refer to kittens, following the rule that small household pets are puppies. Someone who is attentive might make comparable comments about the rules of pronunciation he follows. If all adults were to die and Johnny and his cohorts to survive, they would continue to follow their private and individual rules, except that now these would be rules of a perfectly normal human language which differs from standard English in these (and other) respects. In that case, however, we would not normally say that Johnny is following a rule, because the term is rarely used for observance of norms and standards. Thus, only linguists would say that Mary is following Principle (C) of binding theory in examples (1) and (2), or following the intricate and complex rules of referring to objects when she talks about her house.

When we attribute rule-following in the normal way – say, to Johnny in the case above – we do not mean to suggest that the rule-followers are (or could be) aware of following the rules or choosing to do so. Those who speak of "the fact that linguistic meaning involves deliberate rule-following" are using the term "rule-following" in a technical sense of philosophical discourse, not in the conventional way (Baldwin 1993: 187, citing P. Pettit). I think the same is true of other terms of philosophical discourse, including "knowledge," "content," and "reference," among others. For some discussion, see publications cited earlier, and Chapter 2 of this volume.

Within the naturalistic theory of (I-)language – internalist and individualist – conclusions can be drawn about what one ought to do, but only in uninteresting hypothetical imperatives (if you want to rhyme something with "tower" or refer to daffodils, use "flower" not "book"). Such normativity, a regular consequence of knowledge, abounds in a naturalistic setting, but not the kind that arises when we ask whether Jones should change his usage of "arthritis" to conform to that of the doctor, a question of a very different kind, with no definite answer apart from specification of one or another region in a highly intricate space of human interests and concerns.

A related matter is the notion of language as a "community property" of some kind, as when we say that Hans and Maria speak German even though they cannot understand one another, and Hans does not speak Dutch though he understands quite well the Dutch spoken right across the border. Or when we say that Pierre and his son Jean, monolingual speakers of French who have moved to New York, are learning English, which Jean will succeed in doing though Pierre only partially so. Or that Johnny, with his "mistakes" about "brang," "puppy," and the pronunciation of his name, speaks no language at all (an odd gap in normal usage), though he will speak English some day and has "partial knowledge" of it today, and his current I-language would be a normal language if it perpetuates as described. A vast range of such usages are not problematic in ordinary life, but are of little interest for the effort to understand what language is and how it is used. It is not a matter of idealization; there are no sensible idealizations, any more than we reify *areas* in clarifying what is meant by the statement that John lives near Mary but far from Bill. Sometimes these usages are codified in "national languages," sometimes even imposed by force. Attempts to relate notions of "common language" to cultures simply make matters worse. A person will typically be part of many communities and cultures, with only weak correlations among the forms of association. Jones may participate in a common culture – with shared values, beliefs, understanding, etc. – with a monolingual speaker of some language he knows not a word of, perhaps to a greater extent than with his identical twin, with whom he grew up and whose speech is virtually indistinguishable from his own. None of this has anything to do with successful communication. We need not assume shared pronunciations or meanings to account for this, any more than we assume shared shapes to account for people who look alike.

Again, one may describe the innumerable situations that arise, and study of them is legitimate and useful. If pursued seriously, such study presupposes what is learned from naturalistic inquiry into the language faculty. However, attempts to base theories of pronunciation or meaning (with common pronunciations and common meanings) on alleged community properties can only lead to confusion. Such attempts again illustrate the kind of dualism that would never be taken seriously beyond the domain of the mental.

Another form of dualism that has arisen in the discussion of language acquisition is illustrated by a curious debate on "innatism" or "the innateness hypothesis." The debate is one-sided: no one defends the hypothesis, including those to whom it is attributed (me, in particular). The reason is that there is no such hypothesis. There are certain proposals about the initial state of the language faculty (LAD, UG). These are not questioned by the critics. Rather, they regard the enterprise as somehow faulty, apparently on some dualist assumption. Similar questions are not raised when proposals are made about other aspects of growth, and no reason has been given as to why they are appropriate here. Alternative theses of a very general nature have been put forth: for example, that "general learning mechanisms" suffice, with no need to assume specific properties of the language faculty. Such theses cannot be discussed until we are told what these mechanisms are. Specific proposals that have been made are hardly worth considering on naturalistic grounds, so they must be motivated by some other demands, dualist in nature.

Quine's behaviorism is a variant of this form of dualism.[5] He argues that "the behaviorist approach is mandatory" (Quine 1990: 37) for the study of language because, in acquiring language, "we depend strictly on overt behavior in observable situations" (p. 38). By similar argument, the nutritionist approach is mandatory in embryology because, in the passage from embryo to mature state, the organism depends strictly on nutrition provided from outside; just as linguists must be behaviorists, so biologists must be nutritionists, restricting themselves to observation of nutritional inputs. The fallacy in the latter argument is apparent; the same fallacy undermines the former. Only radical dualist assumptions allow the matter even to be discussed. Perhaps the actual study of language is conceptually flawed but, in order to establish this, it does not suffice to demand that the linguist abandon naturalistic inquiry – as Quine and his followers do – and adopt stipulations that are arbitrary apart from their historical antecedents, plainly irrelevant.

Closely related is Quine's radical translation paradigm. In the naturalistic study of interaction among organisms (cells, insects, birds, dolphins, . . .), we try to discover what internal states make the interaction possible, yielding the interpretations given to signals. In the study of human language, that path is interdicted. The study of interaction must keep within stipulated bounds: the investigating scientist is permitted to register noises in a specific way, to pick out some features of the situation, to test assent or dissent to the inquiry "Is this an X?," and to carry out elementary induction, but nothing more. Various hints are given as to the features admissible, the choice of X, etc. Quine alleges further that this is also the epistemic situation of the child acquiring language and the person in a communication interchange. The three cases are entirely different in character: the child comes equipped with the initial state of the language faculty (LAD, UG); the person in a communication interchange, with the properties of the attained state; the linguist, with the science-forming faculty and the result of earlier inquiry into language. It is not, however, important to sort this out, because there is a more fundamental problem: the radical dualism of the entire approach. Nothing remotely similar would be tolerated in the study of other organisms, or aspects of humans that do not fall under the traditional descriptive category of the "mental."

From this paradigm, widely adopted and discussed, far-reaching conclusions are drawn about language and thought. It appears to be a pointless intellectual exercise if intended to shed light on the nature of communication, acquisition, or the study of language and thought. At least, no satisfactory justification has been offered for it, to my knowledge, nor any explanation of why the approach should be adopted (or even considered) in this unique case. If the goal is to sharpen understanding of the concepts of belief, intention, meaning, and the like, the criteria for evaluation are more obscure but it is hard to see why the specific stipulated conditions should be privileged in this conceptual inquiry.

The paradigm underlies other dualist moves. Adapting it to his own concerns, Davidson argues that the goal of the descriptive study of meaning is to construct a theory that "is a model of the interpreter's linguistic competence," but that it "does not add anything to this thesis to say that if the theory does correctly describe the competence of an interpreter, some mechanisms in the interpreter must correspond to the theory" (Davidson 1986b: 438). Like Quine, he stipulates what is to count as relevant evidence: "what is open to observation is the use of sentences in context," nothing more. Theories may introduce "reference and related semantic notions," but there "can be no question about the correctness of these theoretical concepts beyond the question of whether they yield a satisfactory account of the use of sentences" (Davidson 1990: 300). Similar positions have been developed by Dummett and others (see Davidson 1986b; 1990a; on Dummett's version, see Chomsky 1986).

Again, comparable ideas would not be taken seriously in the study of other systems. Only if we keep to the radical translation paradigm or some other arbitrary constraint is evidence restricted to the use of sentences by the speaker (or some selected community). Approaching the topic as in the sciences, we will look for all sorts of evidence. For example, evidence from Japanese will be used (and commonly is used) for the study of English; quite rationally, on the well-supported empirical assumption that the languages are modifications of the same initial state. Similarly, evidence can be found from studies of language acquisition and perception, aphasia, sign language, electrical activity of the brain, and who knows what else. Furthermore, it adds a great deal to postulate mechanisms in the interpreter that "correspond to the theory," since it is precisely that move that subjects the theory to a wide variety of evidence beyond the stipulations of radical translation. Davidson's injunction simply bars naturalistic inquiry into the nature of the interpreter. Efforts to verify and improve the postulated account are declared illegitimate, or perhaps irrelevant for some reason. The same holds of many other variants.

In his historical reconstruction of the origins of the "Theory–Theory," Stephen Stich observes that with "the decline of Cartesian dualism, philosophers began looking for a way to locate the mental *within* the physical, identifying mental events with some category of events in the physical world" (Stich 1983: 14). That quest could have taken two directions, he observes: an attempt "to define mental vocabulary in *neurological* terms" (p. 14), or an analysis of mental concepts in terms of behavior, leading to philosophical behaviorism. The latter prevailed, he argues. What has just been reviewed is one highly influential strand, with no redeeming features, as far as I can see. The other direction has also been pursued, but also tainted by unjustified dualism.

Before turning to that, a few comments on this way of framing the issues. First, the reasons for the collapse of Cartesian dualism are somewhat misconstrued: as noted, it was the theory of body that was refuted, leaving no intelligible mind–body problem, no notion of "physical," etc. In this realm, we have only the naturalistic approach: to construct explanatory theory in whatever terms are appropriate, and to face the unification problem. Second, it is, for the moment, only a hope that "neurological terms" are relevant for the unification problem. Finally, there is no reason to try to define the "mental vocabulary" of ordinary discourse in a naturalistic framework, just as no one contemplates that for "physical vocabulary," at least in the modern period. Stich reaches a similar conclusion, but it is not clear why it even requires argument, dualist prejudice aside.

Naturalistic inquiry into the mind yields theories about the brain, its states and properties: UG, for example. No one knows how to begin to relate these theories to properties of atoms, cells, neurons, or other known structures of the brain. The disparity between theories of the mind and what has been learned about neurophysiology "creates a crisis for those who believe that the nervous system is precise and 'hardwired' like a computer," biologist Gerald Edelman (1992: 27f.) concludes; and for connectionist and neural net theories as well. The varied individual histories of the nervous system and the "enormous individual structural variation" of brains provide "the coup de grace (actually multiple coups)!" (Edelman 1992: postscript) to attempts to construct computational or neural net theories of the mind. Apparently Edelman takes this to be true no matter how successful such studies might be, now or ever, by the standards of science (explanation, insight, etc.).

By similar logic, one could have argued not long ago that there is a terrible crisis for the study of matter and organisms in terms of colors, valence, the solid state, and a multitude of other properties; and earlier, for the investigation of electricity and magnetism, planetary and celestial motion, etc. Virtually the whole of science was in crisis because of the huge gap between what had been learned about these topics and the principles of the mechanical philosophy (or even much more recent physics). The crisis Edelman perceives is real, but misplaced.

As for the "enormous variation" in structure of brains and experience, that tells us little. Not many years ago, languages appeared to differ from one another as radically as neural structures do to many a trained eye today, and were considered mere reflections of infinitely variable experience. Any complex system will appear to be a hopeless array of confusion before it comes to be understood, and its principles of organization and function discovered. Edelman argues that introducing considerations of meaning will somehow overcome the alleged problems of "formalist" approaches. These he seriously misunderstands – so his few comments indicate – but more important is the mistaken view of semantics. Simple semantic properties pose all the problems Edelman perceives in syntactic theories and constructions. They are rule-governed, sharply delineated, and fixed in relative independence of experience and known aspects of neural structure; hence they too induce the "crisis" caused by the gap between the apparent algorithmic, digital character of language and the observed variability and continuous flux of individual experience and neural structure. We face a typical problem of unification in the sciences, which may, as often in the past, require that the more "basic" science be fundamentally recast if it is to be integrated with successful explanatory theory at other levels.

Various remedies have been proposed to deal with the "crisis." One is the proposal that "the mental is the neurophysiological at a higher level." That could turn out to be true, but it is now a hypothesis about the neurophysiological, not a characterization of the mental; the shoe is on the wrong foot, in the light of what is at all understood. Another is the version of "eliminative materialism" that holds that we should concentrate on neurophysiology, which has all the merit of a proposal some time ago that chemistry should be abandoned in favor of the study of solid particles in motion, or that embryologists should follow the same course. There is a substantial literature asking what it would imply if neural-net (connectionist) models could account for the phenomena that have been explained in terms of computational–representational systems. Such discussion may appear to be naturalistic in temper, but that is hardly clear. Few biologists would be intrigued by the suggestion that unstructured systems with unknown properties might some day make it possible to account for development of organisms without appeal to complex constructions in terms of concentration of chemicals, the cell's internal program, production of proteins, and so on.

In some domains – language in particular – successful theories are commonly of the computational–representational type, a fact that causes considerable uneasiness. To relieve it, computer models are often invoked to show that we have robust, hard-headed instances of the kind: psychology then studies software problems. That is a dubious move. Artifacts pose questions that do not arise in the case of natural objects. Whether some object is a key or a table or a computer depends on designer's intent, standard use, mode of interpretation, and so on. The same considerations arise when we ask whether the device is malfunctioning, following a rule, etc. There is no natural kind or normal case. These questions do not arise in the study of organic molecules, the wings of chickens, the language faculty, or other natural objects. The belief that there was a problem to resolve, beyond the normal ones, reflects an unwarranted dualism; the proposed cure is worse than the disease.

These remarks barely skim the surface of dualist elements in much of the most sophisticated and influential thinking about language and mind. These should either be justified or abandoned. The critique of naturalistic approaches also seems to me to be flawed. There is, I think, good reason to examine more closely doctrines that have been assumed too casually, and if they do not withstand such analysis, to ask why they seem so compelling.

5   Language as a natural object

I would like to discuss an approach to the mind that considers language and similar phenomena to be elements of the natural world, to be studied by ordinary methods of empirical inquiry. I will be using the terms "mind" and "mental" here with no metaphysical import. Thus I understand "mental" to be on a par with "chemical," "optical," or "electrical." Certain phenomena, events, processes, and states are informally called "chemical" (etc.), but no metaphysical divide is suggested thereby. The terms are used to select certain aspects of the world as a focus of inquiry. We do not seek to determine the true *criterion of the chemical*, or the *mark of the electrical*, or the *boundaries of the optical*. I will use "mental" the same way, with something like ordinary coverage, but no deeper implications. By "mind" I just mean the mental aspects of the world, with no more interest in sharpening the boundaries or finding a criterion than in other cases.

I'll use the terms "linguistic" and "language" in much the same way. We focus attention on aspects of the world that fall under this informal rubric, and try to understand them better. In the course of doing so we may – and apparently do – develop a concept that more or less resembles the informal notion of "language," and postulate that such objects are among the things in the world, alongside of complex molecules, electrical fields, the human visual system, and so on.

A naturalistic approach to linguistic and mental aspects of the world seeks to construct intelligible explanatory theories, taking as "real" what we are led to posit in this quest, and hoping for eventual unification with the "core" natural sciences: unification, not necessarily reduction. Large-scale reduction is rare in the history of the sciences. Commonly the more "fundamental" science has had to undergo radical revision for unification to proceed. The case of chemistry and physics is a recent example: Pauling's account of the chemical bond unified the disciplines, but only after the quantum revolution in physics made these steps possible. The unification of much of biology with chemistry a few years later might be regarded as genuine reduction, but that is not common, and has no particular epistemological or other significance: "expansion" of physics to incorporate what was known about valence, the periodic table, chemical weights, and so on is no less valid a form of unification. In the present case, the theories of language and mind that seem best established on naturalistic grounds attribute to the mind/brain computational properties of a kind that are well understood, though not enough is known to explain how a structure constructed of cells can have such properties. That poses a unification problem, but of a familiar kind.

We do not know how eventual unification might proceed in this case, or if we have hit upon the right categories to seek to unify, or even if the question falls within our cognitive reach. We have no warrant simply to assume that mental properties are to be reduced to "neural-network properties," to take a typical claim (see Patricia Churchland 1994). Similar pronouncements have often proven false in other domains and are without any particular scientific merit in this case. If the thesis about neural networks is understood as a research proposal, well and good; we wait and see. If more is intended, rather serious questions arise.

As for the matter of cognitive reach, if humans are part of the natural world, not supernatural beings, then human intelligence has its scope and limits, determined by initial design. We can thus anticipate that certain questions will not fall within their cognitive reach, just as rats are unable to run mazes with numerical properties, lacking the appropriate concepts. Such questions, we might call "mysteries-for-humans" just as some questions pose "mysteries-for-rats." Among these mysteries may be questions we raise, and others we do not know how to formulate properly or at all. These truisms do not charge humans with "feeble intelligence." We do not condemn the human embryo as "feeble" because its genetic instructions are rich enough to enable it to become a human, hence to block other paths of development. Everyone would applaud if "questions shift status from Mysteries We Can Only Contemplate in Awe, to Tough Problems We Are Beginning to Crack" (Patricia Churchland 1994).[1] To demonstrate the shift for matters of traditional concern is no small order, and one may fairly ask whether the horizons remain as remote as ever, perhaps for reasons rooted in the human biological endowment.

Daniel Dennett argues that the notion of "epistemic boundedness," while "doctrinally convenient," is "rhetorically unstable," because "Chomsky and [Jerry] Fodor have hailed the capacity of the human brain to parse, and hence presumably understand, the official infinity of grammatical sentences of a natural language," including those "that best express the solutions to the problems of free will or conscious-ness," which he mistakenly claims I have declared "off-limits" (Dennett 1991: 10). However, even if the solutions can be formulated in human language – which has to be shown, not asserted – the argument is fallacious. First, as is well known, expressions of natural language are often unparseable (not only because of length, or complexity in some sense independent of the nature of the language faculty). Second, even if parsed and assigned an interpretation, they may be utterly incompre-hensible; examples are all too easy to find.

The history of the advanced sciences offers some insights into the quest for unification. Take as a starting point the "mechanical philosophy" that reached its apogee in the seventeenth century: the idea that the world is a machine of the kind that could be constructed by a skilled craftsman. This conception of the world has its roots in common-sense understanding, from which it drew the crucial assumption that objects can interact only through direct contact. As is familiar, René Descartes argued that certain aspects of the world – crucially, the normal use of language – lie beyond the bounds of mechanism. To account for them, he postulated a new principle; in his framework, a second substance, whose essence is thought. The "unification problem" arose as a ques-tion about the interaction of body and mind. This metaphysical dual-ism was naturalistic in essence, using empirical evidence for factual theses about the world – wrong ones, but then, that is the rule.

The Cartesian theory collapsed soon after, when Isaac Newton showed that terrestrial and planetary motion lie beyond the bounds of the mechanical philosophy – beyond what was understood to be body, or matter. What remained was a picture of the world that was "antima-terialist," and that "relied heavily on spiritual forces," as Margaret Jacob puts it (M. Jacob 1988: 97).

Newton's invocation of gravity was sharply condemned by leading scientists. E.J. Dijksterhuis points out that "the leaders of the true mechanistic philosophy regarded the theory of gravitation (to use the words of Boyle and Huygens) as a relapse into medieval conceptions that had been thought exploded, and as a kind of treason against the good cause of natural science" (Dijksterhuis 1986: 479). Newton's "mysterious force" was a return to the dark ages from which scientists had "emancipated themselves," "the scholastic physics of qualities and powers," "animistic explanatory principles," and the like, which admitted interaction without "direct contact." It was as if "Newton had stated that the sun generates in the planets a quality which makes them describe ellipses." In their correspondence, Leibniz and Huygens condemn Newton for abandoning sound "mechanical principles" and reverting to mystical "sympathies and antipathies," "immaterial and inexplicable qualities." Newton seems to have agreed. The context of his famous comment that "I frame no hypotheses" was an expression of concern over his inability to "assign the cause of this power" of gravity, which so departs from "mechanical causes." He therefore had to content himself with the conclusion "that gravity does really exist," its laws explaining "all the motions of the celestial bodies, and of our sea" – though he regarded the principle he postulated as an "absurdity." To the end of his life, Newton sought some "subtle spirit which pervades and lies hid in all gross bodies" that would account for interaction, electrical attraction and repulsion, the effect of light, sensation, and the way "members of animal bodies move at the command of the will." Similar efforts continued for centuries.

These concerns, at the origins of modern science, have something of the flavor of contemporary discussion of the "mind–body problem." They also raise questions about what is at stake. Thomas Nagel observes that "the various attempts to carry out this apparently impossible task [of reducing mind to matter] and the arguments to show that they have failed, make up the history of the philosophy of mind during the past fifty years." The hopeless task is to "complete the materialist world picture" by translating accounts of "mental phenomena" in terms of "a description that is either explicitly physical or uses only terms that can apply to what is entirely physical," or perhaps gives "assertability conditions" on "externally observable grounds" (Nagel 1993: 99). In an instructive review of a century of the philosophy of mind (see also Chapter 4 of this volume), Tyler Burge discusses the emergence of "naturalism" ("materialism," "physicalism") in the 1960s as "one of the few orthodoxies in American philosophy" (1992: 32). The view that there are no mental states (properties, etc.) "over and above ordinary physical entities, entities identifiable in the physical sciences or entities that common-sense would regard as physical" (1992: 31; see also Chapter 4 of this volume).

Such discussions assume, contrary to Newton and his contemporaries, that Newton remained within "the materialist world picture"; that would be true only if we understand "the materialist world picture" to be whatever science constructs, however it departs from "mechanical causes." To put it differently, the discussions presuppose some ante-cedent understanding of what is physical or material, what are the physical entities. These terms had some sense within the mechanical philosophy, but what do they mean in a world based on Newton's "mysterious force," or still more mysterious notions of fields of force, curved space, infinite one-dimensional strings in ten-dimensional space, or whatever science concocts tomorrow? Lacking a concept of "matter" or "body" or "the physical," we have no coherent way to formulate issues related to the "mind–body problem." These were real problems of science in the days of the mechanical philosophy. Since its demise, the sciences postulate whatever finds a place in intelligible explanatory theory, however offensive that may be to common-sense. Only on unjustified dualistic assumptions can such qualms be raised specifically about the domain of the mental, not other aspects of the world.

The anti-materialism of the Newtonians soon became established. By the mid-eighteenth century, Diderot's materialist commitments were apparently a factor in his overwhelming rejection for membership in the Royal Society. Hume wrote that "Newton seemed to draw off the veil from some of the mysteries of nature," but "he shewed at the same time the imperfections of the mechanical philosophy; and thereby restored [Nature's] ultimate secrets to that obscurity in which they ever did and ever will remain" (see Hume 1841 vol. 6: 341, cited in Gay 1977: 130).

That these secrets might remain in obscurity had sometimes been denied. Isaac Beekman, whom Jacob identifies as "the first mechanical philosopher of the Scientific Revolution" (M. Jacob 1988: 52), was confident that "God had so constructed the whole of nature that our understanding . . . may thoroughly penetrate all the things on earth" (M. Jacob 1988: 52–3). Similar theses are propounded with the same confidence today, notably by people who describe themselves as hard-headed scientific naturalists and who typically rephrase Beekman's formula, replacing "God" by "natural selection" – with even less justi-fication, because the *deus ex machina* is better defined in this case, so it is easy to see why the arguments fail.

Though Newton's anti-materialism became scientific common-sense, his qualms were not really put to rest. One expression of them was the belief that nature was unknowable. Another variant held that theoretical posits should be given only an operationalist interpretation. Lavoisier believed that "the number and nature of elements" is "an unsolvable problem, capable of an infinity of solutions none of which probably accord with Nature"; "It seems extremely probable we know nothing at all about . . . [the] indivisible atoms of which matter is composed" (Lavoisier, cited in Brock 1992: 129), and never will, he believed. Ludwig Boltzmann described his molecular theory of gases as nothing but a convenient analogy. Jules Poincaré held that we have no reason to choose between ethereal–mechanical or electromagnetic theories of light and accept the molecular theory of gases because we are familiar with the game of billiards (Brock 1992: 165). The chemist's atoms were considered "theoretical, metaphysical entities," William Brock observes;

interpreted operationally, they provided a "conceptual basis for assigning relative elementary weights and for assigning molecular formulae" (p. 171), and these instrumental devices were distinguished from "a highly controversial physical atomism, which made claims concerning the ultimate mechanical nature of all substances." Unification was only achieved with radical changes in physical atomism: Bohr's model, quantum theory, and Pauling's discoveries (see Chomsky 1986: 251–2, citing Heilbron). The unification finally overcame what had seemed an unbridgeable divide, pre-Planck: "The chemist's matter was discrete and discontinuous, the physicist's energy continuous, [a] nebulous mathematical world of energy and electromagnetic waves . . ." (Brock 1992: 489).

In the mid-nineteenth century, the formulas analyzing complex molecules were considered to be "merely classificatory symbols that summarized the observed course of a reaction"; the "ultimate nature of molecular groupings was unsolvable," it was held, and "the actual arrangements of atoms within a molecule," if that even means anything, is "never to be read" into the formulas (Brock 1992: 254). Kekulé, whose structural chemistry paved the way to eventual unification, doubted that "absolute constitutions of organic molecules could ever be given" (p. 252); his models and analysis of valency were to have an instrumental interpretation only. Until the 1870s, Kekulé rejected the idea that the "rational formulae . . . actually represented the real arrangements of a molecule's atoms." As late as 1886, French schools were not permitted to teach atomic theory because it was a "mere hypothesis," by decision of the Minister of Education, the well-known chemist Berthelot (p. 364).

Forty years later, eminent scientists ridiculed as a conceptual absurdity the proposal of G.N. Lewis that "the atomic shells were mutually interpenetrable" so that an electron "may form part of the shell of two different atoms" – later "a cardinal principle of the new quantum mechanics," Brock notes (1992: 476). It was "equivalent to saying that husband and wife, by having a total of two dollars in a joint account and each having six dollars in individual bank accounts, have got eight dollars apiece," one objection ran (Brock 1992: 477, citing Kasimir Fajans); it was as if the electrons were "sitting around on dry goods boxes at every corner, ready to shake hands with . . . electrons in other atoms," a distinguished Faraday lecturer commented with derision (Brock 1992: 477, citing R.A. Mullikan). America's first Nobel Prize-winning chemist, Theodore Richards, dismissed talk about the real nature of chemical bonds as metaphysical "twaddle." This was nothing more than "a very crude method of representing certain known facts about chemical reactions. A mode of represent[ation]" only (Brock 1992: 466, citing Theodore Richards). The rejection of that skepticism by Lewis and others paved the way to the eventual unification.

It is not hard to find contemporary counterparts in the discussion of the mind–body problem, whatever that is supposed to be. There is, I think, a good deal to learn from the history of the sciences since they abandoned common-sense foundations, always with some uneasiness about just what they were doing. We should by now be able to accept that we can do no more than seek "best theories," with no independent standard for evaluation apart from contribution to understanding, and hope for unification but with no advance doctrine about how, or whether, it can be achieved. As Michael Friedman puts the point, "the philosophers of the modern tradition," from Descartes, "are not best understood as attempting to stand outside the new science so as to show, from some mysterious point outside of science itself, that our scientific knowledge somehow 'mirrors' an independently existing reality. Rather, [they] start from the *fact* of modern scientific knowledge as a fixed point, as it were. Their problem is not so much to justify this knowledge from some 'higher' standpoint as to articulate the new *philosophical* conceptions that are forced upon us by the new science" (Friedman 1993: 48). In Kant's words, mathematics and the science of nature stand in no need of philosophical inquiry for themselves, "but for the sake of another science: metaphysics" (Kant 1783: Section 40).

On this view, the natural sciences – whether the topic is the motion of the planets, the growth of an organism, or language and mind – are "first philosophy." The idea is by now a commonplace with regard to physics; it is a rare philosopher who would scoff at its weird and counterintuitive principles as contrary to right thinking and therefore untenable. But this standpoint is commonly regarded as inapplicable to cognitive science, linguistics in particular. Somewhere in-between, there is a boundary. Within that boundary, science is self-justifying; the critical analyst seeks to learn about the criteria for rationality and justification from the study of scientific success. Beyond that boundary, everything changes; the critic applies independent criteria to sit in judgment over the theories advanced and the entities they postulate. This seems to be nothing more than a kind of "methodological dualism," far more pernicious than the traditional metaphysical dualism, which was a scientific hypothesis, naturalistic in spirit. Abandoning this dualist stance, we pursue inquiry where it leads.

We also should be able now to adopt an attitude towards the mind–body problem formulated in the wake of Newton's demolition of materialism and the "mechanical philosophy": for example, by Joseph

Priestley, whose conclusion was "not that all reduces to matter, but rather that the kind of matter on which the two-substance view is based does not exist," and "with the altered concept of matter, the more traditional ways of posing the question of the nature of thought and of its relations to the brain do not fit. We have to think of a complex organized biological system with properties the traditional doctrine would have called mental *and* physical" (John Yolton's paraphrase; Yolton 1983: 114).

In Priestley's own words, matter "is possessed of powers of attraction and repulsion" that act at a "real and in general an assignable distance from what we call the body itself," properties that are "absolutely essential to [the] very nature" of matter (Yolton 1983: 111). We thus overcome the naive belief that bodies (atoms aside) have inherent solidity and impenetrability, dismissing arguments based on "vulgar phraseology" and "vulgar apprehensions," as in the quest for the *me* referred to in the phrase "my body." With the Newtonian discoveries, matter "ought to rise in our esteem, as making a nearer approach to the nature of spiritual and immaterial beings," the "odium [of] solidity, inertness, or sluggishness" having been removed (p. 113). Matter is no more "incompatible with sensation and thought" than with attraction and repulsion. "The powers of sensation or perception and thought" are properties of "a certain organized system of matter"; properties "termed mental" are "the result (whether necessary or not) of such an organical structure as that of the brain." It is as reasonable to believe "that the powers of sensation and thought are the necessary result of a particular organization, as that sound is the necessary result of a particular concussion of the air." Thought in humans "is a property of the nervous system, or rather of the brain." Similar conclusions had been drawn by La Mettrie a generation earlier, though on different grounds.

More cautiously, we may say that in appropriate circumstances *people* think, not their brains, which do not, though their brains provide the mechanisms of thought. I may do long division by a procedure I learned in school, but my brain doesn't do long division even if it carries out the procedure. Similarly, I myself am not doing long division if I mechanically carry out instructions that are interpreted as the very algorithm I use, responding to inputs in some code in a Searle-style "arithmetic room." Nothing follows about my brain's executing an algorithm, in this case or that of translation and understanding. *People* in certain situations understand a language; my brain no more understands English than my feet take a walk. It is a great leap from common-sense intentional attributions to people, to such attributions to parts of people or to other objects. That move has been made far too easily, leading to extensive and it seems pointless debate over such alleged questions as whether machines can think: for example, as to "how one might *empirically* defend the claim that a given (strange) object plays chess" (Haugeland 1979), or determine whether some artifact or algorithm can translate Chinese, or reach for an object, or commit murder, or believe that it will rain. Many of these debates trace back to the classic paper by Alan Turing in which he proposed the Turing test for machine intelligence, but they fail to take note of his observation that "The original question, 'Can machines think?,' I believe to be too meaningless to deserve discussion" (Turing 1950: 442): it is not a question of fact, but a matter of decision as to whether to adopt a certain metaphorical usage, as when we say (in English) that airplanes fly but comets do not – and as for space shuttles, choices differ. Similarly, submarines set sail but do not swim. There can be no sensible debate about such topics; or about machine intelligence, with the many familiar variants.

It is perhaps worth comparing contemporary debate with seventeenth- and eighteenth-century discussion of similar topics. At that time too, many people were intrigued by the capacities of artifacts, and debated whether humans might simply be devices of greater complexity and different design. But that debate was naturalistic in character, having to do with properties not subsumed under the mechanical philosophy, so it appeared. Focusing on language use, Descartes and his followers, notably Géraud de Cordemoy, outlined experimental tests for "other minds," holding that if some object passes the hardest experiments I can devise to test whether it expresses and interprets new thoughts as I do, it would be "unreasonable" to doubt that it has a mind like mine. This is ordinary science, on a par with a litmus test for acidity. The project of machine simulation was actively pursued, but understood as a way to find out something about the world. The great artificer Jacques de Vaucanson did not seek to fool his audience into believing that his mechanical duck was digesting food, but rather to learn something about living things by construction of models, as is standard in the sciences. Contemporary debate contrasts rather unfavorably with the tradition, it would seem (Jonathan Marshall 1989; see also Chomsky 1993a; for further comment and for more extensive discussion, see Chomsky 1966).

Similar considerations hold with regard to the intentional terminology commonly used in describing what happens in the world. Thus we say that the asteroid is aiming towards the Earth and the missile is rising towards the Moon, the flower is turning towards the light, the bee is flying to the flower, the chimpanzee is reaching for the coconut,

John is walking to his desk. Some future naturalistic theory might have something to say both about normal usage and about the cases it seeks to address, two quite different topics. Neither inquiry would be bound by "vulgar phraseology [and] apprehensions," just as we do not expect the theory of vision to deal with Clinton's vision of the international market, or expect the theory of language to deal with the fact that Chinese is the language of Beijing and Hong Kong, though Romance is not the language of Bucharest and Rio de Janeiro – as a result of such factors as the stability of empires and the like.

It would be misleading to say that we abandon the *theories* that the asteroid is aiming towards the Earth, that the Sun is setting and the heavens darkening, that the wave hit the beach and then receded, that the wind died and the waves disappeared, that people speak Chinese but not Romance, and so on, replacing them by better ones. Rather, the search for theoretical understanding pursues its own paths, leading to a completely different picture of the world, which neither vindicates nor eliminates our ordinary ways of talking and thinking. These we can come to appreciate, modify and enrich in many ways, though science is rarely a guide in areas of human significance. Naturalistic inquiry is a particular human enterprise that seeks a special kind of understanding, attainable for humans in some few domains when problems can be simplified enough. Meanwhile, we live our lives, facing as best we can problems of radically different kinds, far too rich in character for us to hope to be able to discern explanatory principles of any depth, if these even exist. (For somewhat similar conclusions on different grounds, see Baker (1988) and Charles Chastain's comments.)

The basic contention of Priestley and other eighteenth-century figures seems uncontroversial: thought and language are properties of organized matter – in this case, mostly the brain, not the kidney or the foot. It is unclear why the conclusion should be resurrected centuries later as an audacious and innovative proposal – "the bold assertion that mental phenomena are entirely natural and caused by the neurophysiological activities of the brain," (Patricia Churchland 1994) the hypothesis "that capacities of the human mind are in fact capacities of the human brain" (Paul Churchland 1994); or that "consciousness is a higher-level or emergent property of the brain," "as much of the natural biological order as . . . photosynthesis, digestion, or mitosis," John Searle's recent formulation (1992: 90), which Nagel (1993) describes as the "metaphysical heart" of a "radical thesis" that "would be a major addition to the possible answers to the mind–body problem" if properly clarified (as he considers unlikely). Every year or two a book appears by some distinguished scientist with the "startling conclusion" or "astonishing hypothesis" that thought in humans "is a property of the nervous system, or rather of the brain," the "necessary result of a particular organization" of matter, as Priestley put the matter long ago, in terms that seem close to truism – and as uninformative as truisms tend to be, since the brain sciences, despite important progress, are far from closing the gap to the problems posed by thought and language, or even to what is more or less understood about these topics.

Here, we face typical problems of unification. "The variance of neural maps is not discrete or two-valued but rather continuous, fine-grained, and extensive," Gerald Edelman writes (Edelman 1992: 28), concluding that computational or connectionist theories of the mind must be wrong because of their discrete character. That is no more reasonable than the conclusion, a century ago, that chemistry must be wrong because it could not be unified with what we now know to be a far-too-impoverished physics; in particular, because "the chemist's matter was discrete and discontinuous, the physicist's energy continuous" (Edelman 1992: 27).[2] The disparity is real enough, but it is not, as Edelman sees it, a "crisis" for cognitive science; it is, rather, a unification problem, in which the chips fall where they may.

There is no problem of principle in devising systems that map continuous inputs into very specific discrete outputs; the "all-or-nothing" character of neural interaction is an example. Another illustration is given in a recent study that uses "a thermodynamic computer model to show that great regularity in the position of a subtle feature, a switch from six to four layers, can result from a slight discontinuity in the inputs to the lateral geniculate during development," a "small perturbation" that "markedly affect[s] the overall organization of . . . a large structure," one of many such examples, the author notes. (Stryker 1994: 1244). Whatever the empirical status of particular proposals, the problems of unification of discrete (computational or connectionist) and cellular theories has not been shown to be different in kind from others that have arisen throughout the course of science.

The current situation is that we have good and improving theories of some aspects of language and mind, but only rudimentary ideas about the relation of any of this to the brain. Consider a concrete example. Within computational theories of the language faculty of the brain, there is by now a fairly good understanding of distinctions among kinds of "deviance" – departure from one or another general principle of the language faculty. Recent work on electrical activity of the brain has found correlates to several of these categories of deviance, and a distinctive kind of electrophysiological response to syntactic versus semantic violations (Neville et al. 1991; Hagoort et al. 1993; Hagoort and Brown

1994). Still, the findings remain something of a curiosity, because there is no appropriate theory of electrical activity of the brain – no known reason, that is, why one should find these results, not others. The computational theories, in contrast, are more solidly based from the point of view of scientific naturalism; the analysis of deviance, in particular, falls within an explanatory matrix of considerable scope.

A naturalistic approach to language and mind will seek to improve each approach, hoping for more meaningful unification. It is common to suppose that there is something deeply problematic in the theory that is more solidly established on naturalistic grounds, the "mental one"; and to worry about problems of "eliminationism" or "physicalism" that have yet to be formulated coherently. Furthermore, this dualist tendency not only dominates discussion and debate, but is virtually presupposed, a curious phenomenon of the history of thought that merits a closer investigation.

Putting aside such tendencies, how would a naturalistic inquiry proceed? We begin with what we take to be natural objects, say Jones. We are initially interested in particular aspects of Jones, the linguistic aspects. We find that some elements of Jones's brain are dedicated to language – call them the *language faculty*. Other parts of the body may also have specific language-related design, and elements of the language faculty may be involved in other aspects of life, as we would expect of any biological organ. We put these matters to the side at first, keeping to the language faculty of the brain, clearly fundamental. There is good evidence that the language faculty has at least two different components: a "cognitive system" that stores information in some manner, and performance systems that make use of this information for articulation, perception, talking about the world, asking questions, telling jokes, and so on. The language faculty has an input receptive system and an output production system, but more than that; no one speaks only Japanese and understands only Swahili. These performance systems access a common body of information, which links them and provides them with instructions of some kind. The performance systems can be selectively impaired, perhaps severely so, while the cognitive system remains intact, and further dissociations have been discovered, revealing the kind of modular structure expected in any complex biological system.

Note that "modularity" here is not understood in the sense of Jerry Fodor's interesting work, which keeps to input and output systems; the cognitive system of the language faculty is accessed by such systems, but is distinct from them. It may well be true that "psychological mechanisms" are "composed of independent and autonomous faculties like the perception of faces and of language" (Mehler and Dupoux 1994), but these "mental organs" do not appear to fit within the framework of modularity, as more narrowly construed. Similarly, David Marr's influential ideas about levels of analysis do not apply here at all, contrary to much discussion, because he too is considering input–output systems; in this case, the mapping of retinal stimulations to some kind of internal image.

Jones's language faculty has an "initial state," fixed by genetic endowment. It is generally assumed that the performance systems are fully determined by the initial state – that any state changes are internally directed or the result of extraneous factors such as injury, not exposure to one or another language. This is the simplest assumption, and it is not known to be false, though it may well be; adopting it, we attribute language-related differences in perception (say, our inability to perceive differences of aspiration as a Hindi speaker would) to differences in the phonetic aspects of the cognitive system, without having much faith in the assumption, though there is some evidence for it: thus, under experimental conditions, English speakers detect the Hindi contrasts that they do not "hear" in a linguistic context. The performance systems may well be specialized for language. Even very young infants appear to have something like the adult phonetic system in place, perhaps a special refinement of a broader vertebrate category. Mehler and Dupoux propose the working hypothesis that "newborns are sensitive to *all* contrasts that can appear in *all* natural languages, and in exactly the same way as adults" (Mehler and Dupoux 1994: 167), with "learning by forgetting" (p. 168) under early exposure, so that before the child is a year old, the cognitive system has selected some subpart of the available potential.

On these simplifying assumptions about development, we look just at the cognitive system of the language faculty, its initial state, and its later states. Plainly, there are state changes that reflect experience: English is not Swahili, at least, not quite. A rational Martian scientist would probably find the variation rather superficial, concluding that there is one human language with minor variants. But the cognitive system of Jones's language faculty *is* modified in response to linguistic experience, changing state until it pretty much stabilizes, perhaps as early as six to eight years old, which would mean, if true, that later (nonlexical) changes that have been found, up to about puberty, are inner-directed.

Let us tentatively call a state of the cognitive system of Jones's language faculty a "language" – or, to use a technical term, an "I-language," "I" to suggest "internal," "individual," since this is a strictly internalist, individualist approach to language, analogous in this respect to studies of the visual system.[3] If the cognitive system of Jones's language faculty is in state L, we will say that Jones has the I-language L. An I-language is something like "a way of speaking," one traditional notion of language.

Despite some similarity to standard locutions, however, the terminology here is different, as we expect even in the earliest stages of naturalistic inquiry. The languages of the world describe such matters in various ways. In English, we say that Jones *knows* his language; others say that he speaks it, or speaks with it, and so on. Also, terms for something like language vary, though I know of no serious cross-cultural study. These topics are of interest for natural-language semantics, and other branches of naturalistic inquiry that seek to determine how cognitive systems, including language, yield what is sometimes called "folk science." We speak of flowers turning towards the Sun, the heavens darkening, apples falling to the ground, people having beliefs and speaking languages, and so on; our ways of thinking and understanding – and our intuitive ideas about how the world is constituted – may or may not relate directly to such locutions. The elements of folk science derive from our biological endowment, taking particular forms under varying cultural conditions. There is evidence that young children attribute beliefs and plans to others well before they have terms to describe this; and the same may be true of adults generally, though most languages, it is reported, do not have terms corresponding to the English "belief." These are serious inquiries, not to be undertaken casually; our intuitions about them provide some evidence, but nothing more than that. Furthermore, whatever may be learned about folk science will have no relevance to the pursuit of naturalistic inquiry into the topics that folk science addresses in its own way, a conclusion taken to be a truism in the study of what is called "the physical world" but considered controversial or false (on dubious grounds, I think) in the study of the mental aspects of the world.

So far I have kept to Jones, his brain, its language faculty, and some of its components; all of these are natural objects. Turning to Smith, we discover that the initial state of his language faculty is virtually identical; given Jones's experience, he would have Jones's language. That seems to be true across the species, meaning that the initial state is a species property, to very good first approximation. If so, the *human language faculty* and the (I-)languages that are manifestations of it qualify as natural objects.

If Jones has the language L, he knows many things: for example, that *house* rhymes with *mouse* and that *brown house* consists of two words in the formal relation of assonance, and is used to refer to a structure designed and used for certain purposes and with a brown exterior. We would like to find out how Jones knows such things. It seems to work something like this.

The I-language consists of a computational procedure and a lexicon. The lexicon is a collection of items, each a complex of properties (called "features"), such as the property "bilabial stop" or "artifact." The computational procedure selects items from the lexicon and forms an expression, a more complex array of such features. There is reason to believe that the computational system is invariant, virtually. There is some variation at the parts closely related to perception and articulation; not surprisingly, since it is here that data are available to the child acquiring language – a process better described as "growth" than "learning," in my opinion. That aside, language variation appears to reside in the lexicon. One aspect is "Saussurean arbitrariness," the arbitrary links between concepts and sounds: the genetic program does not determine whether *tree*, the concept, is associated with the sounds "tree" (in English) or "Baum" (in German). The linkage of concept and sound can be acquired on minimal evidence, so variation here is not surprising. However, the possible sounds are narrowly constrained, and the concepts may be virtually fixed. It is hard to imagine otherwise, given the rate of lexical acquisition, which is about a word an hour from ages two to eight, with lexical items typically acquired on a single exposure, in highly ambiguous circumstances, but understood in delicate and extraordinary complexity that goes vastly beyond what is recorded in the most comprehensive dictionary, which, like the most comprehensive traditional grammar, merely gives hints that suffice for people who basically know the answers, largely innately.

Beyond such factors, variation may be limited to formal aspects of language – case of nouns, verbal inflection, and so on. Even here, variation may be slight. On the surface, English appears to differ sharply from German, Latin, Greek or Sanskrit in richness of inflection; Chinese even more so. But there is evidence that the languages have basically the same inflectional systems, differing only in the way formal elements are accessed by the part of the computational procedure that provides instructions to articulatory and perceptual organs. The mental computation seems otherwise identical, yielding indirect effects of inflectional structure that are observable, even if the inflections themselves are not heard in speech. That may well be the basis of language variation, in large measure. Small changes in the way a system functions may, of course, yield what appears to be great phenomenal variety.

The computational procedure has properties that may be unique to it, in substantial part. It is also "austere," with no access to many of the properties of other cognitive systems. For example, it seems to have no "counters." It registers adjacency; thus every other syllable could have some property (say, stress). But it cannot use the notion *three*. There are no known phonological systems in which something happens every third syllable, for example; and syntax seems to observe a property of "structure dependence," unable to make use of linear and arithmetical properties that are much simpler to implement outside the language faculty.

Recent experimental work by Neil Smith and his colleagues bears on this matter. (Smith *et al.* 1993: 279–347). They have been studying a person – called "Christopher" – who seems to have an intact language faculty but severe cognitive deficits, an example of the kind of modularity of mental architecture that has been found repeatedly. Christopher had mastered some 16 languages, and can translate from them to English. The experiments involved Christopher and a control group. Both were taught Berber and an invented system designed to violate principles of language. As expected, Christopher learned Berber easily but, lacking other cognitive capacities, could do little with the invented system. The control group made some progress on the invented system, apparently treating it as a puzzle. But there were some extremely simple rules they did not discover: for example, the rule that placed an emphatic marker on the third word of a sentence. It seems that the "austerity" of the language faculty sufficed to bar discovery of a simple structure-independent rule, within a linguistic context.

Our use of language of course involves numbers; we can understand and identify sonnets, for example. It also involves inference, though it seems that the computational procedure is too austere to use these resources either. The language faculty is both very rich and very impoverished, as any biological system is expected to be: capable of a high-level of achievement in specific domains, and correspondingly unable to deal with problems that lie outside them. As noted earlier, we should expect that to be true of all our faculties, including what might be called the "science-forming faculty," the particular collection of qualities and abilities we use in conducting naturalistic inquiry.

Though highly specialized, the language faculty is not tied to specific sensory modalities, contrary to what was assumed not long ago. Thus, the sign language of the deaf is structurally much like spoken language, and the course of acquisition is very similar. Large-scale sensory deficit seems to have limited effect on language acquisition. Blind children acquire language as the sighted do, even color terms and words for visual experience like "see" and "look." There are people who have achieved close to normal linguistic competence with no sensory input beyond what can be gained by placing one's hand on another person's face and throat. The analytic mechanisms of the language faculty seem to be triggered in much the same ways whether the input is auditory, visual, even tactual,[4] and seem to be localized in the same brain areas, somewhat surprisingly.

These examples of impoverished input indicate the richness of innate endowment – though normal language acquisition is remarkable enough, as even lexical access shows, not only because of its rapidity and the intricacy of result. Thus, very young children can determine the meaning of a nonsense word from syntactic information in a sentence far more complex than any they can produce (Gleitman 1990).

A plausible assumption today is that the principles of language are fixed and innate, and that variation is restricted in the manner indicated. Each language, then, is (virtually) determined by a choice of values for lexical parameters: with one array of choices, we should be able to deduce Hungarian; with another, Yoruba. This principles-and-parameters approach offers a way to resolve a fundamental tension that arose at the very outset of generative grammar. As soon as the first attempts were made to provide actual descriptions of languages 40 years ago, it was discovered that the intricacy of structure is far beyond anything that had been imagined, that traditional descriptions of form and meaning merely skimmed the surface while structuralist ones were almost irrelevant. Furthermore, the apparent variability of languages explodes as soon as one attends to facts that had been tacitly assigned to the unanalyzed "intelligence of the reader." To attain "descriptive adequacy," it seemed necessary to give very intricate accounts, specific to particular languages, indeed to particular constructions in particular languages: complex rules for relative clauses in English, for example. It was, however, obvious that nothing of the sort could be true. The conditions of language acquisition make it plain that the process must be largely inner-directed, as in other aspects of growth, which means that all languages must be close to identical, largely fixed by the initial state. The major research effort since has been guided by this tension, pursuing the natural approach: to abstract from the welter of descriptive complexity certain general principles governing computation that would allow the rules of a particular language to be given in very simple forms, with restricted variety.

Efforts to resolve the tension in this way led finally to the principles-and-parameters approach just outlined. It is more a bold hypothesis than a specific theory, though parts of the picture are being filled in, and new theoretical ideas are leading to a vast expansion in relevant empirical materials from typologically diverse languages.

These ideas constitute a radical departure from a rich tradition of some 2,500 years. If correct, they show not only that languages are cast to very much the same mold, with a near invariant computational procedure and only restricted lexical variation, but also that there are no rules or constructions in anything like the traditional sense, which was carried over to early generative grammar: no rules for formation of relative clauses in English, for example. Rather, the traditional constructions – verb phrase, relative clause, passive, etc. – are taxonomic artifacts, their properties resulting from the interaction of far more general principles.

The principles-and-parameters approach dissociates two notions that fell together under the concept of I-language: there is a clear conceptual distinction between the state of the language faculty, on the one hand, and an instantiation of the initial state with parameters fixed, on the other. Apart from miracles, the objects so identified will always differ empirically. The actual state of one's language faculty is the result of interaction of a great many factors, only some of which are relevant to inquiry into the nature of language. On more theory-internal grounds, then, we take an I-language to be an instantiation of the initial state, idealizing from actual states of the language faculty. As elsewhere in naturalistic inquiry, the term "idealization" is somewhat misleading: it is the procedure we follow in attempting to discover reality, the real principles of nature. Only in the study of mental aspects of the world is this considered illegitimate, another example of pernicious dualism that should be overcome.

Progress along these lines has opened up new questions, notably, the question to what extent the principles themselves can be reduced to deeper and natural properties of computation. To what extent, that is, is language "perfect," relying on natural optimality conditions and very simple relations? One theory holds that, apart from the phonetic features that are accessed by articulatory–perceptual systems, the properties of an expression that enter into language use are completely drawn from the lexicon: the computation organizes these in very restricted ways, but adds no further features; that is a considerable simplification of earlier assumptions, which would, if correct, require considerable rethinking of the "interface" between the language faculty and other systems of the mind. Another recent theory, proposed in essence by Richard Kayne (1994), is that there is no parametric variation in temporal order. Rather, order is a reflex of structural properties determined in the course of computation: all languages are of the basic form subject–verb–object, on these assumptions. Other recent work seeks to show that possible expressions that would be interpretable at the interface, if formed, are

barred by the fact that other computations with the same lexical resources are more economical. On these matters, see Chomsky (1993b)
and Chomsky (1995b) and sources cited there.

On such assumptions, we expect that languages are "learnable,"
because there is little to learn, but are in part "unusable," for one
reason, because conditions of global economy may yield high levels of
computational complexity. That languages are "learnable" would be a
surprising empirical discovery; there is no general biological or other
reason why languages made available by the language faculty should be
fully accessible, as they will be if languages are fixed by setting of simple
parameters. The conclusion that languages are partially unusable, however, is not at all surprising. It has long been known that performance
systems often "fail," meaning that they provide an analysis that differs
from that determined by the cognitive system (the I-language). Many
categories of expressions have been studied that pose structural problems
for interpretation: multiple embedding, so-called "garden-path sentences," and others. Even simple concepts may pose hard problems of
interpretation: words that involve quantifiers or negation, for example.
Such expressions as "I missed (not) seeing you last summer" (meaning
I expected to see you but didn't) cause endless confusion. Sometimes
confusion is even codified, as in the idiom "near miss," which means
"nearly a hit," not "nearly a miss" (analogous to "near accident").

The belief that parsing is "easy and quick," in one familiar formula –
and that the theory of language design must accommodate this fact – is
erroneous; it is not a fact. The problem, however, is to show that those
parts of language that are usable are properly determined by the theories
of computation and performance, no small matter.

Questions of this sort bring us to the borders of current inquiry.
These are questions of a new order of depth, hence of interest, in the
study of language and mind.

Other questions have to do with interface properties: how do the
performance systems make use of expressions generated by the I-
language? Some features of these expressions provide instructions only
to articulatory and perceptual systems; thus one element of a linguistic
expression is its *phonetic form*. It is generally assumed that these instructions are common to both articulation and perception, which is not
at all obvious, hence interesting if true. Other properties of the expression provide instructions only for conceptual–intentional systems; this
element of the expression is usually called *logical form*, but in a technical
sense that differs from other usages; call it *LF* to avoid misunderstanding. Again, it is assumed that there is only one such array of
instructions, and that it is dissociated from phonetic form. These

assumptions are even more implausible, and hence, if true, very interesting discoveries.

On such assumptions, the computational procedure maps an array of lexical choices into a pair of symbolic objects, phonetic form and LF, and does so in a way that is optimal, from a certain point of view. The elements of these symbolic objects can be called "phonetic" and "semantic" features, respectively, but we should bear in mind that all of this is pure syntax and completely internalist. It is the study of mental representations and computations, much like the inquiry into how the image of a cube rotating in space is determined from retinal stimulations, or imagined. We may take the semantic features S of an expression E to be its *meaning* and the phonetic features P to be its *sound*; E *means* S in something like the sense of the corresponding English word, and E *sounds* P in a similar sense, S and P providing the relevant information for the performance systems.

An expression such as "I painted my house brown," is accessed by performance systems that interpret it, on the receptive side, and articulate it while typically using it for one or another speech act, on the productive side. How is that done? The articulatory–perceptual aspects have been intensively studied, but these matters are still poorly understood. At the conceptual–intentional interface the problems are even more obscure, and may well fall beyond human naturalistic inquiry in crucial respects.

Perhaps the weakest plausible assumption about the LF interface is that the semantic properties of the expression focus attention on selected aspects of the world as it is taken to be by other cognitive systems, and provide intricate and highly specialized perspectives from which to view them, crucially involving human interests and concerns even in the simplest cases. In the case of "I painted my house brown," the semantic features impose an analysis in terms of specific properties of intended design and use, a designated exterior, and indeed far more intricacy. As is mentioned in Chapter 2 if I paint my house brown, it has a brown exterior; I can, however, paint my house brown *on the inside*. The exterior–interior dimension has a marked and unmarked option; if neither is indicated, the exterior is understood. That is a typical property of the lexicon; if I say Jones climbed the mountain, I mean that he was (generally) going up, but I can say that he climbed *down the mountain*, using the marked option. If I am inside my house, I can clean it, affecting only the interior, but I cannot see it, unless an exterior surface is visible (through a window, for example). And I certainly cannot be near my house if I am inside it, even though it is a surface, in the unmarked case. Similarly, a geometrical cube is just a surface, but if we are using natural language, a point inside the cube cannot be near it. These properties hold quite generally: of boxes, igloos, airplanes, mountains, and so on. If I look through a tunnel in a mountain and see a lighted cave within, I do not see the mountain; only if I see its exterior surface (say, from inside the cave, looking through the tunnel at a mirror outside that reflects the surface). The same is true of impossible objects. If I tell you that I painted a spherical cube brown, you take its exterior to be brown in the unmarked case, and if I am inside it, you know I am not near it. And so on, to intricacy that has been far underestimated, and that poses problems of "poverty of stimulus" so extreme that knowledge of language in these regards too can only be assumed to be in substantial measure innately determined, hence virtually uniform among languages, much as we assume without discussion or understanding for other aspects of growth and development.

Quite typically, words offer conflicting perspectives. A city is both concrete and abstract, both animate and inanimate: Los Angeles may be pondering its fate grimly, fearing destruction by another earthquake or administrative decision. London is not a place. Rather, it is *at* a place, though it is not the things at that place, which could be radically changed or moved, leaving London intact. London could be destroyed and rebuilt, perhaps after millennia, still being London; Carthage could be rebuilt today, just as Tom Jones, though perfectly concrete, could be reincarnated as an insect or turned by a witch into a frog, awaiting the princess's kiss, but Tom Jones all along – concepts available to young children without instruction or relevant experience.

The abstract character of London is crucial to its individuation. If London is reduced to dust, *it* – that is, London – can be *re*built elsewhere and be the *same* city, London. If my house is reduced to dust, it (my house) can be rebuilt elsewhere, but it won't be the same house. If the motor of my car is reduced to dust, it cannot be rebuilt, though if only partially damaged, it can be. Pronouns involve dependency of reference, but not necessarily to the same thing; and both referential dependence and the narrower notion of sameness involve roles in a highly intricate space of human interests and concerns. Judgments can be rather delicate, involving factors that have barely been explored.

There are plenty of real examples illustrating such properties of terms of natural language. We have no problem understanding a report in the daily press about the unfortunate town of Chelsea, which is "preparing to move" (viewed as animate), with some residents opposed because "by moving the town, it will take the spirit out of it," while others counter that "unless Chelsea moves, floods will eventually kill it." There is a city called both "Jerusalem" and "al-Quds" (much as London is called

"London" and "Londres"). What is this city? Its site is a matter of no small contention, even a matter of UN Security Council resolutions. The government that claims it as its capital city has been considering plans to move al-Quds, while leaving Jerusalem in place. The chairman of the development authority explained that "We need to find a capital for the Palestinians, we have to find a site for al-Quds" – somewhere northeast of Jerusalem. The proposal is perfectly intelligible, which is why it greatly troubles people concerned about al-Quds. The discussion would pose puzzles of a kind familiar in the philosophical literature, even more so if the proposal were implemented – if we were to suppose that words like "London" or "Jerusalem" refer to things in the world in some public language, and were to try to sharpen meanings and ideas for conditions under which the presuppositions of normal use do not hold, failing to observe some of Wittgenstein's good advice.

Even the status of (nameable) thing, perhaps the most elementary concept we have, depends crucially on such intricate matters as acts of human will, again something understood without relevant experience, determined by intrinsic properties of the language faculty and others. A collection of sticks in the ground could be a (discontinuous) thing – say, a picket fence, a barrier, a work of art. But the same sticks in the ground are not a thing if left there by a forest fire. On such matters, and their significance for Quinean and similar theories of learning, see Chomsky (1975: 43ff., 203).

The matter of space–time continuity has no particular relevance to these issues, contrary to what is sometimes assumed (see Putnam 1993). Discontinuity of things is not at all in question; the United States is discontinuous in space, though it has become a nameable thing (shifting over time from plural to singular usage); an utterance or theatrical performance may be discontinuous in time. As just noted, discontinuous objects are readily understood as nameable things, within a proper matrix of human interests. Whether a city is understood within "folk science" as a (possibly) discontinuous four-dimensional object is a question of fact. The assumption that it is, or that semantic theory should say that it is, requires quite unnatural interpretations of such terms as "move (Chelsea)," "the former (Chelsea)," etc., issues easily overlooked with a narrow concentration on object-reference. The properties and perspectives involved in individuation of cities, houses, and the like remain to be discovered and explained, independent of the question of continuity.

Substances reveal the same kinds of special mental design. Take the term "water," in the sense proposed by Hilary Putnam: as coextensive with "H_2O give or take certain impurities" (Putnam 1992, citing his now classic paper, Putnam 1975). Even in such a usage, with its questionable invocation of natural science, we find that whether something is water depends on special human interests and concerns, again in ways understood without relevant experience; the term "impurities" covers some difficult terrain. Suppose cup_1 is filled from the tap. It is a cup of water, but if a tea bag is dipped into it, that is no longer the case. It is now a cup of tea, something different. Suppose cup_2 is filled from a tap connected to a reservoir in which tea has been dumped (say, as a new kind of purifier). What is in cup_2 is water, not tea, even if a chemist could not distinguish it from the present contents of cup_1. The cups contain the same thing from one point of view, different things from another; but in either case cup_2 contains only water and cup_1 only tea. In cup_2, the tea is an "impurity" in Putnam's sense, in cup_1 it is not, and we do not have water at all (except in the sense that milk is mostly water, or a person for that matter). If cup_3 contains pure H_2O into which a tea bag has been dipped, it is tea, not water, though it could have a higher concentration of H_2O molecules than what comes from the tap or is drawn from a river. Note that this is a particularly simple case, unlike its classic counterparts "earth," "air," and "fire," among many others.

Proceeding beyond the simplest cases, intricacies mount. I can paint the door to the kitchen brown, so it is plainly concrete; but I can walk through the door to the kitchen, switching figure and ground. The baby can finish the bottle and then break it, switching contents and container with fixed intended reference. There is interesting work by James Pustejovsky studying regularities in such systems, drawing from ideas of Julius Moravcsik's, Aristotelian in origin. (See his and other papers in Pustejovsky 1993; 1994; see also Moravcsik 1990; Chomsky 1975.) As we move on to words with more complex relational properties and the structures in which they appear, we find that interpretation is guided in fine detail by the cognitive system in ways that we expect to vary little because they are so remote from possible experience.

Neurologist Rodolfo Llinás puts the matter well when he describes perception as "a dream modulated by sensory input," the mind being a "computational state of the brain generated by the interaction between the external world and an internal set of reference frames" (Llinás 1987: 351). The internal frames that shape the dreams are, however, far more intricate and intriguing than often assumed, even at the level of the lexicon; they are still more so when we turn to expressions formed by the computational procedures.

Spelling out the properties of expressions, we learn more about the instructions at the LF ("semantic") interface, which are interpreted in some manner to think about and talk about the world, along with much else. Important and obscure questions still lie beyond: in what respects, for example, do these properties belong to the language faculty as distinct from other faculties of mind to which it is linked? How do lexical resources relate to belief systems, for example? Such questions remain within the domain of what people know, not what they do. Answers to them would still leave us far short of understanding how the resources of the cognitive systems are put to use. From this welter of issues it is hard to see how to extricate very much that might be subjected to naturalistic inquiry. For some comment on this, see Chapter 2 above.

Note that the properties of such words as "house," "door," "London," "water," and so on do not indicate that people have contradictory or otherwise perplexing beliefs. There is no temptation to draw any such conclusion, if we drop the empirical assumption that words pick out things, apart from particular usages, which they constrain in highly intricate ways.

Should we assume that expressions pick out things, intrinsically? More generally, should the "weakest assumptions" about the interface relations and the way they enter into thought and action be supplemented to include relations that hold between certain expressions and external things? That is commonly assumed, though we have to take care to distinguish two variants: (1) things in the world, or (2) things in some kind of mental model, discourse representation, and the like.[5] If the latter, then the study is again internalist, a form of syntax. Suppose the former, and continue to assume that there are two interface levels, phonetic form and LF.

Suppose we postulate that corresponding to an element "a" of phonetic form there is an external object "*a" that "a" selects as its *phonetic value*; thus the element [ba] in Jones's I-language picks out some entity *[ba], "shared" with Smith if there is a counterpart in his I-language. Communication could then be described in terms of such (partially) shared entities, which are easy enough to construct: take "*a" to be the singleton set {a}, or {3, a}; or if one wants a more realistic feel, some construct based on motions of molecules. With sufficient heroism, one could defend such a view, though no one does, because it's clear that we are just spinning wheels.

The same can be done at the LF interface. Suppose that "a" is constructed by the computational system from one or more lexical choices, where "a" is an LF representation or some further syntactic object computed from it (an expression in some formal language, some kind of mental model, etc.). We could then posit an object "*a" as its *semantic value*, external to the I-language, perhaps shared by Jones and Smith. Again, "*a" could be some arbitrary construction to which we assign the desired properties, or give a touch of realism in a variety of ways. We could then construct truth theories, and develop an account of communication in terms of shared entities – often of a very strange sort, to be sure. As in the case of any theoretical proposal that introduces new entities and principles, what has to be shown is that this one is justified in the usual empirical terms (explanatory power, etc.).

A good part of contemporary philosophy of language is concerned with analyzing alleged relations between expressions and things, often exploring intuitions about the technical notions "denote," "refer," "true of," etc. said to hold between expressions and something else. But there can be no intuitions about these notions, just as there can be none about "angular velocity" or "protein." These are technical terms of philosophical discourse with a stipulated sense that has no counterpart in ordinary language; this is why Frege had to provide a new technical meaning for "Bedeutung," for example. If we rerun the thought experiments with ordinary terms, judgments seem to collapse or, rather, to become so interest-relative as to yield no meaningful results.

Without pursuing the matter here, it is not at all clear that the theory of natural language and its use involves relations of "denotation," "true of," etc. in anything like the sense of the technical theory of meaning.

It is sometimes claimed that such technical notions are required to account for communication or for consideration of truth and falsity. The former belief is groundless (amongst others, see Chomsky 1993a; Chapter 2 above). The latter also seems incorrect. Simply consider the ordinary language terms with which this discussion began: "language" and "mind." Consider two statements about language and mind:

(1)   Chinese is the language of Beijing and Hong Kong, but not Melbourne.

(2)   The mind is its own place, and in itself can make a Heaven of Hell, a Hell of Heaven.

The first is true, but "Chinese" surely has no real world denotatum, in the technical sense, nor need one believe that it does in order to assign truth value. If we are convinced by Milton's argument (*Paradise Lost*), we will agree that the second sentence is true, but without committing ourselves to the belief that the subject, the pronoun, or the reflexive (or the other noun phrases) refers, either to something in the world or in some obscure mental world. At least, there is no compulsion to succumb to such temptations, for reasons put forth in the eighteenth-century critique of the theory of ideas, much enriched in modern ordinary language philosophy. Such properties are typical of the words of natural language, far more so than is believed, I suspect, for reasons already indicated. This is not to deny that such statements can be made with referential intentions, but these are of a far more intricate nature.

In any event, there seems to be no special connection between attribution of truth or falsity and some notion of reference or denotation in anything like the sense of technical discourse.

Consider in contrast another term I have used: *I-language*, which figures in such statements as:

(3)   I-language has a head parameter.

This statement is false if Kayne's theory (1994) is correct, perhaps true if it is not. In this case, it makes sense to say that the term "I-language" has a real world denotatum, or at least is intended to. The statement belongs to the same kind of discourse as statements about H_2O, acids and bases, the specification of proteins by genes, etc. The sentences do not really belong to natural language; they contain technical terms, such as "I-language," introduced in a quite different way. As the disciplines progress, they depart still further from the common-sense and ordinary-language origins from which inquiry begins.

It is reasonable to suppose that, in the course of such inquiry, we attempt to construct systems in which well-constructed symbolic objects are intended to pick out objects in the world: molecules, I-languages, and so on. These symbolic systems may be called "languages," but that is just a metaphor. They typically do not have properties of natural language, are acquired and used in a completely different fashion, and surely are not instantiations of the initial state of the language faculty. We may articulate symbolic objects of these systems with the phonetics of our language and borrow constructions of our language in using them, even when they contain terms that are invented or based on languages we do not know ("eigenvector," "homo sapiens"), but all of that is irrelevant. The systems may depart in arbitrary ways from natural language, using calculus, chemical notations and diagrams, or whatever.

These symbolic systems may well aim towards the Fregean ideal. According to this approach, there is a "common, public language" with formulas or signals that express shared thoughts. The "language" has a syntax, namely a class of well-formed formulas; there is no "right answer" to the question of how that set is generated. It also has a semantics, based on the technical notion of *Bedeutung*, a relation between symbols and things. Perhaps one property of the science-forming faculty of the human mind is that it aims to construct Fregean systems. If so, that will tell us nothing about natural language. Here there is no counterpart to the notion "common" or "public" language. The syntax is radically different. There a real answer to the question of what is the "right generative procedure"; I-languages are functions regarded in intension. And there appears to be no notion of "well-formed formula" in the sense used, for example, by Quine in his discussions of extensional equivalence and indeterminacy of translation, or by many linguists, psychologists, philosophers, and others who have been concerned about generative capacity, decidability of well-formedness, reduction to context-free grammars, excess strength of certain theories, and other problems that cannot even be formulated for natural language, as far as we know. On misunderstandings about these matters and their origins, see Chomsky 1980; 1986.

As for semantics, insofar as we understand language use, the argument for a reference-based semantics (apart from an internalist syntactic version) seems to me weak. It is possible that natural language has only syntax and pragmatics; it has a "semantics" only in the sense of "the study of how this instrument, whose formal structure and potentialities of expression are the subject of syntactic investigation, is actually put to use in a speech community," to quote the earliest formulation in generative grammar 40 years ago, influenced by Wittgenstein, Austin and others (Chomsky 1955/1975; 1957: 102–3). In this view, natural language consists of internalist computations and performance systems that access them along with much other information and belief, carrying out their instructions in particular ways to enable us to talk and communicate, among other things. There will be no provision for what Scott Soames calls "the central semantic fact about language, . . . that it is used to represent the world," because it is not assumed that language is used to represent the world, in the intended sense. (Soames (1989) cited by B. Smith (1992) as the core issue for philosophers or language).

I have only sketched the surface, hoping to convey some picture of how one might study language as a natural object, where such inquiry has led, and what kinds of problems lie at the horizon. Perhaps I might end with just a word on its limits, even if extended to considerably broader scope. Some indication of possible limits has already been suggested; general issues of intentionality, including those of language use, cannot reasonably be assumed to fall within naturalistic inquiry, I believe. The matter can be further clarified by returning to Cartesian dualism, the scientific hypothesis that sought to capture, in particular, the apparent fact that normal language use lies beyond the bounds of any possible machine. The Cartesian framework was undermined by the discovery that even the behavior of inorganic matter lies beyond these bounds. The arguments can, however, be reconstructed, although now without metaphysical implications, the concept of matter having disappeared. So restated, they still seem to pose a complete mystery. They are, for example, unaffected by the transition from the complex artifacts that intrigued the Cartesians to today's computers, and the brain sciences shed little light on them.

Possibly, as some believe, these problems are unreal. Possibly they are real but we have not hit upon the way to approach them. Possibly "that way," whatever it is, lies outside our cognitive capacities, beyond the reach of the science-forming faculty. That should not surprise us, if true, at least if we are willing to entertain the idea that humans are part of the natural world, with rich scope and corresponding limits, facing problems that they might hope to solve and mysteries that lie beyond their reach, "ultimate secrets of nature" that "ever will remain" in "obscurity" as Hume supposed, echoing some of Descartes's own speculations.

6 Language from an internalist perspective

I would like to expand on some remarks on the study of language and mind presented earlier in this book, especially in Chapter 5. To begin with, I want to distinguish an *internalist* from a *naturalistic* approach. By the latter I mean just the attempt to study humans as we do anything else in the natural world. Internalist naturalistic inquiry seeks to understand the internal states of an organism. Naturalistic study is of course not limited to such bounds; internalist inquiry into a planet or an ant does not preempt or preclude the study of the solar system or an ant community. Non-internalist studies of humans can take many forms: as phases in an oxygen-to-carbon-dioxide cycle or gene transmission, as farmers or gourmets, as participants in associations and communities, with their power structures, doctrinal systems, cultural practices, and so on. Internalist studies are commonly presupposed in others with broader range, but it should be obvious that the legitimacy of one or another kind of inquiry does not arise.

To clarify further, I am keeping here to the quest for theoretical understanding, the specific kind of inquiry that seeks to account for some aspects of the world on the basis of usually hidden structures and explanatory principles. Someone committed to naturalistic inquiry can consistently believe that we learn more of human interest about how people think and feel and act by studying history or reading novels than from all of naturalistic inquiry. Outside of narrow domains, naturalistic inquiry has proven shallow or hopeless, and perhaps always will, perhaps for reasons having to do with our cognitive nature.

The aspects of the world that concern me here I will call its mental and linguistic aspects, using the terms innocuously – in the manner of "chemical," "electrical," or "optical" – to select a complex of phenomena, events, processes, and so on that seem to have a certain unity and coherence. By "mind," I mean the mental aspects of the world. In none of these cases is there any need for antecedent clarity, nor any reason to believe that the categories will survive naturalistic inquiry where it can make some progress.

134

By "naturalism" I mean "methodological naturalism," counterposed to "methodological dualism": the doctrine that in the quest for theoretical understanding, language and mind are to be studied in some manner other than the ways we investigate natural objects, as a matter of principle. This is a doctrine that few may espouse, but that dominates much practice, I believe. (For some recent discussion, see Chomsky 1986; and Chapters 2 and 3 above.)

One branch of naturalistic inquiry studies common-sense understanding. Here we are concerned with how people interpret object constancy, the nature and causes of motion, thought and action, and so on ("folk science," in one of the senses of the term). Perhaps the right way to describe this is in terms of beliefs about the constituents of the world (call them "entities") and their organization, interaction, and origins. Assume so. It is an open question whether, and if so how, the conceptual resources of folk science relate to those involved in the reflective and self-conscious inquiry found in every known culture ("early science"), and to the particular enterprise we call "natural science." For convenience, let's refer to the study of all such matters as "ethnoscience."

It is also an open question how the conceptual resources that enter into these cognitive systems relate to the semantic (including lexical) resources of the language faculty. Do people attribute beliefs if they speak languages that have no such term, the great majority, it appears? Can someone lacking the terms recognize *savoir faire*, *Schadenfreude*, *machismo*, or whatever is expressed by the countless locutions that challenge translators? If I say that one of the things that concerns me is the average man and his foibles, or Joe Sixpack's priorities, or the inner track that Raytheon has on the latest missile contract, does it follow that I believe that the actual world, or some mental model of mine, is constituted of such entities as the average man, foibles, Joe Sixpack, priorities, and inner tracks? When the press reports that a comet is aiming towards Jupiter and that lobster fishermen are overfishing New England waters, does that mean that the writers and readers think that comets have intentions and lobsters are fish? These are questions of fact about the architecture of the mind, improperly formulated no doubt, because so little is understood.

If intuition is any guide, there seems to be a considerable gap between the semantic resources of language literally interpreted and thoughts expressed using them. I am happy to speak of the Sun setting over the horizon, comets aiming directly at Jupiter, and waves hitting the shore, receding, and disappearing as the wind dies. But I'm not aware of having beliefs that correspond literally to the animistic and intentional terminology I freely use, or that conflict with anything I understand about relativity and the motions of molecules. Nor does the world, or my mental universe, seem to me to be populated by anything like what I describe as things that concern me. Psychologists and anthropologists exploring language–thought relations (for example, the Sapir–Whorf hypothesis) find such problems hard and challenging; ready answers are offered in much of the contemporary philosophical literature, but on grounds that seem to me less than persuasive.

In fact, radically different answers are offered. Take language as an example. Donald Davidson writes that "we all talk so freely about language, or languages, that we tend to forget that there are no such things in the world; there are only people and their various written and acoustical products. This point, obvious in itself, is nevertheless easy to forget" (Davidson 1990b). To most philosophers of language, it is equally obvious that there *are* such things in the world as languages: indeed, "common, public languages" – Chinese, German, etc. – of which, some hold, we have "a partial, and partially erroneous, grasp" (Dummett 1986: 468). Hilary Putnam, among many others, takes the alleged fact to be as obvious as its denial is to Davidson, along with equally obvious facts about the things in the world that correspond to noun phrases rather freely, so it seems, so that the world contains whatever we might refer to as something that interests or bothers us, including the alleged denotata of words we do not know (Davidson 1990b; Putnam 1992 and 1998a).[1]

A third position is that conclusions about such matters are rarely obvious: answers have to be found case by case, and the questions require more careful formulation in the first place. The ethnoscientist seeks to determine what people take to be constituents of the world, however they may talk about it. A different inquiry seeks the best theory of language and its use, and the states, processes, and structures that enter into it.

The questions arise in the simplest cases: nameable objects, substances, artifacts, actions, and so on. I take the thing in front of me to be a desk, but could be convinced that it is a hard bed for a dwarf that I am misusing as a desk; that's a matter of designer's intent and regular use. From one point of view, I take it to be the same thing whatever the answer; from another point of view, a different thing. Factors entering into such choices are diverse and complex. I take the contents of the cup on the desk to be tea, but if informed that it came from the tap after passing through a tea filter at the reservoir, I conclude that it is really water, not tea (see also Chapter 5, p. 128). Again, it is the same thing for me in either case from one point of view, a different thing from another. Some sticks I pass on the road are not a thing at all, unless it is explained to me that they were specifically constructed as some kind of object, whether by people or, perhaps, beavers. What is a thing, and if so what thing it is, depends on specific configurations of human interests, intentions, goals, and actions; an observation that is, in one form, as old as Aristotle. It could be that in such cases I do not change my beliefs about the constituents of the world as identification changes – that in my own variant of "folk science," the entities that hold up my computer and fill the cup, and that I pass on the road, remain as they were independent of the explanations, which place them in unexpected relations to designs, intentions, uses, and purposes.

As the study of the language faculty and other cognitive systems progresses, we may come to understand in what respects my picture of the world is framed in terms of things selected and individuated by properties of my lexicon, or even involves entities and relationships describable at all by the resources of the language faculty. Some semantic properties do seem specifically linked to language, developing as part of it, closely integrated with its other aspects, even represented in natural ways within its morphological and syntactic structures. Terms of language may indicate positions in belief systems, which enrich further the complex perspectives they afford for viewing the world. Some terms, particularly those lacking internal relational structure, may do little more than that; notably "natural kind terms," though the phrase is misleading, since they have little if anything to do with the kinds of nature. Akeel Bilgrami observes that analysis of lexical resources in terms of "a linguistic agent's perspective on things," resisting dubious notions of independent reference, leads naturally to linking the study of meaning to "such things as beliefs as mediating the things in the world with which we stand in causal relations" and to the "radically local or contextual" notion of content that he develops in rejecting "the entire current way of thinking which bifurcates content into wide and narrow." These seem to me fruitful directions to pursue (see Bilgrami 1993: 62; on natural kind terms, see Bromberger 1992a).

The study of semantic resources of the language faculty is not ethnoscience, and both enterprises, of course, are to be distinguished from naturalistic inquiry into the range of topics that natural language and folk science address in their own ways. The observation is a truism in the case of falling apples, plants turning towards the light, and rockets aiming towards the heavens; here no one expects ordinary language or folk science to enter into attempts to gain theoretical understanding of the world, beyond their intuitive starting points. In contrast, it is considered a serious problem to determine whether "mentalistic talk and mental entities [will] eventually lose their place in our attempts to describe and explain the world" (Burge 1992: 33). The belief that mentalistic talk and entities will lose their place is "eliminationism" or "eliminative materialism," which Burge identifies as a major strand of the effort "to make philosophy scientific"; perhaps wrong, but an important thesis.

Why it is important is unclear. If we replace "mental" by "physical" in the thesis it loses its interest: "physicalistic talk and physical entities" have long ago "lost their place in our attempts to describe and explain the world," if by "physicalistic" and "physical" we mean the notions of common discourse or folk science, and by "attempts to describe and explain the world" we mean naturalistic inquiry. Why should we expect anything different of "mentalistic talk and mental entities"? Why, for example, should we assume that psychology "seeks to refine, deepen, generalize and systematize some of the statements of informed common sense about people's mental activity" (Burge 1986a: 8)[2]. Though chemistry, geology, and biology have no comparable concerns. No one expects ordinary talk about things happening in the "physical world" to have any particular relation to naturalistic theories; the terms belong to different intellectual universes. These facts are not taken to pose a body–body problem, nor has anyone proposed a thesis of "anomalism of the physical" to deal with them. The same should, then, be true of such statements as "John speaks Chinese" or "John took his umbrella because he expected rain" – though one may hope, in all cases, that science might yield some understanding and insight in the domains opened to inquiry by common-sense perspectives.

There seems no basis here for any mind–body problem and no reason to question Davidson's thesis that there are no psychophysical laws that connect mental and physical events in an appropriate explanatory scheme; for similar reasons, there are no physico-physical laws relating ordinary talk about things to the natural sciences, even if the particular events described fall within their potential descriptive range. Distinctions between mental and other aspects of the world, in these respects, seem unwarranted, except in one respect: our theoretical understanding of language, mind, and people generally is so shallow, apart from limited domains, that we can only use our intuitive resources in thinking and talking about these matters.

It is not that ordinary discourse fails to talk about the world, or that the particulars it describes do not exist, or that the accounts are too imprecise. Rather, the categories used and principles invoked need not have even loose counterparts in naturalistic inquiry. That is true even of the parts of ordinary discourse that have a quasi-naturalistic cast. How people decide whether something is water or tea is of no concern to chemistry. It is no necessary task of biochemistry to decide at what point in the transition from simple gases to bacteria we find the "essence of life" and, if some such categorization were imposed, the correspondence to common-sense notions would matter no more than for *the heavens*, or *energy*, or *solid*. Whether ordinary usage would consider viruses "alive" is of no interest to biologists, who will categorize as they choose in terms of genes and conditions under which they function. We cannot invoke ordinary usage to judge whether François Jacob is correct in telling us that "for the biologist, the living begins only with what was able to constitute a genetic program" (1974: 304), though "for the chemist, in contrast, it is somewhat arbitrary to make a demarcation where there can only be continuity." Similarly, the concept "human being," with its curious properties of psychic continuity, does not enter the natural sciences. The theory of evolution and other parts of biology do try to understand John Smith and his place in nature; not, however, under the description "human being" or "person" as construed in ordinary language and thought. These notions are interesting for natural-language semantics and ethnoscience, but not for the branches of human biology that seek to understand the nature of John Smith and his conspecifics or what distinguishes them from apes and plants (for a contrary view with regard to these examples, see Putnam 1992).

The special sciences also go their own ways. To borrow Jerry Fodor's example of a meandering river eroding its banks, the earth sciences do not care under what circumstances people take it to be the same river if the flow is reversed or it is redirected on a different course, or when they regard something projecting from the sea as an island or a mountain with a watery base. The same should be expected in the case of such notions as *language* and *belief*, and terms of related semantic fields in various languages and cultural settings.

The particular natural sciences are commonly recognized to be largely artifacts and conveniences, which we do not expect to carve nature at its joints; F. Jacob's comment is typical. The observation is uncontroversial for the "hard sciences," but has been strongly challenged in the case of language. There has been much heated debate over what the subject matter of linguistics *really is*, and what categories of data are permitted to bear on it. A distinction is made between *linguistic evidence* that is appropriate for *linguistics*, versus *psychological* and other evidence that is not. Such discussions, which can be found in all the relevant disciplines, are foreign to naturalistic inquiry. An empirical observation does not come with a notice "I am for X," written on its sleeve, where X is chemistry, linguistics, or whatever. No one asks whether the study of a complex molecule belongs to chemistry or biology, and no one should ask whether the study of linguistic expressions and their properties belongs to linguistics, psychology, or the brain sciences.

Nor can we know in advance what kinds of evidence might bear on these questions. Thus some current research suggests that studies of electrical activity of the brain may provide evidence bearing on them, a conceptual impossibility according to a considerable part of the literature, which also puts forth other odd contentions: for example, that studies of perceptual displacement of clicks might provide evidence about phrase boundaries, whereas observations about anaphora in Japanese, which provide far stronger evidence on naturalistic grounds, do not constitute evidence for factual theses at all because of some lethal form of indeterminacy (for example, Quine 1987). Or that we should keep to – or even be interested in – "Grandma's view" about the domain of linguistics, though presumably not chemistry (Devitt and Sterelny 1989). Or that studies of processing, acquisition, pathology, injury, genetic variability, and so on cannot in principle be used as evidence about the existence and status of elements of linguistic representation (Soames 1989), contrary to what practicing linguists have long believed; for example Edward Sapir and Roman Jakobson in classic work, or recent studies of priming effects in processing and their implications concerning unarticulated elements. All such moves reflect some form of dualism, an insistence that we must not treat the domain of the mental, or at least the linguistic, as we do other aspects of the world.

Methodological dualism has sometimes been explicitly advocated, or so it appears. Consider Michael Dummett's thesis that scientific accounts fall short of philosophical explanation for conceptual reasons. To take his example, suppose that a naturalistic approach to language succeeds beyond our wildest dreams. Suppose it provides a precise account of what happens when sound waves hit the ear and are processed, is fully integrated into a scientific theory of action, and solves the unification problem, integrating the theories of cells and computational processes. We would then have a successful theory of what Jones knows when he has acquired a language: what he knows about rhyme, entailment, usage appropriate to situations, and so on. But no matter how successful, Dummett writes, these discoveries would "contribute nothing to philosophy," which requires an answer to a different question: not how knowledge is stored or used, but "how it is delivered." The naturalistic account would be a "psychological hypothesis," but not a "philosophical explanation," because it does not tell us "the form in which [the body of knowledge] is delivered" (Dummett 1991; 1993: xi). For the sciences, the account tells everything that can be asked about the form in which knowledge is delivered, but philosophy calls for a kind of explanation unknown in naturalistic inquiry.

Understood in the above way, philosophy appears to exclude much of the core of traditional philosophy: Hume, for example, who was concerned with "the science of human nature," and sought to find "the secret springs and principles, by which the human mind is actuated in its operations" (1748/1975: 14, Section 9), including those "parts of [our] knowledge" that are derived "by the original hand of nature" (1748/1975: 108, Section 85), an enterprise he compared to Newton's. Had Hume achieved these goals, he would have established "psychological hypotheses," in Dummett's terms, but would not yet have contributed anything to philosophy. "Philosophical explanation" requires something more than a discovery of the "secret springs and principles" of the mind and how they function.

If I understand Dummett, philosophical explanation crucially involves access to consciousness. Imagine then a Martian creature M exactly like us except that M can become aware of how its mind is "actuated in its operations." When we ask M whether it is following the rules of phonology in constructing rhymes, or Condition (B) of Binding Theory in determining referential dependence, M reflects and says (truly), "Yes, that's just what I'm doing" – by assumption, exactly what you and I are doing. For M, we would have a "philosophical explanation"; we would understand the form in which the knowledge is delivered, and could properly attribute knowledge to M. But we would not have crossed the bridge to "philosophical explanation" and attribution of knowledge for the human who operates exactly as M does, though without awareness. As Quine, John Searle, and others put it, we would be allowed to say that M is following rules and is guided by them, whereas the human cannot be described in these terms. To avoid immediate counterintuitive consequences, Searle insists further on a notion of "access in principle" that remains entirely obscure (see Chapter 4 of this volume).

Are these proposals substantive or merely terminological? The latter, it seems to me; I do not see what substantive issue arises. It might be added that the proposals radically deviate from ordinary usage, for whatever that may be worth. In informal usage, we say that my granddaughter is following the rules for regular past tense and certain irregular verbs when she says "I rided my bike and brang it home," though these rules are not accessible to consciousness, for children or adults, any more than those that Quine, Searle, and others disqualify. Saul

Kripke's "Wittgensteinian" concept of rule-following in terms of community norms is virtually the complement of ordinary usage, which typically attributes rule-guided behavior in cases of deviation from such norms, as in the example just given. In contrast, only a linguist would be likely to say that my granddaughter is following the rules of Binding Theory, conforming to the community (in fact, the human community, very likely).

In the study of other aspects of the world, we are satisfied with "best theory" arguments, and there is no privileged category of evidence that provides criteria for theoretical constructions. In the study of language and mind, naturalistic theory does not suffice: we must seek "philosophical explanations," delimit inquiry in terms of some imposed criterion, require that theoretical posits be grounded in categories of evidence selected by the philosopher, and rely on notions such as "access in principle" that have no place in naturalistic inquiry. Whatever all this means, there is a demand beyond naturalism, a form of dualism that remains to be explained and justified.

Philosophical demands are sometimes motivated by the problems of error and first-person authority. Defending a position much like the one advanced here, Barry Smith concludes that it still falls short of "a philosophically satisfying account" for such reasons; it fails to "tell us what counts as using . . . words correctly, that is, in accordance with certain normative patterns of use," and to account for our authoritative knowledge of syntax and meaning in our own language. So "philosophical work . . . is vital to complete the overall project," work that goes beyond "scientific psychology" (including internalist linguistics) (B. Smith 1992: 134–5).

These conclusions seem to me unwarranted. Consider a typical example. Suppose that Peter, a normal speaker of English, says "John expects to like him." I conclude that he intends to refer to two different people: John, and someone else picked out by the pronoun *him*. If Peter embeds the same expression in the context "Guess who _____," so that he said "Guess who John expects to like him," I do not know whether or not he intended to refer only to John. In "John expects to like him," *him* is not referentially dependent on *John*; in "Guess who John expects to like him," the question is open. There is a good explanation of such facts in terms of an internalist linguistic theory, call it T.

Suppose T to be true of the Martian M and of us. M can tell us that he draws these conclusions on the basis of T, which he can recognize and even articulate; I cannot, although I operate exactly as M does. Given M's conscious access to the rules it follows, some are inclined to feel that we have an account of M's being "effortlessly authoritative" about the facts informally described; but the internalist naturalistic account "makes a puzzle" or a "total mystery" of this first-person authority in Peter's case. Lacking M's conscious access, how can Peter "understand . . . particular expressions," say the ones in question, about which he is "effortlessly authoritative," Crispin Wright asks? (Wright 1989: 236). He suggests Wright's project as a necessary supplement.

Suppose that we put the matter differently. The kind of account that can be offered today, including T, does not "make a mystery" of first person authority, though it does *leave* a mystery, about both M and Peter. For both, we have an account that meets the conditions of the sciences (questions of precision and accuracy aside), but we lack any insight into the nature of consciousness, something not relevant to the matter of rule-following and first-person authority, though interesting in its own right.

Peter follows the rules of T because that is the way he is constructed, just as he sees the setting of the Sun and the waves dashing against the rocks; his first-person authority is exhausted by this fact. As for what we call "error," there are many possible kinds. Peter may depart from some external standard – say, using "disinterested" to mean "uninterested," or using his native dialect in a formal lecture. He may choose to violate the rules, perhaps using the word "chair" to mean *table* in a code – knowing that in his own language it means *chair*. In doing so, he makes use of faculties of mind beyond the language faculty. He may misinterpret an expression, in that his performance system yields an interpretation different from the one his internal language imposes; there are well-known categories of such cases, which have been fruitfully studied. Running through other possibilities, we seem to find no relevant limits to internalist psychology.

Others use different terms for what seem to be the same points. Thus Thomas Nagel argues that a full naturalistic theory of language, its use, and acquisition would not describe a "psychological mechanism" but "simply a physical mechanism – for it is incapable of giving rise to subjective conscious thought whose content consists of those rules themselves" (1993: 109). The crucial distinction, again, lies in access to consciousness in principle. The point seems the same as Dummett's, but with different terminology: "psychological" replacing "philosophical." Here the problem of understanding "access in principle" and "content of thought" is compounded by the obscurity of the notion "physical mechanism," which had some meaning in pre-Newtonian physics, but not since.

Unless offered some new notion of "body" or "material" or "physical," we have no concept of naturalism apart from methodological naturalism.

More conventional usage refers to a different doctrine: "metaphysical naturalism," which Burge describes as "one of the few orthodoxies in American philosophy" in recent years (1992: 32); in other variants, materialism, physicalism, eliminativism, "the naturalization of philosophy," and so on. These doctrines are intelligible only insofar as the domain of the physical is somehow specified.

One leading advocate, Daniel Dennett, formulates the doctrine in this way: the "naturalization of philosophy," which he describes as "one of the happiest trends in philosophy since the 1960s," holds that "philosophical accounts of our minds, our knowledge, and our language must in the end be continuous with, or harmonious with, the natural sciences." In a discussion of contemporary naturalism, T.R. Baldwin cites this statement to illustrate the thesis of "metaphysical naturalism" (1993, citing Dennett's introduction to a book on the topic by Ruth Millikan). Like other formulations, it poses some problems. What are "philosophical accounts" as distinct from others, particularly in this "naturalized" sense of philosophy? And what are the natural sciences? Surely not what is understood today, which may not be "continuous and harmonious" with tomorrow's physics. Some Peircean ideal, perhaps? That doesn't seem promising. What the human mind can attain in the limit? That at least is a potential topic of inquiry, but it leaves us in even worse shape in the present context. If "metaphysical naturalism" is understood as a hope for eventual unification of the study of the mental with other parts of science, no one could disagree, but it is a thesis of little interest, not "a happy trend in philosophy."

Take the version of this doctrine expressed by Quine (whom Burge identifies as the source of the contemporary orthodoxy). In his most recent formulation, the "naturalistic thesis" is that "the world is as natural science says it is, insofar as natural science is right." What is "natural science"? Quine's total answer is: "theories of quarks and the like." What counts as like enough? There are hints at answers but they seem completely arbitrary, at least by ordinary naturalistic criteria (Quine 1992; for further discussion, see Chapter 4 of this volume).

Suppose we identify the mind–body problem (or perhaps its core) as the problem of explaining how consciousness relates to neural structures. If so, it seems much like others that have arisen through the history of science, sometimes with no solution: the problem of explaining terrestrial and planetary motion in terms of the "mechanical philosophy" and its contact mechanics, demonstrated to be irresolvable by Newton, and overcome by introducing what were understood to be "immaterial" forces; the problem of reducing electricity and magnetism to mechanics, unsolvable and overcome by the even stranger assumption that fields are real physical things; the problem of reducing chemistry to the world of hard particles in motion, energy, and electromagnetic waves, only overcome with the introduction of even weirder hypotheses about the nature of the physical world. In each of these cases, unification was achieved and the problem resolved not by reduction, but by quite different forms of accommodation. Even the reduction of biology to biochemistry is a bit of an illusion, since it came only a few years after the unification of chemistry and a radically new physics.

These examples do differ from the consciousness–brain problem in one important way: it was possible to construct intelligible theories of the irreducible phenomena that were far from superficial, while in the case of consciousness, we do not seem to progress much beyond description and illustration of phenomena (Freudians, Jungians, and others might disagree). The matter is seen more sharply in the case of language. The normal use of language involves a "creative aspect" which, for the Cartesians, provided the best evidence for the existence of other minds. Neither the computational properties of the language faculty nor the creative aspects of use can be related in interesting ways to anything known about cells, but the two topics differ in that, for the computational properties, there are intelligible explanatory theories, while for the creative aspects of use, there is only description and illustration. If so, the crucial issue is not real or apparent irreducibility, a common phenomenon in the history of science, but the fact that we can only stare in puzzlement at such aspects of mind as consciousness and expression of thought that is coherent and appropriate but uncaused, a characteristic feature of core problems of philosophy, Colin McGinn has argued (McGinn 1993).

Furthermore, apart from the fact that literal reduction is hardly the norm as science has proceeded towards unification, there is uncertainty as to whether it even makes sense as a project. Silvan Schweber writes that recent work in condensed matter physics, which has created phenomena such as superconductivity that are "genuine novelties in the universe" (Schweber 1993: 35) has also raised earlier skepticism about the possibility of reduction to "an almost rigorously proved assertion," leading to a conception of "emergent laws" in a new sense (p. 36). Whatever the validity of the conclusion, it is at least clear that philosophical doctrines have nothing to say about it; even less so in the domain of mind and brain, where vastly less is understood.

A naturalistic approach simply follows the post-Newtonian course, recognizing that we can do no more than seek the best theoretical account of the phenomena of experience and experiment, wherever the quest leads.

As in other branches of science, we expect to leave the concepts of common-sense understanding behind. Take a concrete example, the case of a woman called "Laura" studied by Jeni Yamada. Laura's language capacities are apparently intact, but her cognitive and pragmatic competence is limited. She has a large vocabulary that she uses in appropriate ways, though apparently without much understanding. Yamada suggests the analogy of young children who use color words in the proper places "to dress up discourse," but without grasping their referential properties. Laura knows when she should describe herself and others as sad or happy, but apparently without capacity to feel sad or happy; she's a kind of behaviorist. Does she *know* or *understand* or *speak* English? The question is meaningless. Usual assumptions about people do not hold in Laura's case; the presuppositions of ordinary usage are not satisfied. Naturalistic theories of language and mind may provide concepts that apply to Laura, but these depart from ordinary language. These concepts, incidentally, are part of an internalist theory of language and mind, the only kind we have. We cannot ask, for example, about the "broad content" of Laura's speech unless the technical notion is extended to this case (Yamada 1990).

Take a somewhat different case: my four-year-old granddaughter. Does she speak English? What we say in ordinary discourse is that she has a partial knowledge of the language that she will ultimately attain if events follow the expected course, though what she now speaks is not a language at all. But if all adults were to die, and children her age were miraculously to survive, what they speak would be perfectly normal human languages, ones not found today. This teleological aspect of the common-sense notion of language is among the many curious and complex features that render the concept inappropriate for the attempt to understand language and its use, just as biology does not concern itself with the psychic continuity of persons and the earth sciences do not care what people call the same river, or a mountain, or an island. These are truisms in the case of "the physical"; and "the mental" as well, dualistic assumptions aside.

The same holds of attribution of belief. It is a reasonable project of natural science to determine whether people (in particular young children) interpret what happens in the world in terms of such notions as belief and desire, falling from the heavens towards the Earth, turning towards the light, and so on; and the conditions under which they use such intentional and objectual discourse in various languages (perhaps a different matter, as noted). Quite independently, we may ask whether the theory of people, meteors, and flowers should involve such notions. The current answer is "definitely not" in the case of flowers and meteors, and unknown in the case of people, because we do not know much at all. Let us consider a third kind of problem, which does not fall within either framework: the problem of determining when we *should* attribute belief, or rising and turning and aiming towards – when we *are justified* in doing so? To quote one recent formulation, we ask what are "the philosophically necessary condition[s] of being a true believer"; access to consciousness is usually invoked at this point, and Quinean indeterminacy is commonly held to arise for belief, though not the other cases, for which no "philosophical demand" is raised at all (Clark and Karmiloff-Smith 1993). No one seeks to clarify the philosophically necessary conditions for a comet to be truly aiming at the Earth – failing to hit it, if we are lucky, another intentional attribution.

Similarly, we are invited to explore the criteria for determining where to draw the line between comets aiming at the Earth and Jones walking towards his desk; on which side should we place barnacles attaching to shells and bugs flying towards the light? Such questions do not belong to ethnoscience or the study of the lexicon, nor to naturalistic inquiry in other parts of the sciences. Again, it seems that the quest is for "philosophical explanations," whatever they may be.

The same questions arise about debates over manifestation of "intelligence" and "language use." In the case of vision, locomotion, and other systems one might seek homologies or evolutionary connections. But mental properties are not approached in such ways. Something different is at stake in the debates about whether machines think, or translate Chinese, or play chess. We ask whether an imagined Martian or a programmed computer could understand Chinese, but not whether an extraterrestrial creature or a camera could see, like humans. There is a substantial literature on whether a person mechanically carrying out an algorithm with coded inputs and outputs can properly be said to be translating English to Chinese, but none on the analogous questions that could be raised about mimicking the computations and algorithms that map retinal stimulation to visual image or reaching for an object. It is taken to be a crucial task for the *theory of meaning* to construct notions that would apply to any creature however constituted, real or imagined; but this is not a task at all for the theory of vision or locomotion. Curiously, this is also not considered a task for the theory of phonology, though the questions have as much merit here – none, I think. Similarly, no one asks what would count as a circulatory system, or a molecule, in some world of different objects or different laws of nature.

The discussions are not only dualistic in essence, but also, it seems, without any clear purpose or point: on a par with debates about whether the space shuttle flies or submarines set sail, but do not swim; questions of decision, not fact, in these cases, though assumed to be substantive in the case of the mind, on assumptions that have yet to be explained – and that, incidentally, ignore an explicit warning by Alan Turing in the classic paper that inspired much of the vigorous debate of the past years.

When we turn to language, the internalism–externalism issues arise; though again only for the theory of meaning, not for phonology, where they could be posed in the same ways. Thus we are asked to consider whether meanings are "in the head," or are externally determined. The conventional answer today is that they are externally determined by two kinds of factors: features of the real world, and norms of communities.

What notion of meaning is being investigated? Rational reconstruction of actual translation practice is a goal sometimes suggested, but proposals are not seriously evaluated in these terms, and the significance of the project is also unclear. Another stated goal is to determine the meaning of a word (but apparently, not the sound of a word) in a "shared public language," a notion that remains to be formulated in some coherent terms.[3] Plainly, the goal is not to discover the semantic features of the word "meaning" in English or similar expressions, if they can be found, in other languages. Does the inquiry belong to ethnoscience, an investigation of our conceptual resources? The inquiries that are conducted do not seem to be well designed for this purpose. The questions also do not have to do with naturalistic inquiry into the nature of language and its use, which will develop in its own ways. What other possibility is there? The answer is not clear.

In fact, some curious moves take place at this point. Consider the Twin-Earth thought experiment designed by Hilary Putnam, which has provided much of the motivation for externalist assumptions. In one version, we are to explore our intuitions about the *extension* or *reference* of the word "water" on Twin-Earth, where speakers identical to us use it to refer to XYZ, which is not H_2O. But we can have no intuitions about the question, because the terms *extension, reference, true of, denote,* and others related to them are technical innovations, which mean exactly what their inventors tell us they mean: it would make as little sense to explore our intuitions about tensors or undecidability, in the technical sense.

Suppose we pose the thought experiment using ordinary language. Suppose, for example, that Twin-Oscar comes to Earth, is thirsty, and asks for *that*, pointing either to a glass of Sprite or of what comes from the faucet – some odd mixture of H_2O, chlorine, and I hate to think what else, differing significantly from place to place (but called "water").

Is he making a mistake in both cases? In one case? Which one? Suppose he refers to stuff from the faucet that passed through a tea filter at the reservoir (and therefore is *water* for Oscar), and to the chemically identical substance that had a tea bag dipped into it (so it is not *water* for Oscar, but *tea*). In which case (if either) is Twin-Oscar mistaken? Turning to "content of belief," if Twin-Oscar continues to ask for what comes from the faucet to quench his thirst, calling it "water," has he changed his beliefs about water – irrationally, since he has no evidence for such a change? Or is he behaving rationally, keeping his original beliefs about water, which allow for the stuff on Earth to be water (in Twin-English) in the first place? If the latter, then beliefs about water are shared on Earth and Twin-Earth, just as on either planet, beliefs may differ about the very same substance, taken to be either water or tea as circumstances vary, even with full and precise knowledge that the objects of the different beliefs have exactly the same constitution. I have my intuitions, which would be relevant to the study of the lexicon and ethnoscience, but which undermine the intended conclusions of the thought experiment.

There are numerous other problems. The Twin-Earth problem is posed by withdrawing the presuppositions of discourse on which normal usage rests. It is akin to asking whether Laura understands English. Furthermore, if the argument applies to "water," then why not to "earth," "air," and "fire," which had a comparable status in one early tradition? What is "same substance" in these cases? Or consider "the heavens." I use the term with an indexical character, to refer to what I see on a cloudless night: something different in Boston and Tasmania. With ordinary presuppositions withdrawn, as on Twin-Earth, I might decide (in some circumstances) to use "water" the same way. The dimensions of choice are so varied that it is not surprising that "most ears not previously contaminated by philosophical theory" provide no clear judgments in the standard cases, as Stephen Stich has observed. That would not be a decisive objection in a richer theoretical context, but it is a warning sign that should not be ignored when we have little beyond alleged examples (Stich 1983; for some comment, see Chapter 2 of this volume).

Putnam's response to such problems seems to me unconvincing. He agrees that words do not refer, so intuitions about *reference of words* have to be reformulated in some different way. He adopts the Peircean position that "*reference* [in the sense of 'true of'] is a triadic relation (person X refers to object Y by sign S)," where the Y's are "real objects in the world" (Putnam 1992: 382). Furthermore, "That there is a relation between our words and things in the world is fundamental to our existence; thought without a relation to things in the world is empty" (1992: 383).[4] Thus a word refers to (is true of) a real object in the world when people use the word to refer. Since people use the word "Chinese" to refer to the language spoken in Beijing and Hong Kong, that is "a real object in the world," and the same should hold of "the mind," "the average man," "Joe Sixpack," "free trade," "the heavens," etc., as well as of adjectives, verbs, and other relational expressions, it would seem.

Such super-Whorfian conclusions aside, several problems arise. First, accepting this formulation, the externalist arguments collapse, including the Twin-Earth experiment, the case of "the division of linguistic labor,"[5] and others. When Twin-Oscar, visiting Earth, asks for a cup of water, referring to what is in the cup as "water," then we conclude, following Putnam's revision, that *water* in Twin-English is true of H_2O, so that meanings are back in the head. The other arguments fail for similar reasons.

Second, the revision is not helpful, since the Peircean thesis involves an invented technical notion of *reference*, so we are back where we were, with intuitions that we cannot have. In ordinary usage, "reference" is not a triadic relation of the Peircean sort. Rather, person X refers to Y by expression E under circumstances C, so the relation is at least tetradic; and Y need not be a real object in the world or regarded that way by X. More generally, person X uses expression E with its intrinsic semantic properties to talk about the world from certain intricate perspectives, focusing attention on particular aspects of it, under circumstances C, with the "locality of content" they induce (in Bilgrami's sense). Indeed the components of E may have no intrinsic semantic relation at all to what Jones is referring to, as when he says the performance at Jordan Hall was remarkable, referring to Boston and his favorite string quartet.

Putnam writes that he thinks "Chomsky knows perfectly well that there is a relation between speakers, words, and things in the world." So there sometimes is, abstracting from circumstances of use, in more or less the sense in which a relation holds of people, hands, and rocks, in that I can use my hand to pick up a rock. But that leaves us a long way from establishing anything remotely like the conclusions Putnam wants to reach.

From the natural-language and common-sense concepts of *reference* and the like, we can extract no relevant "relation between our words and things in the world." When we begin to fill out the picture to approach actual usage and thought, the externalist conclusions are not sustained except that, in the welter of uses, some will have the desired properties; in special circumstances, we may indeed understand *water* in the sense of "same liquid," where "liquid" and "same" are the kinds of notions that science seeks to discover, and satisfy other externalist assumptions. Thinking about the world is no doubt "fundamental to our existence," but this does not seem to be a good way to gain a better understanding of the matter.

The philosophical inquiry seems oddly framed in other respects as well. Thus the word "water" is a collection of phonetic, semantic, and formal properties, which are accessed by various performance systems for articulation, perception, talking about the world, and so on. If we deny that its meaning is in the head, why not also that its phonetic aspects are in the head? Why does no one propose that the *phonetic content* of "water" is determined by certain motions of molecules or conventions about "proper pronunciation"? The questions are understood to be absurd or irrelevant. Why not also in the case of meaning?

The literature suggests some answers. Thus, Putnam's conclusions about "water" and H_2O are in part motivated by the problem of intelligibility in scientific discourse. As he points out, we do not want to say that Bohr was talking utter nonsense when he used the term "electron" in pre-quantum theoretic days, or that all his statements were false. To avoid such absurd conclusions, Putnam argues that Bohr was referring to *real* atoms and electrons, which perhaps some experts finally can tell us about (or maybe not). If reference is determined by meaning, then meanings aren't in the head, as Twin-Earth experiments are supposed to show.

The argument, however, is not persuasive, for reasons beyond those already mentioned. Jay Atlas has pointed out that nuclear engineers distinguish "light water" from "heavy water," only the former being H_2O. Taking them as experts, have we been misusing "water" all along, really meaning light water? (For extensive discussion, see Atlas 1989.) Pre-Avogadro, chemists were using "atom" and "molecule" interchangeably. To render what they were saying intelligible, do we have to assume that they were referring to what are now called "atoms" and "molecules" (or what they *really* are, which no one today may know)? After the Bohr model of the atom was available, it was proposed that acids and bases be understood as potential acceptors or donors of electrons, which made boron and aluminum chlorides acids alongside of sulphuric acid, opening up "a whole new area of physical inorganic chemistry," a standard history of the science observes (Brock 1992: 482). Were earlier scientists *really* referring to boron as an acid? Must we assume that in order to render their views intelligible? To take a simpler example, closer to home, must we assume that structural phonologists, 40 years ago, were referring to what generative phonologists call phonological units, though they hotly denied it – and rightly so? Structuralist phonology is surely intelligible; without assuming that there are entities of the kind it postulated, much of the theory can be reinterpreted today, with many results carried over.

What is required in all such cases is some degree of shared structure. In none of them is there any principled way to determine how much must be shared, or what "similarity of belief" is required. Sometimes it is useful to note resemblances and reformulate ideas, sometimes not. The same is true of the earlier and later Bohr. Nothing more definite is required to maintain the integrity of the scientific enterprise or a respectable notion of progress towards theoretical understanding.

Putnam objects that mere structural similarity "is very different from saying that either theory *describes*, however imperfectly, the behavior of the elusive extra-mental phenomena we refer to as *electrons*" – or *light water*, *atoms* and *molecules*, *acids* and *bases*, *phonemes*, etc. That is true, but not relevant. In all cases, including the current theories, we have to add whatever it is that distinguishes theories about the world from science fiction. We take such theories to describe extra-mental phenomena, however imperfectly, whether they involve Apollo and the Sun, Galen's four humors and the atoms of Democritus, Descartes's tubes with animal spirits, . . . , and on to today's attempts. In no case, however, is there any convincing reason to adopt a theory of *real reference* of the kind that has been based on externalist arguments of this nature.

These considerations aside, discussions about *reference* in the sciences have no particular bearing on human language and common-sense understanding unless we add the further assumption that such words as "electron," "base," "eigenvector," "phoneme," and so on belong to English and other natural languages, presumably along with expressions in which they appear, perhaps also formulas, diagrams, etc. Putnam has assumed that the lexicon is homogeneous in this sense. Thus in defending meaning holism, he argues that the theory of meaning must deal with "the hardest case"; he gives the example of "momentum," which was once defined in a way now taken to express a falsehood. However we interpret this, it has no bearing on the inquiry into language unless we assume that "momentum" in the physicist's sense enters the lexicon by the same mechanisms of the language faculty that allow a child to pick up such words as "house" and "rise," and has the properties of lexical entries determined by the language faculty. That seems dubious, to say the least.

Putnam is right to say that I "agree that there is such a relation as reference," in the technical sense, or at least may be, but misses my point: it is reasonable to suppose that naturalistic inquiry aims to construct symbolic systems in which certain expressions are intended to pick out things in the world.[6] There is, however, no reason to believe that such endeavors inform us about ordinary language and common-sense understanding. It seems to me surprising that Putnam should take the position he does, given his eloquent critique of "scientism."

Putting meaning aside, are the contents of thought externally determined? We cannot sensibly ask such questions about *content*, wide or narrow; these are, again, technical notions. But we can ask whether we attribute thoughts to people on grounds that do not keep to their internal state. That we do is clear without exotic examples. If Jones tells me he is mourning those who died in the trenches at Verdun 50 years ago, I can properly say that he is really talking about (thinking of) the First World War, not the Second World War; or, alternatively, that he is mistaken about the Second World War, which is what he is talking about (thinking of). In the first case, I am attributing to him a state that is not internal; the attribution is based on my beliefs, not his. There is no real question as to whether psychology deals with Jones's state as specified in this case. That is, again, a question of decision; in this case, it is about the invented technical term "psychology." Similarly, if Anna Karenina is modeled on a real person, Tolstoy might have been thinking, talking, having beliefs, etc. about her, and some of his knowledgeable readers as well; and as for Smith, who knows nothing about this, I might decide one way or another, as circumstances vary. However this turns out, it tells us nothing about the "real" subject matter of psychology, though these could be reasonable topics for internalist inquiry into how people talk about the world, inquiry that seeks to find out about the internal states that lead people to describe others in various ways as they interpret circumstances variously.

In this context too, the thought experiments designed to support anti-internalist conclusions often seem based on questionable assumptions. Take, for example, Lynne Rudder Baker's locust–cricket example, slightly simplified (Baker 1988). Suppose that Jones speaks ordinary English, and Smith does too except that, in his speech community, crickets are called *locusts*. Suppose J learns his language from Jones, and S from Smith, and they learn the term "locust" from the same pictures, ambiguous between locusts and crickets, along with "information which by chance pertains to both locusts and crickets." Since the intentions of the instructors are different, it "seems straightforward," Baker concludes, that J has "acquired the belief that locusts are a menace and [S] acquired the belief that crickets are a menace" (1987: 121), though J and S are in the same internal state.

Under these assumptions, J and S will generalize the same way so, if presented with an unambiguous locust, they will each call it "a locust," although S will be making an error because the beliefs he expresses are about crickets, not locusts. Suppose S moves to an island with speakers of an unrelated language, and his descendants learn exactly his language, indefinitely, all records and cognates having disappeared; similarly J. The J and S progeny are now indistinguishable in their language and its use, and the history is unrecoverable so they could never learn otherwise. Nevertheless, it should seem straightforward that they have different beliefs, and that the S progeny are making many errors in using their word "locust," always talking about and thinking of crickets. It could be, in fact, that we are of the S-progeny type, that somewhere in the mists of prehistory our ancestors acquired the word that became "locust" under the conditions of S, their instructor having intended to refer to some different species X, so that the beliefs we express using the word "locust" are really about X's and are often mistaken.

Nothing of the sort seems at all straightforward to me, even the first step. But it's also not clear why it matters. Suppose we accept Baker's intuitions. What would this tell us about language, belief, and thought? At most, that sometimes we might attribute beliefs (etc.) to X in terms of other people's beliefs and intentions; but that is clear from simple and ordinary cases. Again, inquiry into the ways we attribute belief as circumstances vary is a legitimate topic of linguistic semantics and ethnoscience, but the study of how people attain cognitive states, interact, and so on will proceed along its separate course.

A standard externalist argument is that unless the external world determines the contents of the thought of an agent, "it is an utter mystery how that agent's thoughts can be publicly available to another" (Bilgrami 1992: 4). For psychology, the assumption is not needed. In order to account for the way Smith understands what Jones says we need not appeal to entities in the external world that correspond to the phonetic representations in the mind of Smith and Jones (say, some kind of motions of molecules associated with the syntactic entity "bilabial stop"); and external objects are no more required in the case of meanings and thoughts. Other possibilities are certainly available, and are probably correct. Thus it could be that Smith assumes that Jones is identical to him, modulo some modifications M, and then seeks to work out M, a task that may be easy, hard, or impossible. Insofar as Smith succeeds, he attributes to Jones the expression that his own mind constructs, including its sound and meaning, communication being a more-or-less affair.[7] And using a variety of other information, he seeks to ascertain Jones's thoughts, perhaps in a similar way.

To be sure, this is psychology, and the issues are supposed to arise only in folk psychology, for Bilgrami at least. But the conclusions seem no better founded here. We have no reason to believe that Mary interprets the interactions of Smith and Jones by postulating "publicly available" entities that fix thoughts, meanings, or sounds. Furthermore, it is not clear that a mystery about communication would even be relevant to folk psychology, which need not and commonly does not face the task of resolving such problems.

Examples of the Twin-Earth type serve as one prong of conventional externalist theories of language and thought. The other prong involves deference to authority and experts, community norms, and so on. Meanings are not "in the head" because they are fixed in such terms, it is argued. Again, we may ask where the concept of meaning under investigation belongs. It is plainly not part of some scientific inquiry into language and its use, or into the lexical entry for "meaning" and "language" in English. Is it speculative ethnoscience, a study of "the commonsense psychological explanation of human behavior," as Bilgrami (1992: 3) describes the project while rejecting this prong of the argument (rightly, I believe)? Perhaps that is what is intended but, if so, the conclusions seem highly variable, as conditions vary, with nothing of much clarity emerging.

Whatever the inquiry may be about, it crucially relies on a notion of "common, public language" that remains mysterious. If it is the notion of ordinary discourse, it is useless for any form of theoretical explanation. In the empirical study of language, it has long been taken for granted that there is nothing in the world selected by such terms as "Chinese," or "German," or even much narrower ones. Speaking the same language is much like "living near" or "looking like"; there are no categories to be fixed. The fact that ordinary language provides no way to refer to what my granddaughter is speaking is fine for ordinary life, but empirical inquiry requires a different concept. In that inquiry, her language faculty is in a certain state, which determines (or perhaps *is*) her "language." Communities, cultures, patterns of deference, and so on, are established in human life in all sorts of ways, with no particular relation to anything we call "languages" in informal discourse. There is no meaningful answer to the question whether Bert should refer to the pain in his thigh as arthritis; or whether he should use the word "disinterested" to mean "unbiased," as the dictionary says, or "uninterested," as virtually every speaker believes; or whether he should pronounce words as in Boston or London.[8]

There is simply no way of making sense of this prong of the externalist theory of meaning and language, as far as I can see – or of any of the work in theory of meaning and philosophy of language that relies on such notions, a statement that is intended to cut a rather wide swath.

In brief, though naturalism does not entail an internalist approach, it does seem to leave no realistic alternative. And in actual empirical inquiry, that approach is regularly adopted, even when that is denied, a matter I have discussed elsewhere; as is familiar, to determine what scientists are doing, we investigate their practice, not what they say about it.

As noted earlier, the issue of legitimacy of inquiries that go beyond internalist limits does not arise. This should be the merest truism. Accordingly, I am constantly surprised to read that I and others deny it. Thus, a recent text on sociolinguistics opens with the remarkable claim that "modern linguistics has generally taken for granted that grammars are unrelated to the social lives of their speakers" (Romaine 1994: vii), an absurd idea, advocated by no one, which the author attributes to my insistence that "questions of power . . . are not the sorts of issues which linguists should address" (p. 1) – that I should not engage in activities that occupy a good part of my time and energy, for example. The book ends with the conclusion that "linguistic differences enact and transmit inequalities in power and status" (p. 225) – there are, for example, prestige dialects – a discovery that is held to refute my contention that the study of such matters is not illuminated by what is presently under-stood about the nature of language.

Similar pronouncements abound in the literature, often put forth with much passion and indignation. They appear to be based on a belief that I have indeed expressed: that people should tell the truth. In particular, they should not claim special insight in areas of human concern unless the claims are true; and if they are, they should impart that special knowledge, which is rarely difficult. Posturing about such matters merely serves to intimidate and marginalize, reinforcing "in-equalities in power and status." Furthermore, to make very clear the limits of understanding is a serious responsibility in a culture in which alleged expertise is given often unwarranted prestige. If inquiry in areas of basic human concern can draw from authentic discoveries about language, vision, or whatever, well and good, but that has to be shown, not proclaimed. As for sociolinguistics, it is a perfectly legitimate inquiry, externalist by definition. It borrows from internalist inquiry into humans, but suggests no alternative to it, to my knowledge. How much its findings illuminate issues of power and status is a separate question.

To cite another case, Putnam interprets my comments (actually, tru-isms) about "shared public language" as implying that unless "cultures can be defined essentialistically," we should "forget about them and return to the serious business of computer modeling" (Putnam 1992: 385) – by which he seems to mean naturalistic inquiry into the language faculty, to which computer modeling might make some contribution, though it has never been a particular interest of mine. But the problems faced by uncritical reliance on this notion are not overcome by invocation of "culture" or "cultural artifacts"; and recognition of simple facts about Chinese, English, etc. – and about the irrelevance of culture to the matters in question – in no way suggests the conclusion he draws. Cultures cross-cut anything that might reasonably be called "languages" in all sorts of ways, and "cultural studies" leave the problems where they were.

Putnam's statement that *"Languages and meanings are cultural realities"* (his emphasis; p. 385) is accurate in one sense, which is why (like everyone else) I describe the way the terms are understood in the cultures we more or less share in terms of structures of power and authority, deference patterns, literary monuments, flags and (often mythical) histories, and so on. Such terms as "language" are used in different ways in other speech communities; and our terms *belief, meaning*, etc. commonly lack any close counterpart. But these "cultural realities" do not contribute to understanding how language is acquired, understood, and used, how it is constituted and changes over time, how it is related to other faculties of mind and to human action generally. Neither the empirical study of language itself, nor Putnam's "cultural studies (history, anthropology, sociology, parts of philosophy)," when seriously pursued, make use of the notion of "shared public language" of ordinary usage, apart from informal comment; in various contexts, an anthropologist may speak of the Chinese, or Chinese–Japanese, or East Asian culture area, of the culture of scientists speaking entirely different languages, of the culture of slum-dwellers in New York, Cairo, and Rio, and so on in an intricate array that lacks any interesting relation to the languages spoken, or what are called "languages" in ordinary usage or in our literary cultures and others.

Such languages often are "cultural artifacts" in a narrower sense: partially invented "standard languages" that few may speak and that may even violate the principles of language. It is in terms of such artifacts that "norms" and "correct usage" are determined in many cultures, matters of little interest to "cultural studies," if only because they are too transparent. There is little interest in studying the behavior of the French Academy, for example.

In cultural studies, as in informal usage, we say, perfectly intelligibly, that John speaks the same language as Bill, looks like Bill, and lives near

Bill. But we are not, therefore, misled into believing that the world is divided into objective areas or places, or that there is a shape that John and Bill share; or a common language. The problem is not open texture or lack of "sharp boundaries," as Putnam believes, any more than in the case of "area" or "era." "Standard languages" are in fact quite sharply determined (for example, by the French Academy). In other usages too the boundaries of "language" are reasonably sharp, as these things go, determined by such matters as colors on maps and the like. But ordinary usage provides no notion of "shared public language" that comes even close to meeting the requirements of empirical inquiry or serious philosophical reflection on language and its use, and no more adequate notion has been proposed. Nor is there an explanatory gap that would be filled by inventing such a notion, as far as is known.

A central point of the article on which Putnam is commenting is that "Many questions, including those of greatest human significance one might argue, do not fall within naturalistic inquiry; we approach them in other ways" (see Chapter 2 of this volume, p. 19). There is no implication there, or elsewhere, that we should keep to "the serious business of computer modelling," but only that we should keep to "serious business," whatever the domain.

Is there a problem with internalist (or individualist) approaches to other domains of psychology? So it is widely claimed, but on dubious grounds, I think. Take the study of hearing. One long-standing question is how the auditory cortex determines the location of a sound. There does not seem to be any "auditory map," as there is a visual and somatosensory map. Some recent work suggests that the auditory cortex registers sound location not by spatial arrangement of neurons, but by a temporal pattern of firing in a kind of "Morse code" (Barinaga 1994). The discussion is worded in the usual mixture of technical and informal discourse. Someone reading it might be misled into thinking that the theory of auditory perception is externalist, making crucial reference to "solving problems" posed by the external world of sounds. But that is an illusion. The auditory system doesn't "solve problems" in any technical sense of this term and, if they knew how to do so, the researchers might choose to stimulate the receptors directly instead of using loudspeakers – much as they did in the computer model which, in fact, provided the main evidence for their theory of sound localization, which would work as well for a brain in a vat as for an owl turning its head to face a mouse in the brush.

The same considerations apply to the study of visual perception along lines pioneered by David Marr (1982), which has been much discussed in this connection. This work is mostly concerned with operations carried out by the retina or, loosely put, the mapping of retinal images to the visual cortex. Marr's famous three levels of analysis – computational, algorithmic, and implementation – have to do with ways of construing such mappings. Again, the theory applies to a brain in a vat exactly as it does to a person seeing an object in motion. The latter case has indeed been studied, in work of Marr's collaborator Shimon Ullman (1979). His studies of determination of structure from motion used tachistoscopic presentations that caused the subject to see a rotating cube, though there was no such thing in the environment; "see," here, is used in its normal sense, not as an achievement verb. If Ullman could have stimulated the retina directly, he would have done that; or the optic nerve. The investigation, Ullman writes, "concerns the nature of the internal representations used by the visual system and the processes by which they are derived." The account is completely internalist. There is no meaningful question about the "content" of the internal representations of a person seeing a cube under the conditions of the experiments, or if the retina is stimulated by a rotating cube, or by a video of a rotating cube; or about the content of a frog's "representation of" a fly or of a moving dot in the standard experimental studies of frog vision. No notion like "content," or "representation of" figures within the theory, so there are no answers to be given as to their nature. The same is true when Marr writes that he is studying vision as "a mapping from one representation to another, and in the case of human vision, the initial representation is in no doubt – it consists of arrays of image intensity values as detected by the photoreceptors in the retina" (Marr 1982: 31) – where "representation" is not to be understood relationally, as "representation of."

Technical presentations talk about algorithms "breaking down" under some conditions, and giving the "correct answer" in others – where the "correct answer" may be, for example, the strong three-dimensional percept given by a random dot stereogram. They may also speak of "misperception" in the case of the person or frog in the experiments, though perhaps not when a photoreceptor on a street light is activated by a searchlight rather than the Sun. And they speak of the brain as "solving problems" and as "adapted to normal situations" in which the visual system "represents" objective features of the external world. Such informal usages conform to Tyler Burge's starting point: "the premise that our perceptual experience represents or is about objects, properties, and relations that are *objective*" (Burge 1986c: 125) a premise that goes beyond an individualist–internalist approach. But these usages are on a par with an astronomer warning that a comet is aiming directly towards the Earth, implying no animist, intentional physics.

The internalist study of language also speaks of "representations" of various kinds, including phonetic and semantic representations at the "interface" with other systems. But here too we need not ponder what is represented, seeking some objective construction from sounds or things. The representations are postulated mental entities, to be understood in the manner of a mental image of a rotating cube, whether it is the consequence of tachistoscopic presentations or a real rotating cube, or stimulation of the retina in some other way; or imagined, for that matter. Accessed by performance systems, the internal representations of language enter into interpretation, thought, and action, but there is no reason to seek any other relation to the world, as might be suggested by a well-known philosophical tradition and inappropriate analogies from informal usage. Misperception raises no difficulties for this approach; it is a matter of how people assign interpretations to interactions they observe – to the reactions of a frog or person in an experiment, a photoreceptor that is "deceived," etc. – a fair topic for internalist inquiry into the psychology of the person who is deciding what to call a "misperception."

For psychology and ethnoscience, little seems at stake in these debates. Suppose Jones is a member of some ordinary community, and J is indistinguishable from him except that his total experience derives from some virtual reality design; or let J be Jones's Twin in a Twin-Earth scenario. They have had indistinguishable experiences and will behave the same way (insofar as behavior is predictable at all); they have the same internal states. Suppose that J replaces Jones in the community, unknown to anyone except the observing scientist. Unaware of any change, everyone will act as before, treating J as Jones; J too will continue as before. The scientist seeking the best theory of all of this will construct a narrow individualist account of Jones, J, and others in the community. The account omits nothing, including the way in which members of the community attribute mental states (beliefs, meanings, perceptual contents, etc.), if they do.

Suppose that the community contains a philosopher P with the externalist intuitions of recent discussion. The theory will assign to P the corresponding internal state. It will now predict correctly that P, taking J to be Jones, will attribute to J the mental states he did to Jones; and that if aware of the J–Jones interchange when it occurs, P will attribute different mental states to J. Not sharing P's intuitions, I don't know how P would attribute mental states as J lives on in the community, in a world of "objective" things (does J now come to share Jones's beliefs?). But whatever the answer, the theory will describe P's internal states accordingly. If I am a member of the community too, the theory will assign to me a different internal state, in which no fixed answers are given about attribution of beliefs and meanings to J (and nothing interesting about contents, perceptual or other, because I take the technical innovations to mean what their designers say), various judgments being given as circumstances vary.

This account deals with Jones, J, other community members, and people with various intuitions about attribution of mental states; it is incomplete insofar as these intuitions are as yet unknown but, otherwise, nothing seems missing from it, and it can readily be extended to the usage of other languages and cultures, as they differ. It can be converted easily enough into a non-individualist theory, more cumbersome and adding no new insight. That step would be inappropriate for naturalistic inquiry, and it is unclear what other purpose it might serve.

Talk about organs or organisms "solving problems," or being adapted to their functions, is to be understood similarly: as metaphoric shorthand. There is no question as to whether the wings of a butterfly are designed to "solve the problem" of flight; they evolved as thermoregulators, and still serve that purpose. If we were to learn that they reached their current state before they were ever used to fly, they would still now have the function of flight and would serve that purpose. The human visual system is maladapted to seeing in the dark, but is not a failure, for that reason. The spine of large vertebrates is badly designed from an engineering standpoint, as most people know from their personal experience; but it is neither a success nor a failure. Human languages are in part unusable, but none the worse for that; people use the parts that are usable. It has very recently been discovered that while insects seem marvellously adapted to particular kinds of flowering plants, in fact insects achieved virtually their present diversity and structure millions of years before flowering plants existed. When they appeared, "there was already waiting for them an encyclopedia of solutions waiting for the problems to be solved," Richard Lewontin (1990) points out, intending to stress the meaninglessness of these intuitive categories for biology. It is, correspondingly, a misreading of informal talk to conclude that Marr's theory of vision attributes "intentional states that represent objective, physical properties" because "there is no other way to treat the visual system as solving the problem that the theory sees it as solving" (Burge 1986a: 28–9). The theory itself has no place for the concepts that enter into the informal presentation, intended for general motivation. The statement "the idea that we classify our perceptual phenomenology without specifying the objective properties that occasion it is wildly out of touch with actual empirical theories of perception as well as with common sense" (p. 38) is correct in some circumstances with regard to common sense, but misleading with regard to empirical theories of perception, which are concerned with how things work and with perceptual reports and intuitive classifications only as evidence bearing on this matter.[9] See also Labandeira and Sepkoski 1993; Burge 1986a.

Studying any organic system, a biologist naturally takes into account environmental interactions and physical law that are likely to have influenced mutations, reproductive success, and the course of development. For motivation and intuitive guidance, the biologist might speak of systems as having "evolved to solve certain problems forced on them by the environment," with "Different species [setting] different problems and solv[ing] them differently" (Burge 1986a: 28). But this is informal talk, and if it is discovered that the course of evolution was not what had been thought, as in the case of insects and flowers, the actual theory of sensory processing and other systems is not modified, with different attributions and individuation, and revised descriptions of intentional content, mistakes, functions, purposes, problems solved, and so on. Similarly, suppose it were discovered that our ancestors had been constructed in an extraterrestrial laboratory and sent to Earth by space ship 30,000 years ago, so that natural selection played virtually no role in the formation of the kidney, visual system, arithmetical competence, or whatever. The technical sections of textbooks on the physiology of the kidney would not be modified, nor the actual theory of the functions computed by the retina or of other aspects of the human visual and other systems.

The critique of internalism (individualism) gains no more force from the observation that, in normal environments, internal processes are reliably correlated with distal properties (object boundaries, and so on). In other environments they correlate with different properties, which may be distal properties or direct retinal (or deeper internal) stimulation. We can say, if we like, that "where the constraints that normally enable an organism to compute a cognitive function are not satisfied, it will fail to represent its environment" (Egan, no date); but that "failure" is our way of describing some human end that we impose for reasons unrelated to naturalistic inquiry, much as in the case of the failure of a comet to hit Jupiter, as we hoped it would. Nor is it relevant that consideration of "representation" in normal environments allows us to associate the system under analysis with the informally described cognitive function of vision. It's no task of science to conform to the categories of intuition, or to decide whether it is still "vision" in abnormal environments, or if parts of the brain normally used for other purposes take over some of the analysis of visual images, as they sometimes do. The study of perception naturally begins with informally presented "cognitive tasks," but cares little whether something similar to them is discovered as it progresses.

Informal discussion of evolutionary processes makes use of such locutions as "solving problems," but again that is not to be taken too seriously. Physical law provides narrow channels within which complex organisms may vary, and natural selection is doubtless a factor in determining the distribution of traits and properties within these constraints. *A* factor, not *the* factor, at least if we follow Darwin's sensible strictures. Much concerned by the misinterpretation of his ideas, Darwin firmly denied that he attributed "the modification of species exclusively to natural selection," emphasizing in the last edition of *Origin of Species* that "in the first edition of this work, and subsequently, I placed in a most conspicuous position – namely, at the close of the Introduction – the following words: 'I am convinced that natural selection has been the main but not the exclusive means of modification'. This has been of no avail. Great is the power of steady misrepresentation" (cited in Gould 1982: 45). Darwin took explicit note of a range of possibilities, including nonadaptive modifications and unselected functions determined from structure.

We cannot sensibly estimate the weight that will be assigned to natural selection as a mechanism of evolution as more is learned about complex systems, the operation of physical law, the factors in spontaneous self-organization in living as in other physical systems, and so on (see Waldrop 1990; Bradley 1994).[10] The status of internalist approaches is unaffected by such considerations, whether we are thinking of ants and the kidney, or language and mind.

Virtually every aspect of the study of language and mind seems to me to involve unjustified non-naturalist assumptions. (For more extensive discussion, see Chapter 4 of this volume.) If this discussion is on the right track, one would want to ask why such ideas appear so compelling. The answer could be that our common-sense picture of the world is profoundly dualistic, ineradicably, just as we can't help seeing the setting of the Sun, or sharing Newton's belief in the "mechanical philosophy" that he undermined, or watching the wave that "flees the place of its creation," as Leonardo put it, independently of what we may know in some other corner of our minds. If so, and if metaphysical dualism has been undermined, what is left is a kind of methodological dualism, an illegitimate residue of common sense that should not be allowed to hamper efforts to gain understanding into what kind of creatures we are.

7   Internalist explorations

As I write, the sky is darkening and the radio warns that a storm is heading towards Boston, expected to bring heavy rain and strong winds, flooding of rivers and coastal areas, damage to trees and homes, and loss of power. The preceding statement, call it S (and pretend it to be spoken), is manifested in an external medium and understood in various ways by speaker and hearers. Informally, we say it has sound and meaning. S is also related to inner states of speaker and hearers, which enter into the ways they interpret it. Communication depends on similarity among these states. In such ways, language engages the world.

These topics have been studied for millennia from many points of view. They are also matters of interest in ordinary life, and there are varying cultural and linguistic practices concerning them, sometimes called "common sense" or "folk science." Plainly, the study of the topics themselves is not the study of such practices. The earth sciences are not bound by ideas and attitudes expressed in S, and the same holds for Hume's "science of human nature," which seeks to discover "the secret springs and principles, by which the human mind is actuated in its operations" (1748/1975: 14, Section 9).

While the issues are clear enough for the earth sciences, they are more convoluted when we turn to the science of human nature, which counts among its concerns the investigation of common sense (what we might call ethnoscience). Nevertheless, it proceeds on its own course. Inquiry may begin with ordinary notions of *language, sound, meaning, wind, river*, etc. but without expecting them to be a reliable guide beyond a superficial level.

I am interpreting Humean "science of human nature" as individualist and internalist. It comes nowhere near exhausting the study of how humans function in the social and physical worlds. The broader inquiries presuppose, if only tacitly, ideas about the inner states that enter into thought and action, and commonly use what they can from the internalist study of systems of the mind/brain. Interchange flows in other directions as well, as in the study of other organisms. In the case of human

164

language, the least remote analogues are perhaps in insects (see Griffin 1994; Austad 1994). Investigation of such properties as "displaced reference" in bee communication will attend to the (internal) nature of bees, their social arrangements, and their physical environment, mutually supportive inquiries.

Apparent conflicts should be resolved by clarity about the enterprise being pursued. Take, say, discussion of wide and narrow content, specification of mental representations, or individuation of thought and belief. If the inquiry falls within ethnoscience, we ask how people think and talk about such matters – recognizing, however, that the question cannot be raised directly for "content" and "mental representation," used here in a technical sense; that "thought" and "belief" are words of English without close counterparts even in similar languages, whatever significance that may have (for comment, see Rhum 1993); and that common-sense accounts of what people do are not to be construed as a form of theoretical explanation. Here we find ourselves in a morass that is largely unexplored. In the science of human nature, different questions arise. We look into the theoretical framework in which such notions as *content* and *thought* are formulated and assess its descriptive adequacy and explanatory force. It comes as no surprise that common-sense notions are not of much use, and that pickings remain thin.

Accordingly, one should be cautious about putting much weight on how "cognitive science appeals to the meaning of mental representations" to express generalizations about cognitive processes and action, and "to help explain these generalizations." Similarly, the shift from "*linguo*semantics" to "*psycho*semantics" on grounds that "psychological natural kinds" are likely to better "fulfill the purposes of psychological explanation" (Lormand 1996: 52, 53) is significant only as far as psychological explanation reaches. Quite far in some domains (for example, visual perception), but rarely in dealing with behavior.

The term "cognitive science" is sometimes used for the empirical study of cognitive capacities (vision, language, reasoning, etc., components of the science of human nature that may not form a unitary discipline); and sometimes for reflection on the nature of mind. In the latter sense, it may be plausible to hold that "Kant's central methodological innovation, the method of transcendental argument, has become a major, perhaps the major, method of cognitive science" (Brook 1994: 12); but not the former. In both cases, Jerry Fodor's "First Law of the Non-Existence of Cognitive Science" (Fodor 1987: 107) is pertinent, though for different reasons.

Psychological generalizations also come in several varieties. Consider, for example, the discoveries about "what infants know": enough to distinguish the mother's language from a different one a few days after birth; to individuate physical objects in terms of common fate and other complex properties not many months later; and much else (see Mehler and Dupoux 1994; Spelke 1990). The science of human nature tries to account for such accomplishments in terms of inner states, sorting out innate and environmental factors, constructing explanatory theory at any appropriate level. Here we have substantive research programs concerning a particular biological organism. Call this category of generalizations PG_1.

Consider the psychological generalization PG_2: if Peter wants X, thinks that obtaining X requires doing Y, and is easily capable of Y, then he will typically do Y. PG_2 differs from PG_1 in many ways. It purports to explain behavior; the generalizations of PG_1 do not. The empirical content of PG_1 is easy to detect; not so PG_2, which holds of any organism we choose to describe in such terms. Unlike PG_1, PG_2 is evaluated by reflection, not empirical inquiry, and opens no research programs – except, perhaps, into ordinary use of the terms and concepts of rationality. PG_1 falls within the science of human nature, but that is less clear for PG_2. The idea that "cognitive science" tries to express and explain PG_2 is correspondingly obscure, as are efforts to ground such "intentional laws" and to explore their implementation in computational or other mechanisms.

Study of PG_1 falls together with other branches of science. "Let chemical affinity be received as a first principle, which we cannot explain any more than Newton could explain gravitation," the eighteenth-century British chemist Joseph Black recommended, "and let us defer accounting for the laws of affinity, till we have established such a body of doctrine as he has established concerning the laws of gravitation" (cited in Schofield 1970: 226). Unification with fundamental physics was delayed until the twentieth century, while chemistry proceeded to establish a rich body of doctrine, its "triumphs . . . built on no reductionist foundation but rather achieved in isolation from the newly emerging science of physics" (Thackray 1970: 279). A similar course is reasonable with regard to PG_1.[1] PG_2 however, suggests few ways to proceed to a body of doctrine, hence to eventual unification.

Mental and physical reality

When chemistry had achieved a sufficient "body of doctrine," one might have chosen to call its constructs *physical* (though some eminent scientists did not); even more so after physics had changed enough to permit unification, departing even more radically from common-sense notions of the physical so as to "free itself" from "intuitive pictures" and "give up visualizability totally," in Heisenberg's phrase (cited by Holton 1996). The lessons carry over to mental aspects of the world, including mental representations and processes that might be postulated by the science of human nature.

Cartesian dualism had raised substantive questions: a mechanical concept of *physical* was proposed and arguments were offered to show that it was incomplete. The questions – though not the problems that had given rise to them – dissolved with the collapse of mechanism and we "accustomed ourselves to the abstract notion of forces, or rather to a notion hovering in a mystic obscurity between abstraction and concrete comprehension," as Friedrich Lange (1925: 308), in his classic scholarly study, summarized this "turning-point" in the history of materialism, which deprives the doctrine of much significance. A century before, Hume had taken the dimmer view that by showing "the imperfections of the mechanical philosophy," Isaac Newton had "restored [Nature's] ultimate secrets to that obscurity in which they ever did and ever will remain" (Hume 1841 vol. 6: 341). Efforts to grapple with the component of the obscurity called *mental* led some to the conclusion that "it is the organization of the nervous system itself" that "freely exercises in a healthy state all the properties" of mind (La Mettrie, cited in Wellman 1992: 147). But the problems that had troubled the Cartesians were never addressed, and no substantial "body of doctrine" was developed. (For discussion, see Chomsky (1966; 1968) and later publications, including Chomsky (1995a); on Newton's struggles with the basic problem, see Dobbs and Jacob 1995.)

Apart from its theological framework, there has been, since Newton, no reasonable alternative to John Locke's suggestion that God might have chosen to "superadd to matter a faculty of thinking" just as he "annexed effects to motion, which we can in no way conceive motion able to produce" (1975: book IV, Chapter 3, Section 6, p. 541). As Joseph Priestley later elaborated, drawing "the obvious conclusion to the thinking-matter debate" (Yolton 1983: Chapter I, VI, especially p. 113), we take those properties "termed mental" to be the result of "such an organical structure as that of the brain," superadded to others, none of which need be comprehensible in the sense sought by earlier science. While European materialism took a different tack, at its heart "lay the assertion, based on one reading of Newtonian physics, that motion is inherent in matter, that all of nature is alive, that soul and body are one, all material, all entirely of this world" (M. Jacob 1991: 200; Chomsky 1995a).

With the notion of *the physical* abandoned, never to be replaced, we can go no further than to ask whether mental aspects of the world, or

others, "can be accommodated within the framework of physical explanation, as presently conceived," being:

> fairly sure that there will be a physical explanation for the phenomena in
> question, if they can be explained at all, for an uninteresting terminological
> reason, namely that the concept of 'physical explanation' will no doubt be
> extended to incorporate whatever is discovered in this domain, exactly as it was
> to accommodate . . . numerous other entities and processes that would have
> offended the common sense of earlier generations. (Chomsky 1968: 98)

The study of language tries to develop bodies of doctrine with an eye to
eventual unification. Its constructs and principles can properly be
"termed mental," and assumed to be "the result of organical structure"
– how, it remains to discover. On these aspects of the way language
engages the world, there is little more to say.[2]

The faculty of language

There is reason to believe that humans have a specialized "organ"
dedicated to the use and interpretation of language, call it "the faculty
of language" (FL). We can take FL to be common to the species,
assuming states that vary in limited ways with experience. Interacting
with other systems (cognitive, sensorimotor), these states contribute to
determining the sound and meaning of expressions. Study of these
topics may not capture common-sense notions of sound and meaning,
sameness of meaning, repetition, etc.; and there is no clear question as
to whether they count as theories of sound and meaning, as in the case
of motion, rivers, life, and so on.

For concreteness, consider the expressions of example (1):

(1)   a   John was (too) clever to catch.
        b   John was (too) clever to be caught.
        c   John was (too) easy to catch.
        d   John was (too) easy to be caught.

If Peter's FL has attained the appropriate state, he knows that with
"too" included, (1a) and (1b) are true if John was so clever that one
could not catch him (John), and that, with "too" deleted, (1a) is
"deviant," requiring some non-standard mode of interpretation (while
(1b) is differently interpreted). He knows further that (1c) is true if it
was (too) easy to catch John (who wasn't "easy"); and that with or
without "too," the obvious analogies fail for (1d), also deviant. The
study of FL seeks to encompass such observations under broader
generalizations of the category PG_1 and to discover the principles and

structures that underlie them. Though not explaining Peter's behavior, these elements of inner states should contribute to an account of how he thinks and acts, insofar as there is one. There is a reasonably successful theory that addresses such facts on the assumption that FL is a computational system with largely invariant principles. Tentatively adopting it, we attribute to Peter the corresponding mental states, representations, and processes (to which he has no conscious access).[3]

Suppose Peter's FL is in state L. We may then say that Peter has (speaks, understands, . . .) the language L. Here the term "language" is used in a technical sense: call L an "I-language" – "I" to suggest internal and individual, and also intensional, in that L is a specific procedure that generates infinitely many expressions of L. One such expression of Peter's I-language, call it RA_P, enters into determining how Peter might interpret the radio announcement reported in the statement S above. RA_P resembles expressions generated by the minds of the announcer and other listeners, if they understand the announcement more or less as Peter does. The part of the science of human nature that concerns itself with FL, the states it assumes, and the expressions these I-languages generate, we could call "I-linguistics."

The notion of I-language seems to be about as close as I-linguistics comes to the various common-sense notions of language. Though unproblematic for ordinary life, these are intricate and obscure. One description of ordinary English usage, as good as any I know, is that it takes a language to be "an (intentional) object of (mutual) belief, appropriately studied hermeneutically within a sociology of language" (Pateman 1987: 73); though the notion is no more likely to be useful for sociology of language beyond the surface than the phrases of S are for the earth sciences: say, the term "coastal area," which has something like the status of "language," except that it is much less amorphous, shifting, and multidimensionally interest-relative. The ordinary terms are often used as shorthand, as in discussing general properties of Chinese versus Italian (for neither of which is there much in the way of mutual belief). We also say that Peter does or does not speak the same language as I do, or live in the same place. But the world does not consist of such areas or languages in any sense that interests the earth sciences or I-linguistics.

Even to speak of Peter as having the I-language L is a severe simplification; the state of any person's faculty of language is some jumble of systems that is no more likely to yield theoretical understanding than most other complex phenomena of the natural world. Peter is said to be multilingual when the differences among his languages happen to interest us for one or another reason; from another point of view, everyone is multiply multilingual.

In English usage, having a language is called "knowing a language," a fact that has led to attempts to impose various conceptions of the nature of knowledge, and to determine to what entity Peter stands in a cognitive relation when he has L. For reasons discussed elsewhere, I think the questions are misconceived, though others are worth pursuing. Thus, when Peter has L, he knows many things: for example, that "chase" rhymes with "lace" and entails "follow." To spell all this out is a meaningful and important pursuit; and there are others about the nature of knowledge of X generally, the cognitive content of knowing how, the relations of knowledge to ability, and so on. (For some discussion, see Chomsky 1975; 1986.)

The expressions of L are constructed from lexical items, each a collection of properties; the simpler words of S come close. We speak informally of the sound and meaning of a word, the way it is pronounced, and what it means. The nearest I-linguistic paraphrase refers to the properties of a lexical item LI that are involved in sound and meaning: its phonological and semantic features (call them its *I-sound* and *I-meaning*, respectively). LI consists of these, along with formal features (not necessarily distinct) involved in the computational processes that form larger structures. And it may have more complex internal structure. There is no separate substratum, the word, in which the properties inhere, and any feature change yields a different LI. Putting aside many interesting issues, let us assume that the language includes a lexicon which is the set of LIs, and that the lexicon is accessed by the computational procedures that form expressions.[4]

The meaning of words has elicited a good deal of attention and controversy; that any such thing as I-meaning ("semantic representation," "narrow content") even exists is now commonly denied. Comparable questions about I-sound have rarely been raised. The empirical disciplines seem to me to study them in much the same way: in particular, to assume that both involve invariant universal features of which LIs are constituted (and hence are not radically holistic). I will tentatively assume that postulation of I-sound and I-meaning is legitimate, returning to reasons for denying it.

FL attains state L with little if any effect of instruction, training, or decision, passing through characteristic stages and partially stabilizing at fixed periods. To borrow Hume's phrase, the operations of the mind proceed "by a natural transition, which precedes reflection, and which cannot be prevented by it" (1740/1948: 147, Book I, Part III, Section 13). In these respects too FL seems similar to other bodily organs. The lexicon continues to change in certain ways, and is subject to a degree of conscious choice (as are other parts of language, marginally). Thus the lexicon of my language includes the word "dour," which rhymes with the final word of S, "power." Peter's language may have a different word with the same meaning but rhyming with "poor." I might abandon my usage and adopt Peter's, or adopt a somewhat different meaning while keeping the I-sound fixed; by decision, or without and beyond awareness. Such events fall within what Tyler Burge calls that "vast ragged network of interdependence, established by patterns of deference which lead back to people who would elicit the assent of others (1986b: 702, 703)," and which, along with various power relations, social arrangements, personality factors, and much else, "set a norm for conventional linguistic understanding," as informally construed. Whether "they also provide linguistic meaning," as Burge suggests, seems to me a matter of terminology, not fact. Also, it is unclear to me how one might learn about such a heterogeneous complex except by chipping away at parts that lend themselves to closer inquiry. In any event, I-linguistics goes no further than to say that, in the case in question, I have added a new item to my lexicon, perhaps abandoning usage of an older one; and more generally, seeks only to isolate certain factors, crucial it seems, that enter into the awesome complexity of human affairs.

It is often held that "people's spontaneous judgments, or their intuitions, as philosophers call them," constitute the subject matter for linguistics and for the theory of reference, which aim to systematize "grammatical intuitions" and "reference intuitions."[5] One can define projects at will, but it is hard to see the interest in systematization of some category of judgments, or other selected data.

Take the study of reference, in its two aspects: the study of how people use language to talk about things and of their ideas about such matters. For these endeavors, judgments might provide evidence, perhaps reliable or useful, perhaps not. A serious investigation of either topic might explore cross-cultural similarities, poverty of stimulus considerations, psycholinguistic experiment, brain scans, or anything else that can be devised. Neither endeavor is the study of judgments, though we could think of them as studies of intuitions in a different sense: what they really are, a topic for which intuitive judgments serve at best as a source of information. (Stich (1996) looks at the matter somewhat differently.)

Intuitive judgments are data, nothing more; they might become evidence within the framework of some explanatory theory. The judgments reported in connection with (1) have been used as evidence to support the conclusion that the complement of the adjective is clausal with three empty categories: the null subject, an empty operator O, and the trace of O, notions explained within the theory and justified independently if the account of example (1) is to have any force. About these matters, speakers have no intuitive judgments, any more than they do about tensors and undecidability.

Forced intuitive judgments with ordinary expectations withdrawn have to be considered with particular caution. Suppose we ask Peter whether a Martian speaks his language if it shares his judgments concerning example (1) and other expressions but uses different principles or has a different biochemistry; or whether a Peter-duplicate created this instant can talk about rivers or water. Judgments become unclear, fading towards insignificance as thought experiments strip away background beliefs presupposed in the ordinary use of language, moving to the realms of Twin-Earth, Swampmen, and other strange worlds (see Stich 1983: 62; Fodor 1994: Appendix B).[6]

Suppose we adopt a "strange worlds" scenario to investigate what falls under Peter's concepts: does his concept *water* include Twin-Earth XYZ, for example? Would he say – or be right to say – that on Twin-Earth water is XYZ, unlike here? That Twin-Earth doesn't have water, only XYZ? Or either, as conditions of the thought experiment are changed? Or perhaps nothing coherent? Answers might provide evidence for some account of Peter's linguistic states and practices, and ways of thought, and might bear on the initial question about concepts if that technical notion figures in the theoretical account. In isolation, the judgments would tell us little even if they were stable as conditions of the thought experiment vary, which does not seem to be the case.

The study of folk semantics should not lightly assume that practices and conventions of some cultural tradition are a good guide to common-sense understanding, that of the investigator or anyone else.[7] At the very least, it should try to discover the analogues to FL and I-language in this domain, seeking to identify the innate component.

Suppose Peter says that Joe Sixpack voted for a living wage because he's worried about his child's health. Are we entitled to conclude that Peter believes the world to be constituted of such entities as Joe Sixpack, living wages, and health, and relations like voting-for and worrying-about that hold among them? Would the parallel inference be legitimate when Peter says that Tom visited Boston? If Peter says that the bank moved across the street after it was destroyed by fire, does he believe that among the things in the world there are some that can be destroyed but still be around, so that they can move? Similar questions can be asked about the terms of S. Ethnoscience is concerned with folk-scientific conceptions of such matters. The science of human nature tries to find out what is actually happening, to unravel "the anatomy of the mind," in Hume's phrase, and the ways its structures and processes are implicated in thought and action. The inquiries are different, though they might use similar data (perhaps intuitive judgments).

Similarly, inquiry into the meaning of *meaning* or of *sound* might be concerned to discover:

1. the semantic features (I-meaning) of the lexical items "meaning" and "sound" in some variety of English;
2. the ideas people have about the general domain of meaning and sound; or
3. the best theory of language and its use.

(1) is a question about some (rather idiosyncratic) English words; (2) falls within ethnoscience; and (3) within the science of human nature. (1) and (2) pose perfectly serious questions. Thus, pursuing (1), we find that names have no meaning: the question "what does 'Stalin' mean?" makes sense only if one is asking about etymology. We find further that the phrase "what does the expression E mean?" shares properties with "what does John weigh?" and "how does John feel?" rather than "what did John eat (say, mean)?," suggesting that what E means might have some kind of adverbial quality. The study of (1) and (2) has little obvious import for (3). Much the same holds of the study of thought, belief, concepts, etc.

Interpretation of interface levels

Let's turn to questions that fall within (3) above: questions about FL and the states it assumes, and how they are integrated with other components of the mind/brain in language use.

One fairly standard assumption, adapting traditional ideas, is that an expression E of L is a pair <PHON, SEM>, where PHON(E) is the information relevant to the sound of E and SEM(E) to its meaning. PHON and SEM are constructed by computational operations on lexical items. Suppose E is a word in isolation. PHON(E) is generally distinct from its I-sound by virtue of phonological operations, but SEM(E) could be identical with the I-meaning of E, depending on the facts about lexical decomposition and the like. PHON(E) and SEM(E) are elements at the "phonetic level" and "semantic levels," respectively; they are phonetic and semantic "representations." The terms have their technical sense; there is nothing "represented" in the sense of representative theories of ideas, for example.[8] These levels are the "interface" between FL and other systems, providing the information used by the sensorimotor apparatus and other systems of language use.

There has been a great deal of illuminating work about such representations and how they are constructed by operations of the I-language. (On the semantic side, see, *inter alia*, Larson and Segal (1995), Pustejovsky (1995), and sources cited.) This work could be considered syntax in the technical sense; it deals with the properties and arrangements of the symbolic objects. On the sound side, the work is sometimes called phonetics, but with the understanding that the study of phonetic features, syllabic and metrical structures, and so on, only contributes to the more general investigation of how information made available by the I-language is used by the sensorimotor systems, and how the whole complex relates to external events. These are the topics of acoustic and articulatory phonetics, going well beyond I-language. The same practice would be appropriate, I think, with regard to the work often called "natural-language semantics" and "lexical semantics." It can be regarded as part of syntax, but oriented to a different interface and different aspects of language use. Insofar as the relation of rhyme that holds between "chase" and "lace" is based on properties of I-sound, and the relation of entailment that holds between "chase" and "follow" on properties of I-meaning, both fall under syntax, in a traditional sense.

Virtually all work in syntax in the narrower sense has been intimately related to questions of semantic (and of course phonetic) interpretation, and motivated by such questions. The fact has often been misunderstood because many researchers have chosen to call this work "syntax," reserving the term "semantics" for relations of expressions to something extra-linguistic.[9] The earliest work in modern I-linguistics (generative grammar) was concerned with the meanings of such expressions as in example (1) on p. 168, reviving concerns of traditional grammar. We can usefully distinguish aspects of I-language that are more relevant to sound or to meaning; but phonetics and semantics, in the sense of how language engages the world, lie beyond.

Serious questions about the general picture arise at every point, from the assumed architecture of mind to details of implementation. One category of questions has to do with the location of the interface. On the phonetic side, it has to be determined whether sensorimotor systems are in part language specific, hence within FL, so that the interface level should be "beyond" what is usually taken to be phonetic representation; there is considerable disagreement about the matter. On the semantic side, the questions have to do with the relations between FL and other cognitive systems. At either level, one can offer only reasonable guesses, taken as first approximation.

Questions of language–world relation at the phonetic interface have been studied intensively with sophisticated technology, but the problems are hard, and understanding remains limited. Questions about the use of semantic representations are much more obscure. Far less is known about the language-external systems; much of the evidence about them is so closely linked to language that it is notoriously difficult to determine when it bears on language, when on other systems (insofar as they are distinct). Additionally, direct investigation of the kind possible for sensorimotor systems is in its infancy. Nonetheless, there is a huge amount of data about how expressions are used and understood in particular circumstances, enough so that natural-language semantics is one of the liveliest areas of study of language, though questions of language use remain elusive.

Lexical items

I have taken an expression to be a pair <PHON, SEM> constructed from lexical items LI, each a complex of properties, including I-sound and I-meaning. PHON and SEM are interpreted by language-external systems. At these interface levels, there may be no sub-unit corresponding to LI. For the phonetic interface, the point is uncontroversial. A good deal of work in syntax/semantics assumes that LIs may be decomposed and reconstructed in the course of computation of SEM. For example, such items as *who* or *nobody* might yield operator–restrictor–variable constructions at the level SEM, something like: [[QUx, x a person] [John saw x]]. And there may be other ways in which the semantic properties of LIs are modified or distributed. However, for simple words we can generally assume that SEM = I-meaning (perhaps a reflection of our ignorance).

With regard to the semantic component of LIs, alternatives to this picture are common. The questions also tend to be approached somewhat differently in more empirically oriented studies and in conceptual discussions of the nature of meaning and reference. The latter typically regard words and other expressions as phonetic (or orthographic) units, or as dissociated from either sound or meaning; accordingly a word can change its meaning, perhaps even both its sound and meaning, and still be the same word. It is not obvious that these conventions make sense. At least, they have to be explained and justified. The simplest thesis is that an expression E has no existence apart from its properties at the interface levels, PHON(E) and SEM(E) (if these exist).

It is a useful heuristic, I think, to pursue analogies between the sound and meaning sides as far as they plausibly go. Specifically, we may ask whether some light can be shed on issues of semantics by looking at phonetic analogues, which often seem less contentious.

Consider a "Mentalese" alternative to the picture outlined so far. Instead of taking LI to include I-sound and I-meaning, let us assume that one or the other is missing, or perhaps both. Accordingly, either SEM, PHON, or both are missing at the interface levels. To learn a language is to acquire rules that map LI into some other system of mind, Mentalese, which is interpreted to yield (aspects of) sound and meaning. If I-sound is missing, then LI is mapped into P-Mentalese. If I-meaning is missing, then LI is mapped into S-Mentalese. Or both. Language itself has no phonology/phonetics, or no semantics, or neither. These are properties of Mentalese.

On the phonetic side, there are no such proposals, to my knowledge. On the semantic side, they are common. What is their substantive content, on either side?

For concreteness, consider, again, the words given in example (2), or the words "persuade," "force," "remind" for X in example (3):

(2)   chase, lace, follow

(3)   John X-ed Mary to take her medicine.

Suppose the corresponding LIs lack I-sound and that Peter has learned how to map them into regions of P-Mentalese that have phonetic inter-pretation. Peter knows a lot about the regions and their interpretations. Thus "chase" rhymes with "lace"; "persuade" and "force" begin with lip constriction, though in different ways, and "remind" does not; etc. Standard approaches assign these properties to FL, taking them to be represented in PHON. The P-Mentalese alternative adds an extra layer of complexity, and raises new problems, for example: What component of LI indicates the region of P-Mentalese to which it is mapped, if not the I-sound (as conventionally assumed)? At what point in the com-putation of an expression does the mapping to P-Mentalese take place? How are universal and particular properties of sound expressed in the interpretation of P-Mentalese? For good reasons, such questions have not been raised, and we may drop the matter.

Consider the semantic analogue. We now assume that LIs have only I-sound and uninterpreted formal properties, and that Peter has learned how to map them into regions of S-Mentalese, which have semantic interpretation. (For several versions of such views, see Fodor 1990: Chapter 7, a review of Schiffer 1987.) Peter knows a lot about these regions/interpretations too. Thus, if Tom chased Bill then Tom fol-lowed Bill with a certain intention, not conversely; if X = "persuade" in example (3), then John's efforts were a partial success (Mary came to intend to take her medicine, but may not have done so); if X = "force," John succeeded, but differently (Mary took her medicine, whatever her intentions); if X = "remind," John may have failed (Mary may not have been paying attention), but if he succeeded, then Mary came to remember to take her medicine. The earlier picture assigns the relevant properties to FL, taking them to appear in SEM by virtue of operations on LIs and the constructions in which they appear. The S-Mentalese alternative adds an extra layer of complexity and raises new problems analogous to those of the phonetic counterpart. If we take LIs to have neither I-sound nor I-meaning, then both kinds of problem arise.

One can be misled by simple examples, say, "snow is white," or descriptive phrases of S: "the sky is dark," etc. But problems multiply with even the slightest extension of the paradigm. Consider "the rain looks heavy," "the wind feels strong," . . . ; and, in general, example (4):

(4)   X (is, looks, tastes, sounds, feels, smells, . . .) Y

Even such simple sentences impose translation problems, even for very similar languages. How are they to be translated into universal Mentalese?[10]

Answers to such questions might yield empirical consequences within more articulated theories of language and Mentalese, perhaps justifying the additional complexity. Standing alone, the proposals can hardly be evaluated.

Suppose that we develop *denotational* theories of interpretation, either directly for linguistic expressions, or for Mentalese translations. With regard to sound, a standard assumption is that in producing or perceiving E, the sensorimotor systems access PHON(E). Instead, let us now suppose that LI has no I-sound but *P-denotes* some object that is external to the person; call it the *phonetic value* PV of LI (alternatively, of its P-Mentalese image), and suppose some computation on PVs yields the linguistic component of the sound of E, PV(E). PV could be something about the noises associated with utterances (or possible utterances) of E as circumstances vary (perhaps also as speakers vary, insofar as they are sufficiently alike); a construction from motions of molecules, perhaps. The proposal could be elaborated by taking PV to be determined by social and physical factors of various kinds. One might proceed to an account of communication, translation, acquisition, and other processes in these terms. Thus Peter is able to communicate with Tom because the same PV is denoted by their expressions in the language they share (but only partially know).

The proposal leaves all problems where they were, adding a host of new ones. We understand nothing more than before about the relation of E to its external manifestations. The account of communication and other processes is worthless. There is no reason to suppose that such PVs figure in the process by which one person's mind constructs some version of what another is saying. For such reasons, there are no proposals along these lines.

Consider the semantic analogue.[11] We now suppose that LI has no I-meaning but that it (or its S-Mentalese image, perhaps an "idea" or "concept") *S-denotes* a *semantic value* SV(LI) that is external to the person, some construction from what is being talked about when E is uttered (speakers and circumstances varying), perhaps partially determined by social and physical properties. One might again offer an account of communication, translation, acquisition, and other processes in these terms. Thus Peter is able to communicate with John because their expressions S-denote the same SVs in the shared language that they partially know.

We now take the SV for "Joe Sixpack," "living wage," "chase," "persuade," "look," the words of S, and so on (or for the S-Mentalese images) to be Joe Sixpack, living wages, chasing, persuading, looking, the sky, Boston, rivers, damage, loss, power, . . . , while adding something about "who," "nobody," and so on. To account for the semantic properties of E = "Chinese is the language of Beijing and Hong Kong," we take the SVs to be Chinese, language, Beijing, etc. We would ask whether the external object SV("the fate of the Earth") = SV("the Earth's fate") for the common language (or for someone who can be said "to know it"). We could go on to explore intuitive judgments, whatever that might mean within this quasi-technical array.

So far, at least, the original project isn't advanced, merely restated, with many new problems. We have learned nothing more about how expressions are used and interpreted. Adopting one or the other proposal, we still have to account for the properties of expressions: those of examples (1)–(4), for instance. The phonetic and semantic cases are not the same, of course; only similar, but in what may be informative ways.

Suppose we follow a different course, saying that properties of rhyme, inference patterns, etc. do not relate to language (or its Mentalese images), but have to do with our beliefs about Values: the external objects, whatever they are. On the phonetic side, we say that Peter's belief that PV(*chase*) rhymes with PV(*lace*) has a different status from his other beliefs about PVs (say, about their frequency). Similarly for other properties. Such a proposal has never been entertained, and we can again drop the matter.

The counterpart on the semantic side would be to hold that the properties of examples (1)–(4) are accounted for in terms of Peter's beliefs about the world; perhaps strength of belief, in Quinean terms. Such proposals are familiar, even close to orthodoxy. To evaluate them, we have to find out more about how beliefs are fixed in these highly intricate and strikingly uniform ways within and among languages, among other questions. Until they are addressed, the proposals are virtually without substance.

For the present, it seems reasonable to conclude that the situation is much as on the phonetic side: the semantic properties of the words and constructions are determined by the ways they are constituted, with a rich innate contribution. The problem is to discover the properties of I-sound and I-meaning (whether for LIs, or their S-Mentalese counterparts), the ways they can be combined, the computations that yield interface representations and how these are interpreted by language-external systems. In both domains, there are many open problems, but substantive progress as well.

Consider a different approach: the sound and meaning of an expression reduce in part to relations of the sort discussed in connection with examples (2) and (3). For LI, we have some (finite) pattern of relations to other expressions, phonetic relations R_P and semantic relations R_S, perhaps supplemented with P- and S-denotational properties. Similarly for more complex expressions. For "chase," R_P consists of the properties *rhymes with "lace", begins the same way as "child", has the same number of syllables as "pin"*, etc.; and R_S consists of the relations to "follow," "intend," etc., and other conceptual and inferential roles.

On the phonetic side, the move again seems pointless. The standard feature-composition approach suffices to express R_P along with other phenomena: the relation of components of "chase" to articulatory gestures and noises, their distributional properties (for example consonant–vowel interactions), and so on. Furthermore, $R_P(chase)$ shares properties with $R_P(W)$ for other words W. Numerous facts of this sort are expressible under the standard view that LI is constituted of its properties, which enter into determining its phonetic relations to other expressions and much else. For such reasons, the proposal has never been entertained.[12]

On the semantic side, again, there are such proposals, and similar questions arise. Thus, $R_S(persuade)$ shares properties with $R_S(raise)$: "causative" properties, which have been extensively studied in many languages, with nontrivial results. A sensible version of LI should express such facts. It should also capture distributional properties that are not (sensibly) stated in terms of inferential and conceptual roles; for example, the fact that "deny," "doubt," "refuse," and so on occur with polarity items ("any," "ever," etc.) in ways that "assert," "believe," "accept" do not, and that in these respects the former are similar to "not," "few" (versus "many"). Standard approaches seek properties of I-meaning and SEM in terms of which a wide array of facts can be expressed and explained, including inferences and their shared and dissimilar properties.

So conceived, semantic and phonetic interpretation are somewhat analogous. The expression E consists of the interface representations PHON(E) and SEM(E), computed from LIs. PHON(E) provides information that is used by sensorimotor systems for articulation and perception; SEM(E), information that is used by conceptual–intentional systems to engage the world in different ways as the language user thinks and talks in terms of the perspectives made available by the resources of the mind.

The referential use of language can attend in various ways to the component elements of I-meaning and SEM. Individuation commonly turns on such factors as design, intended and characteristic use, institutional role, etc. If something looks to me just like a book but I learn that it was designed to be a paperweight and is characteristically used that way, I could come to agree that it is a paperweight, not a book. Suppose the library has two indistinguishable copies of *Middlemarch*, Peter takes out one, and Tom the other. If we attend to the material component of the LI, they took out different books; if we focus on its abstract component, they took out the same book. We can attend to both simultaneously, using words with an abstract/concrete character, as in the expressions "the book that he is planning will weigh at least five pounds if he ever writes it," or "his book is in every store in the country." Similarly, we can paint the door white and walk through it. Or consider the word "bank" (savings, river). We can say that:

1. The bank burned down and then it moved across the street;
2. The bank, which had raised the interest rate, was destroyed by fire; and
3. The bank lowered the interest rate to keep from being blown up.

Referential dependence is preserved across the abstract/concrete divide. Thus (1) means that the building burned down and then the institution moved; similarly (2), (3). But we cannot say that:

4. The bank burned down and then it eroded; or
5. The bank, which had raised the interest rate, was eroding fast; or
6. The bank raised the interest rate without eroding.

Sentence (4) does not mean that the savings bank burned down and then the river bank eroded.

The facts are often clear, but not trivial. Thus, referentially dependent elements, even the most narrowly constrained, observe some distinctions but ignore others (pronouns, relatives, the "empty category" that is the subject of "being blown up" and "eroding"). In the case of "bank," the natural conclusion is that there are two LIs that happen to share the same I-sound (homonymy), and that one of them, "savings bank," is polysemous, like "book": it provides a way of looking at the world that combines abstract and concrete properties, allowing referential dependence across these perspectives. (On some traditional problems, often obscure and complex, see Lyons 1977: Section 13.4.) Such properties can be investigated in many ways: language acquisition, generality among languages, similar items within the language, invented forms, zeugma, and so on. If systematic similarities and differences persist, conclusions about lexical structure are supported. There is no *a priori* reason to expect that language will have such properties; Martian could be different.

The question, "to what does the word X refer?," has no clear sense, whether posed for Peter, or (more mysteriously) for some "common language." In general, a word, even of the simplest kind, does not pick out an entity of the world, or of our "belief space" – which is not to deny, of course, that there are banks, or that we are talking about something (even some thing) if we discuss the fate of the Earth (or the Earth's fate) and conclude that *it* is grim; only that we should not draw unwarranted conclusions from common usage. The observations extend to the simplest referential and referentially dependent elements (pronouns, *same*, *re*("build"), etc.); or to proper names, which have rich semantic–conceptual properties derived in large part from our nature, with some overlay of experience. Something is named as a person, a river, a city, with the complexity of understanding that goes along with these categories. Language has no logically proper names, stripped of such properties; one must beware of what Peter Strawson called "the myth of the logically proper name" (Strawson 1952: 216) in natural language, and related myths concerning indexicals and pronouns. We can think of naming as a kind of "world-making," in something like Nelson Goodman's (1978) sense, but the worlds we make are rich and intricate and substantially shared thanks to a complex shared nature. Even the conscious efforts of the sciences and the arts are guided by such properties – fortunately, or they could accomplish nothing. (For some further discussion, see Chomsky 1975; 1995a.)

An approach to semantic interpretation in such terms has a traditional flavor. Seventeenth-century rationalist psychology held that innate "cognoscitive powers" enable people "to understand or judge of what is received by the sense," which only gives the mind "an occasion to exercise its own activity" to construct "intelligible ideas and conceptions of things from within itself" as "rules," "patterns," exemplars," and "anticipations" that provide relations of cause and effect, whole and part, symmetry and proportion, characteristic use (for all "things artificial" or "compounded natural things"), unity of objects and other Gestalt properties, and in general "one comprehensive idea of the whole".[13] "It is manifest," Hobbes held, that "Names are signs not of things but of our cogitations," "our conceptions" (1889: 16f.); the technical notion "sign of X," holding of words, is better construed in such a way. These "conceptions" can be intricate, as we see from our manner of individuation in terms of constitution, form, origin, and other properties. A man

will always be the same, whose actions and thoughts proceed all from the same beginning of motion, namely, that which was in his generation; and that will be the same river which flows from one and the same fountain, whether the same water, or other water, or something else than water, flow from thence [as in the classical case of the ship of Theseus, Hobbes adds]; and that the same city, whose acts proceed continually from the same institution. (p. 16f.)

The inquiry into personal identity from Locke to Hume was concerned with organic unity, a broader notion. A tree or an animal "differs from a mass of matter," Locke noted, by virtue of the "organization of parts in one coherent body, partaking of one common life" with "continued organization" that comes from within, unlike artifacts. The identity of an oak resides in "a sympathy of parts" contributing to "one common end" of "support, nourishment and propagation" of the form, Shaftesbury added. Hume largely agreed, though taking "the identity, which we ascribe to the mind of men," and "the like kind . . . that we ascribe to vegetables and animal bodies," to be "only a fictitious one" established by the imagination, not Shaftesbury's *peculiar nature belonging to this form*." John Yolton makes a strong case that the core of the theory of ideas from Descartes to Reid took ideas to be "not things, but ways of knowing," "not signs of the corpuscular structure, but signs in terms of which we know of or are acquainted with experience," so that "The world as known *is* the world of ideas, of significatory content" (Yolton 1984: 213ff.; other quotes here and below from Mijuskovic 1974: 97–113).

Hume's conclusion gains more force as we look more closely at the intricacy of the concepts. "[*Person*] is a forensic term," Locke observed, "appropriating actions and their merit; and so belongs only to intelligent agents, capable of a law, and happiness, and misery," as well as accountability for actions, and much else. Individuation of rivers and cities involves factors well beyond origin. The flow of a river can be reversed, or it may be diverted to a different course or even divided into streams that may later converge, or changed in all sorts of other ways, and yet remain the same river, under appropriate circumstances. The press reports intelligibly that scientists "have discovered the source of the Amazon" in an unexpected place, the sole source, though usually "rivers start off as myriad little ones." Locke notes that the oak remains the same when a branch is lopped. Suppose the oak is transplanted elsewhere and replaced in its original location by the branch, which grows into a replica of the tree while the transplanted oak withers and dies – but is still the original tree, according to the fictitious identity established by innate cognoscitive powers. This barely touches the surface. Proceeding further, we find that these powers impose a rich framework of interpretation and understanding, which we would expect to be only marginally influenced by experience, as in the case of other complex organic structures.

From such ideas about internally generated modes of cognition to which experience conforms, it is a short step to an analysis in terms of semantic features, or what Julius Moravcsik calls the "(generative) factors" of lexical structure (Moravcsik 1975; 1990).[14] Recasting the enterprise in these terms, we try to unravel the anatomy of the mind, including FL and the systems at the interface, and to discover how experience and social interaction are shaped in terms of these internal resources.

Some questions of legitimacy

It is commonly held that this version of the science of human nature is needlessly complex, or misguided in principle. On one view, the evidence adduced for principles of FL "is much more simply accounted for by the . . . hypothesis" that FL indeed is "innate in human brains" but we need only say that there is "a hardware level of explanation in terms of the structure of the device" and "a functional level of explanation, describing which sorts of languages can be acquired" (Searle 1992: 244). Or, we should dispense with FL altogether in favor of the "competing hypothesis" that the innate structures of the brain "have as their original and still primary function the organization of perceptual experience, the administration of linguistic categories being an acquired additional function for which evolution has only incidentally suited them," thus overcoming the problem of accounting for the evolution of language among "other advantages" (Paul Churchland 1981: 86).[15]

That there is a "hardware level" is not in contention, if by that we mean that atoms, cells, and so on are presumably involved in "the structure of the device" FL that is "innate in human brains." For the moment, we can only follow Joseph Black's good advice and construct a "body of doctrine" about FL; with progress towards unification there could be more to say – perhaps, as in the case of chemistry, that current assumptions about the "hardware" are misconceived. The "body of doctrine" is concerned with "which sorts of languages can be acquired" and also their properties, their interactions with other systems, the manner of their acquisition and use, unification problems, and anything else that lends itself to useful investigation. Working this out, we seem to be led back to the "deep unconscious rules" that Searle regards as dispensable. Searle is right that there is "no further predictive or explanatory power . . . by saying that there is in addition [to the hardware and functional level] a level of deep unconscious rules" (1992: 244–5) of FL. But what has been proposed is quite different: specific structures and principles of FL, which yield at least a partial account of properties of language. Similarly, chemistry is uninteresting if it says only that there are deep structural properties of matter, anything but as a body of doctrine about these is developed. At best, the debate is rather reminiscent of past controversy over whether chemical properties, molecular structure, etc. should be attributed to matter or regarded simply as calculating devices; all pointless, as largely agreed in retrospect, and falling under Burge's apt observation that questions of ontology and the like are "epistemically posterior to questions about the success of explanatory and descriptive practices" (Burge 1986a: 18; see also Chomsky 1986: 250f.; 1995a; note 2).[16]

Paul Churchland's proposal could become a "competing hypothesis" if spelled out sufficiently to say something about the most elementary properties of language (discrete infinity, structure dependence, etc.) and on to the properties of example (1) and others like them.[17] It would also be necessary to deal with the fact that we do not find, as apparently predicted, uniformity of cognitive development and attained structures across domains, similarities of language use among species with similar modes of organizing perceptual experience, no dissociation of function under disabilities, homogeneity of brain structure, and so on.

A more considered challenge is presented by Hilary Putnam in his critique of "MIT mentalism," in part the view outlined so far (which he attributes to Fodor and to me; Putnam 1986a; 1986b).[18] His goal is to "destroy the theory of innate semantic representations," call it TISR, which asserts:

(5)   a   "There are 'semantic representations' in the mind/brain."
       b   "These are innate and universal."
       c   "All our concepts are decomposable into such semantic representations." (Putnam 1986b: 18)

TISR holds further that the mind is a "Cryptographer": "the mind thinks its thoughts in Mentalese, codes them in the local natural language, and then transmits them" to a hearer who "has a Cryptographer in his head too, of course, who thereupon proceeds to decode the 'message'" (Putnam 1986b: 20) in the *lingua mentis*.

TISR goes well beyond I-linguistics. That representations generated by I-language map into a *lingua mentis* is a separate hypothesis. Statement (5c) also goes beyond the study of language, which has to do with FL, not other cognitive systems, which could be (and I suppose are) different in character. Statement (5b) requires clarification. Only the elements of which representations are constructed are taken to be innate (hence universal, available generally though perhaps unrealized). Thus the components and mode of composition of phonetic representation are presumably innate, but the representations are not; they differ for English and Japanese, even among siblings. The same is true of whatever is involved in fixing meaning – "semantic representations," or something else. Languages differ in this regard, one of the many problems that bedevil translators. There is no controversy about this, nor, presumably, about the thesis that the elements of whatever is involved in fixing meaning are innate. It is hard to imagine an alternative.

There are empirical grounds for believing that variety is more limited for semantic than for phonetic aspects of language. Phonetic data are available to the child in abundance, and the gap between target attained and data available seems narrower than for semantic subsystems. If so, variety is more easily tolerated. The study of meaning has to face the fact that extremely limited exposure in highly ambiguous circumstances suffices for children to come to understand the meanings of words and other expressions with remarkable delicacy, far beyond anything that the most comprehensive dictionaries and grammars begin to convey, with refinements and intricacy that are barely beginning to be understood. For such reasons, empirical inquiry has sought to discover semantic properties that are innate and universal.

These problems have to be faced whether one adopts an I-linguistic (or more broadly, TISR) framework or any other. Putnam's position seems to be that mechanisms of general intelligence suffice. Hence these must have the innate structure required to carry the mind from the data available to the cognitive systems attained. For language, the problem is now displaced from FL to general intelligence. We now face the problems that confront the "competing hypothesis" that everything reduces somehow to perceptual organization. The prospects look as unappealing as before, but there is nothing to discuss until something specific is proposed.

For language, the thesis that Putnam aims to destroy is now reduced to (6):

(6)   a   "There are 'semantic representations' in the mind/brain."
       b   They are constructed of elements that are innate.

Statement (6b) is innocuous if (6a) holds. But (6a) has nothing particular to do with "MIT mentalism." Empirical semantics generally assumes something similar. Suppose nonetheless that (6a) is false. Thus, neither FL nor any other system of the mind/brain involves "semantic representations." But some internal state is involved in how we understand sentences, say S or the examples in (1). The alternative to (6), then, holds that such states do not involve "semantic representations." Apparently, the intended alternative keeps the assumptions about states of the mind/brain relating to sound, and perhaps also those concerning the structural properties of FL that enter into establishing the meaning of expressions, but not "semantic representations." The specific intricate knowledge that the child has acquired and uses is represented in the mind/brain somehow, but not in the manner developed in studies of natural-language semantics, now cutting a very broad swath. That is not unlikely; current phonetic theory may also turn out to be wide of the mark. But again, comment is impossible.

Putting this aside, let's look at Putnam's critique of (6a). It has several strands. One is that "meaning is holistic." In the Quinean formula, sentences meet the test of experience "as a corporate body," and revision can strike anywhere. For the sciences, the formula seems fair enough; Rudolf Carnap apparently agreed, though preferring a different formulation (see Uebel and Hookway 1995). However, the questions here have to do with human language, a biological object, not with the sciences that humans construct, using different faculties of mind, so it appears.

Putnam holds, however, that "the language of ordinary life" has the same holistic properties as the sciences. The reason is that everyday discourse relies on unstated assumptions, so that "if language describes experience, it does so as a network, not sentence by sentence" (1986b: 23). But language does not "describe experience," though it may be used to describe or misdescribe it, or in countless other ways. The fact that hidden assumptions enter into use of language tells us nothing relevant here.

Another strand of Putnam's critique turns on scientific practice. Right or wrong, these arguments do not bear on human language, or other aspects of human thought, except on assumptions about uniformity of mind that surely require justification, so far lacking. Other parts of the argument rely on conclusions about *lingua mentis* and "public language," and intuitions about synonymy, translation, and other matters, none of which would be relevant here even if tenable (throughout, I am skeptical; see Chomsky 1995a).

The rest of the argument has to do with "Chomsky's innateness hypothesis." I have never understood what that is supposed to be. It is often refuted, but never formulated or defended, to my knowledge. Presumably, cognitive capacities, like all others, are rooted in biological endowment, and FL (if it exists) is some kind of expression of the genes. Beyond that, I know of no innateness hypothesis, though there are specific hypotheses about just what is innate.

Putnam seems to identify the "innateness hypothesis" with:

1. the thesis that the *lingua mentis* is innate; and
2. the thesis that "the mental vocabulary" is innate.

I-linguistics is not committed to (1) or (2) – at least, insofar as I understand these theses; admittedly, not very far. Whatever their content, furthermore, they are presumably distinct: the *lingua mentis* is not the mental vocabulary, just as English is not its vocabulary.

Putnam then turns to the arguments that are widely alleged to undermine not only "MIT mentalism" but also an approach to the study of meaning and reference that reaches from Aristotle to Mill, Russell, Frege, and Carnap, the tradition that holds (7a) and (7b):

(7)　　a　"When we understand a word or any other 'sign', we associate that word with a 'concept'."
　　　　b　The concept determines the reference of the word (or sign).

Putnam takes (7) to be refuted by the fact that reference is determined in part by "the division of linguistic labor" and the "contribution of the environment."

I-linguistics has no commitment to (7); nor could it, without some explanation of the technical notions. At most, I-linguistics is committed to (8):

(8)　　a　When X understands the word W, X makes use of its properties.
　　　　b　The properties might include I-sound and I-meaning and, if so, the latter play a part in determining what X refers to in using W.

Beyond that, the chips fall where they may.

The critique of (7) does not seem to bear on at least the I-linguistic component of "MIT mentalism," but let us look at it anyway. To illustrate the division of linguistic labor, Putnam considers the word "robin" in British and American English. Suppose Peter$_{GB}$ in Britain and Peter$_{US}$ in the United States are in relevant respects the same, and are unaware that (9):

(9)   "The word 'robin' does not refer to the same species of bird in Britain and in the United States."

Peter$_{GB}$ and Peter$_{US}$ have the same word "robin" in their I-languages, but it has different extensions because *"reference is a social phenomenon"* involving reliance on experts. We must therefore abandon the traditional thesis (7).

Taking (9) to be a statement of fact about language–world relations, we want to determine whether it is true. We first have to understand its terms: specifically, the phrases "the word 'robin'" and "refer," a relation alleged to hold between "the word 'robin'" and a biological species. Let's grant (much too quickly) that we understand well enough what is meant in speaking of "the word 'robin'," an entity in a "public language" (as intended). What about "refer"? People use words to refer to things in various ways, but English has no term "refer" or "reference" used in the sense of (9);[19] nor do similar languages, one reason why Frege had to make up technical terms and why there is much variation as to how to translate them, some preferring Latin words that make clear the technical status. Some work has to be done, then, to make it possible to evaluate (9) as an empirical claim.

The context (resort to thought experiments, etc.) suggests that (9) is to be understood within the study of folk theories. If so, the conclusions have no obvious bearing on I-linguistics; or perhaps even on the tradition, if understood as offering a kind of rational reconstruction. Let us ask nevertheless whether (9) is well grounded within the study of folk theory. To avoid the (as yet unexplained) technical terms, let us select some ordinary English counterpart, perhaps (10):

(10)   Peter$_{US}$ uses the word "robin" to refer to one species of bird, and Peter$_{GB}$ to refer to a different species.

Is (10) true? The birds Peter$_{US}$ has called robins are different in all sorts of ways from the ones Peter$_{GB}$ has called robins, but that's also true of Peter$_{US}$ and his friend Charles, who have been neighbors all their lives. We have to know much more to evaluate (10).

Suppose we ask what Peter$_{US}$ would say if he went to Britain and saw the red-breasted things there. By assumption, he would call them robins, so this gets nowhere. Suppose Jones would say that Peter$_{US}$ is making a mistake when he calls the birds in Britain robins (I wouldn't). We are then learning something about Jones that is of no relevance here.

Jones may be assuming something like thesis (9). Perhaps Jones holds that Peter$_{US}$'s concept *robin* doesn't cover the species in Britain; and that Earthly Oscar's concept *water* doesn't cover Twin-Earth XYZ. But now we are back to the original query: how do we find out whether Jones's claims are true?

Suppose that Peter$_{US}$'s cousin Bill lives in a part of the United States where the birds called robins belong to a different subspecies. If Peter$_{US}$ visits Bill and calls the thing on his lawn a robin, is he making a mistake? Can he understand Bill's talk about robins? Suppose that Peter$_{US}$'s wife Mary grew up in his neighborhood but spent part of her childhood in Britain. What is Mary referring to when she talks about robins? As cases vary, judgments do too, in all sorts of ways, and are often highly uncertain.

The case does not seem problematic for "MIT mentalism." By assumption, the above characters, alike in relevant respects, would have the same judgments about what is a robin. Further conclusions about whether they are right or wrong, or how "the word 'robin'" is used to refer in "public languages," or about their beliefs, raise other questions that may or may not be worth investigating once given a clear enough formulation. There seems little more to say.

To illustrate "the contribution of the environment," Putnam adduces Twin-Earth and other arguments, all based on assumptions about what "a typical person would say" under various circumstances. Again, the arguments have no direct bearing on a theory of language T that adopts thesis (8). The most they could show is that T (or TISR) does not yield a full explanation of linguistic behavior or capture ordinary usage, but that is obvious in advance.

The arguments (for "water") are based on the assumption that water is H_2O. To assess the status of this statement we have to know to what language it belongs. Not English, which has no word "H_2O." Not chemistry, which has no word "water" (though chemists use the word informally). We could propose that chemistry and English belong to some "superlanguage," but it remains to explain what this means (see Bromberger 1996).

Putting such qualms aside, is it true that a typical speaker relies on constituency in deciding whether to call something water? Suppose two glasses G and G′ are on the table, G filled from the tap and G′ from a well. Suppose a tea bag is dipped in G′. The contents of G and G′ could be chemically identical: maybe tap water comes from a reservoir that uses a "tea filter" to remove contaminants. Knowing that the contents are identical, I would say that the stuff in G is water, not tea; and that the stuff in G′ is tea, not water. I suspect this is typical. Constitution is a factor in deciding whether something is water, but not the only one.[20]

The situation recalls the case of "book" and others like it. Here too we can arrange circumstances so that we will attend to constitution, not other factors, in deciding what we are talking about. Under such circumstances, we might call the contents of both G and G′ water. Empirical study might show that constitution is more of a core factor for "water" than for "book"; presumably so, but that would still have no bearing on (8). In ordinary cases, there are no answers except in terms of complex and varying circumstances and interests that yield what Akeel Bilgrami (1992) calls "locality of content." If, for example, Mary believes that there is water on Mars, and something is discovered there that she regards as water although it has the internal constitution of heavy water or XYZ, there is no general answer as to whether her belief is right or wrong.

Reference to expert use adds new quandaries. A recent technical article opens by saying that "Glass, in the popular and basically correct conception, is a liquid that has lost its ability to flow," and goes on to conclude that "most of the universe's water exists in the glassy state (in comets, . . .)," as "naturally occurring glassy water" (Angell 1995: 1924). Suppose the tea–water scenario just described took place on Twin-Earth, where they happen to make their glasses from tails of Earthly comets. Suppose Earthly Oscar arrives on Twin-Earth and asks for water, pointing to G. Is he right if he is referring to the glass and wrong if he is referring to its contents? My judgments are reasonably clear, and I suspect typical.

Looking at the issues from a different standpoint, take Albert and Bill to be relevantly alike, and A, B to be indistinguishable apples, A an object of Albert's experience, B of Bill's. Each thinks about, looks at, and takes a bite of their respective apples, leading to identical state changes throughout. Shall we say that the thoughts, visual images, tastes, weight changes, and so on are the same for Albert and Bill but "directed" to different things? Or different for Albert and Bill, the external objects A, B being "part of" the thoughts, etc.? Hearing indistinguishable renditions of the statement S, do Albert and Bill have the same auditory and understanding experiences directed to different objects, or different ones incorporating the objects? Ordinary English may tolerate the "externalist" usage for thought and understanding rather than weight changes, though what we would learn from this is unclear. The science of human nature is too primitive for the question to arise. An internalist picture seems appropriate, though incomplete in the uninteresting sense that a study of Albert and Bill in their environments takes the latter into account.

Ordinary examples are often more complex. Take a version of Kripke's puzzle. Suppose that Peter says: "I used to think that Constantinople and Istanbul were different cities, but now I know they are the same," adding: "but Istanbul will have to be moved somewhere else, so that Constantinople won't have an Islamic character." (For real examples of this kind see Chomsky 1995a.) Has he adopted new lexical items? New beliefs? Something different? If, referring to Istanbul, he says "*it* will have to be moved and *re*built elsewhere" (while remaining the *same* city), how are we to interpret the italicized items – which behave differently in curious ways as examples vary? (Chomsky 1995a; see also Chapter 5, p. 127 above). We can only proceed sensibly as indicated earlier, it seems.

Consider the issue of fallibility: clearly we want to be able to say that Peter might be mistaken in calling something an X. Thus Peter might misdescribe the contents of G′ as water, not knowing that it is tea, not water. Or he might mistake a paperweight for a book. Perhaps Peter is mistaken by his own lights: he would not call it X if he were aware of the facts. Or perhaps we are adopting a standpoint that relies on constitution to decide whether he is right or wrong, so what Peter takes to be water might *be* something else, maybe heavy water, or XYZ. Such moves are standard in the sciences, but that they are appropriate for natural language and, if so, in what respects, has to be shown. It would be necessary to outline the theoretical framework in which the questions are being posed, and if it uses such notions as *concept*, to define them in non-question-begging ways; not, say, by stipulating that concepts are specified by internal constitution. There is no clear question, hence no straightforward answers.

Suppose that young Charlie has experiences that lead him to recognize that his usage differs from that of adults in his community.[21] Suppose at Stage 1 he referred to streamlined aquatic animals as fish and very large ones as whales. Finding that adults adopt a different usage for the nearest counterparts (pronouncing the words differently too), he moves to Stage 2, adapting himself to adult usage, consciously or not. How do we describe what happened?

Some might be inclined to say that what Charlie thought about whales and fish in Stage 1, and the way he used the words and pronounced them, was wrong. By Stage 2, he had corrected himself. He is improving his knowledge of English, the language of his community (ordinary usage provides no way of referring to his linguistic system at Stage 1). Search for further understanding can follow the usual two courses. We can seek to learn more about how people talk and think about such matters, or about what is actually happening.

An I-linguistic account is straightforward, though incomplete, in part because of its scope, in part because of lack of understanding within its scope. In Stage 1, Charlie has I-language L_1 with lexical items "fish$_1$," and "whale$_1$." In Stage 2, his I-language L_2 has "fish$_2$" and "whale$_2$," differing somewhat in properties. The phonological features are different (by assumption); but the status of the semantic features is unclear. Do the new items have different features, incorporating the new criteria for referring to aquatic animals? Do they select different regions in a *lingua mentis*, conceptual space, belief system? Something else? What Charlie calls things will change in various ways, depending on accidental facts: for example, whether the large aquatic animals with which he had some acquaintance in Stage 1 happened to be mammals or tuna fish. We could look for principles that enter into whatever happened and ask to what extent it could have followed another course had circumstances differed. So little is known about these topics that we can only speculate, but no obvious problems of principle arise. The enterprise would not be carried forward by invoking "the real meaning (denotation)" of words in a "common language" that is partially known and shared, "the collective mind," "words" that remain constant as pronunciation and usage varies, and other such notions that remain mysterious.

Suppose we approach the matter in terms of a notion of reference in a common language, perhaps a causal theory. We would then have to determine whether or not the denotations of "whale" or "fish" remained constant as Charlie changed what he calls things (including the objects of his earlier experience), and what happened to the content of his thoughts. If the technical notions are clarified, it might be possible to formulate significant empirical questions about how people think about these matters in one or another cultural and linguistic setting. For the science of human nature, it does not seem to me a very promising course.

Consider finally a case discussed by Burge (1986b), illustrating an interesting genre. Suppose A shares with other English speakers the word "sofa" and relevant experiences with things they call sofas. But he comes to believe that sofas "function not as furnishings to be sat on but as works of art or religious artifacts," and are not "preeminently *for*" sitting. A and others agree about which things of their common experience are sofas, but disagree about the function of sofas; they may also disagree about whether sofas have really been used for sitting (A thinking that others are deluded about this). If A's doubts prove well founded, Burge concludes "the conventional meaning of 'sofa' would have to change," but "it might remain appropriate . . . to attribute propositional attitudes involving the notion of sofa" (1986b: 715), as just described.

How might such events be described in the internalist framework, extending it now to the assumption that there is an I-conceptual and I-belief system alongside of I-language?

Initially, A and others have the same LI "sofa," the same I-concept *sofa*, and the same I-beliefs about sofas. Call this shared complex SOFA. Within it, sofas are identified as artifacts with certain physical properties and functions. For A, SOFA changes to SOFA′ with a shift of beliefs about what sofas are for. Someone else, call him B, might change his beliefs about constitution, concluding that sofas are typically flat surfaces with iron spikes, though still used for sitting; for B, SOFA changes to SOFA″. All agree about which of the things around them are sofas, but A differs from others on the function, and B on the constitution, of the category to which these things belong.

So far, there is no difficulty in describing the events and the (I)-mental states of the participants. We have said nothing, however, about what happened to conventional meaning, thoughts, and beliefs as the story unfolds; or about where in SOFA the changes took place.

The first question cannot be addressed until the notions are clarified. The second could be relevant here, but it is still unanswerable. By assumption, changes in the I-belief component of SOFA took place, but this leaves open the question whether A and B changed the LIs of their I-languages or some other aspect of the complex SOFA. Whatever the answer, a straightforward account seems available.

Burge argues that it would be "unacceptably superficial" to say that A changed his language when his doubts arose, because "we have no difficulty understanding that he is raising questions about what sofas really are" and know how to investigate the questions. Granting all of this, however, we still don't know whether A changed his I-language, replacing one LI by another. If his I-language remained fixed, he would now be saying that what people thought about sofas was wrong; if it changed as indicated, he would now be saying that people were mistaken in calling these things sofas – they were really something else. Either way, we can understand his questions and know how to investigate them. There are empirical issues lurking here, and perhaps they can be extricated. However, it is not clear that anything more is at stake.

Similar questions arise about whales and fish. Suppose whales are considered to be fish in Peter's community, but he decides that a different classification would make more sense, and revises his usage accordingly. Again, we have no difficulty understanding that he is raising questions about whales and fish (what they "really are," perhaps, though it is not obvious that this is the most apt locution), and know how to investigate those questions.

Inquiry into such cases in their dazzling variety seems to yield answers that vary widely under slight changes of assumed circumstances, arousing some skepticism about how much can be learned by proceeding in this way. However that may be, such phenomena do not seem to me to bear on the soundness of internalist approaches to linguistic and other mental aspects of human life, as far as they can reach, or to suggest a preferable alternative.

Notes

2 EXPLAINING LANGUAGE USE

1 Davies accepts Tyler Burge's position that work of the Marr school is concerned with "informational" representations with intentional content (hence
with actual causal antecedents), but that position does not seem reconcil-
able with actual experimental practice or theoretical results (for example,
Ullman's rigidity principle); it is hard to see how it could be correct, if only
because – as Davies emphasizes – Marr's work did not reach to 3D model
representation at all. Insofar as the study of visual perception does so (for
example, Elizabeth Spelke's work on object constancy in infancy; Spelke
1990), it keeps to visual experience, not perceptual content in the technical
sense of philosophical discourse (Ullman 1979; Davies 1991).

2 It reveals such a rich vascular system, Richard Lewontin remarks, that to
the fanciful stories concocted about evolution of cognition one might add
the speculation that the brain evolved as a thermoregulator, cooling the
blood as Aristotle thought and yielding human cognition as a by-product
(Lewontin 1990).

3 There is, again, no implication here that the actual performance systems
will correspond closely to informal usage, or philosophical or other technical
discourse.

4 Much less likely, even if the phrase can be given some meaning clear enough
for the question to be sensibly raised.

5 The topic has been widely debated since John Searle's "Minds, brains, and
programs" (Searle 1980). It is not clear that any substantive issue has yet
been formulated.

6 The interstage problem is held to arise only on the assumption of "semantic
holism."

7 These procedures are not to be confused with principles of charity and the
like, if the language-belief distinction is valid; see later in this chapter. To be
even minimally realistic, we should distinguish many cases. Thus, what
Peter does when Mary speaks a closely related language may have little
relation to his procedure when she speaks an unintelligible one. Subsuming
all such processes under "interpretation" or "translation" is not a good
research strategy.

8 On Saul Kripke's development of this approach, and his conclusions about
its relevance to linguistics, see Chomsky 1986a: Chapter 4.1.

9 In *Representation and Reality*, Putnam (1988a) argues against the assumption that the lexical entry includes specific reference to expert judgment. The argument is based on tacit assumptions about common public language and translation that do not seem to me easy to defend, or even formulate. We might, however, accept the conclusion, considering reliance on expert judgment (among other options) to be a general property of a wide range of lexical entries, relating to the ways they enter into belief systems.

10 See Stich 1983. The basic problem – that any criteria we put forth are at once too strong and too weak – was outlined in Scheffler 1955.

11 Technically, we should speak of "I-rhyme," etc.

12 See Lasnik 1989: particularly Chapter 9. Interesting questions arise in the case of (2c) ("backwards pronominalization") with regard to such matters as referential use of definite descriptions and old–new information.

13 Putnam has frequently stressed that standards for inference and justification of belief are inescapably interest-relative. Furthermore, the particular character (and therefore limits) of human understanding impose choices of framework for theory that may be inappropriate, leaving problem areas that are inherently mysteries for humans (a general property of organisms). See Chomsky 1975; McGinn 1991.

14 Not in question, of course, is the fact that what people do depends upon events elsewhere in space and time; the question is whether naturalistic inquiry will be "Markovian" (see Miller and Chomsky 1963: 422ff.), taking only the resulting state of the organism to enter into local current performance. Thus memories may fade or be reshaped, but to understand what a person is doing here and now, we ask what is internally represented, not what may once have happened. Similarly, the growth of a cell to a finger or a bone of the forearm depends on elapsed time, but the study of the process keeps to such indicators as current gradients of chemical concentration that inform the cell of such facts. That is standard, and it seems very reasonable, procedure.

15 Whether the theories should be developed in these terms is another matter. My point is simply to note that if they rely on notions of intended reference, referential dependence, etc., as more than a façon de parler, then something of the sort outlined here seems to be presupposed – not reference to things in (or believed to be in) the world.

16 There are differences in backwards pronominalization; see note 12.

17 The basic point about "systematically misleading expressions" in Ryle's sense is traceable at least to the eighteenth-century critique of the theory of ideas by du Marsais and later Thomas Reid; see Chomsky 1965: 199–200.

18 Or about *perceptual content* in the special technical sense of philosophical discourse; see note 1 and text. The distinction Davies draws between "conservative" and "revisionary" interpretations of the technical notion is not clear, any more than we can distinguish conservative and revisionary interpretations of *electromagnetic force*.

19 Note Stich's observations (1983) about the inability of "most ears not previously contaminated by philosophical theory" to provide judgments at all in many such cases. The observation is not necessarily decisive; perhaps the facts of folk psychology can only be discerned by trained and guided

intuition. With a richer theoretical context, that might be a reasonable surmise. But there is virtually no theoretical context, hence little reason to regard the isolated judgments as meaning much.

3 LANGUAGE AND INTERPRETATION: PHILOSOPHICAL REFLECTIONS AND EMPIRICAL INQUIRY

1 Thus from the last statement quoted, it follows that if I believe that it is raining because I heard it over the radio, so that the complete account of the causal relation of my belief with the world is this interaction, then there is nothing more to know about the relation of my belief that it is raining to the fact that it is or is not raining; there is no further question as to the relation between my beliefs and the world.

2 Though one may, of course, choose to ignore one or another distinction for the purposes of some particular inquiry. The point is that there is no general interpretation of Dummett's "fundamental sense" (no narrower interpretation, for example) that overcomes problems of the kind noted, or any known way to construct such a general concept as a useful idealization, or any reason to try to do so. Note that not every idealization is worth constructing. This one, whatever exactly is intended, apparently is not.

3 I know of only one attempt to come to grips with these problems (Pateman 1987). Pateman develops a notion of language as a "social fact" in a way that seems plausible, but has no relevance to the issues I am discussing here. In his sense, a person who is aware of some of the elementary facts about language and society will speak a great many languages, changing from moment to moment, depending on how he or she chooses to identify with one or another community. A person unaware of such facts will have a considerable range of beliefs (and typically, illusions) about what he or she is doing; beliefs that may play some social role in certain communities.

4 On Kenny's misunderstanding of my rejection of these views, and the consequent irrelevance of his response to it, see Chomsky 1988b.

5 This is, in fact, just the tack taken by Kenny (1984) in the face of conceptual considerations of this sort, though he does not recognize that a substantive change in the understanding of "ability" or "capacity" has been introduced. See Chomsky 1988b.

6 I return directly to some of Quine's qualifications, with regard to these curious doctrines.

7 To focus the discussion, I put aside further complexities; for example, the fact that the resources of the initial state also play a role in determining what counts as evidence and how it is used (or disregarded). Introduction of such further factors would simply strengthen the conclusions.

8 The example is, in fact, a real one. See Chomsky 1986: 61.

9 He suggests also studies of uniformities in language acquisition; the same considerations apply in this case.

10 We might note, incidentally, that the latter phrase is appropriate only insofar as one might refuse to speak of theories as true in physics, only as being useful for some purpose over some domain of phenomena; Quine might reject this conclusion on the grounds of his stipulations with regard to the study of

the mind/brain by the "linguist," in which the normal canons of natural science are (implicitly) held to be unacceptable, as discussed in the text.

11 I place "simplification" in quotes, since the concept is highly misleading. The rule "Front *wh*- phrase," not subject to the coordinate structure constraint and other locality conditions, would indeed be simpler than the actual rule, which is subject to these conditions, for an organism that lacked the conditions (or more properly, the principles from which they derive) as part of its innate structure; for humans, the opposite is true. Whatever sense there may be to the concept "absolute simplicity," independent of the structure of the system under investigation, it is not relevant here. For discussion of these matters, see Chomsky (1955/1975).

12 Quine supposes that the coordinate structure constraint is tied to translatability, assuming that to determine whether it holds in some language we must determine which expressions count as semantic counterparts of English coordinate constructions. The constraint, however, has to do with structures, independent of their semantic relation to coordinate constructions in some other language, and may well derive, at least in significant part, from much more general conditions on locality of grammatical operations that are construction-independent altogether; surely many examples of constraints raising the same issues are of this nature, perhaps all.

13 For discussion of Dummett's version, see Chomsky 1986. Note that Davidson is apparently limiting attention here to what is called "observational adequacy," not "descriptive adequacy," in the linguistic literature; if the theory of linguistic competence were understood in the latter sense, then it would attribute specific mechanisms (at an abstract level, to be sure).

14 See Chomsky (1986: 240) for discussion. Roger Gibson attributes to me the belief that "neither physics nor linguistics has a fact of the matter" (Gibson 1986: 141), a conclusion that I do not accept and that is not suggested by the argument, to which he refers, that the study of language faces no problem of indeterminacy that does not arise throughout the natural sciences. His further effort to establish a difference on ontological grounds, endorsed by Quine in response, fails for the reasons given in the references he cites. We can certainly insist, loudly if we like, that there just *are* chemical elements and (unknown) physical configurations that determine the course of sexual maturation, and there just *aren't* lexical meanings, connections of referential dependency, and phrases, and perhaps this conclusion will someday be shown to have merit; but what is required is an argument. To say that "two conflicting manuals of translation can both do justice to all dispositions to behavior" and are "compatible with all the same distributions of states and relations over elementary particles" (Quine 1981: 23) makes as much sense as saying essentially the same thing about two theories of chemistry or physical maturation; and in the nineteenth century, one could have added, with equal irrelevance, that neither chemical theory could be accommodated within "an already accepted naturalistic–physicalistic theory" (Gibson 1986: 143), if by the latter we mean "fundamental physics," which had to be significantly modified to incorporate the chemist's discoveries. From such considerations, epistemological or ontological, nothing follows with regard to language or anything else.

15 For discussion, see Chomsky (1987) – from which some of these remarks are drawn and sources cited there.

16 Quine (1986: 186) describes the "supposed equipment" as "innate skeletal grammars," apparently confusing the structure of the initial state of the language faculty with that of the mature states attained.

17 The basic assumption was that the theory of body could be given fairly sharp bounds, essentially those of Cartesian contact mechanics. This was undermined by Isaac Newton, and since that time it has been impossible to formulate a coherent mind–body problem in anything like Cartesian terms, or any others, as far as I can see, there being no fixed concept of body.

18 For Quine, grammars differ "extensionally" if "they diverge in net output" (Quine 1986). This familiar usage is seriously misleading, because it is combined with stipulations as to what constitutes "net output" for a grammar. Recall again that Quine is not considering the empirically significant concept of "strong generation" of structural descriptions, but rather "weak generation" of some class K of expressions selected on a basis that seems quite arbitrary. It is K that is the "net output"; but however K may be selected, its properties appear to be of no empirical significance. On these matters, see Chomsky (1955/1975; 1965). Quine has always taken the question of "grammaticality" to be essentially that of "having meaning," and believes that this concept, "for all its shortcomings, is in far better order than" the concept "alike in meaning" (Quine 1986). But insofar as we have any understanding of "grammaticality," it has little to do with "having meaning" and, unlike the various semantic notions that Quine finds problematic, his concepts of "grammaticality" and "having meaning" appear to lack any moderately clear sense, or any status in the study of language.

19 An erroneous assumption since, as noted earlier, the tasks of the child and the linguist are radically different.

20 Insofar as any scientific theories merit this appellation. We may put aside here any questions that apply to scientific inquiry generally. It makes little sense to raise such questions with regard to the "soft sciences." If one is interested in finding answers to questions, rather than just harassing emerging disciplines, one will turn to domains in which answers are likely to be forthcoming; in this case, domains in which there is sufficient depth of knowledge and understanding to guide inquiry in a serious way.

21 For recent reiteration of this idea, see Quine (1986). Here he describes a "brilliant idea" of W. Haas concerning a criterion to establish the distinction he appears to have in mind; the criterion, such as it is, provides a distinction of no known significance for inquiry into the study of language. The widespread belief to the contrary is based in part on a mistaken analogy to formal languages, where the issues are entirely different, and may have been fostered by expository passages in early work in generative grammar that evidently were misleading, though appropriate qualifications were in fact expressed.

22 See Chomsky (1955/1975), where the issues were discussed in terms that seem to me still accurate, and an attempt was made to define such a concept in terms of the principles for assignment of derived constituent structure.

23 For discussion in a linguistic–cognitive context, see Jerne (1985) and, for more extensive discussion, see Piattelli-Palmarini (1986).

24 Nor are "short theories" necessarily theories attainable by humans, or recognizable as intelligible theories by humans, given their specific biologically-determined intellectual capacities.

25 Again, we are assuming familiar idealizations, as discussed elsewhere.

26 Strategies, memory structure, etc. Note that a parser, as conceived in current research, is postulated, rightly or wrongly, to be a real component of the mind/brain, a coherent subsystem of some sort including certain elements of the full interpreter, not others. As throughout, these assumptions are subject to exactly those general questions that arise in all empirical inquiry. The study of the parser is often thought to be somehow immune to general problems that arise in the study of linguistic competence (that is, study of the generative procedure that is taken to be one component of the parser), but this is an error. It is sometimes argued that since evidence is always from performance, we have no justification for using it to determine the nature of underlying competence. By the same (fallacious) argument, we could conclude that we are not justified in using such evidence to determine the nature of the idealized parser, and we would have no basis for supposing that physics is the study of anything beyond meter readings. Data do not come labeled as "evidence for X, not Y."

27 Related considerations help explain why the efforts in Artificial Intelligence about which Daniel Dennett is so enthusiastic are so barren of consequences (see Putnam 1988b; Dennett 1988). Dennett believes that there are or might be substantive results falling under something he calls "engineering," but it is not clear what he has in mind; also, his report of informal discussion several years ago, on which his account is in part based, seems to me rather misleading, to say the least.

28 Note again that there is no reason to suppose that the I-language "weakly generates" some set of well-formed expressions, so that it would make sense to speak of I-languages ("grammars") as "extensionally equivalent" or not in Quine's terms; even if this concept is found to have some sense or significance, now unknown, there is no reason to suppose that formal properties of this set would be of any interest for the study of language structure, meaning, learning, communication, parsing, etc. See Chomsky (1965). There has been vast confusion about these matters, which I will not pursue here.

29 In an odd sense, however. In this case, I am applying a word lacking certain evidence that is relevant to its application, as specified by my internal lexicon. We would not say that Jones is misusing his language when he refers to an object before him as a sphere, not knowing that the hidden part has some different shape.

30 Even by sociolinguists and others who sometimes allege that they are not following this practice. On this matter, see Chomsky 1986: 17–18.

31 Suppose that Jones's lexicon includes deference to some expert, say some speaker of German, in the entry for "arthritis." Then attribution of "belief" to Jones may involve further circumlocution, or we might want to abandon the concept as useless in anything like its familiar sense for psychology. No

matter of much import appears to be at stake. For more on the questions touched on here, see Bilgrami 1987; Segal 1987.

4   NATURALISM AND DUALISM IN THE STUDY OF LANGUAGE AND MIND

1 For discussion of the matter, see Bilgrami 1993. On the (often tacit) presupposition of an internalist-individualist approach in broader inquiries (sociolinguistics, language acquisition, Hilary Putnam's "social division of labor," etc.), see Chomsky (1980: 25f.).

2 The concepts of the "special sciences" (geology, biology, etc.) also do not satisfy the Davidsonian conditions; see Fodor (1987).

3 It is not clear whether Quine would draw this conclusion, because of a distinction he makes between "psychological" and "linguistic" evidence. Thus for determining phrase boundaries, he accepts the former as legitimate but not the latter; the former includes experiments on perceptual displacement of clicks; the latter studies of referential dependency, as in the case of examples (1) and (2), below. The distinction is mysterious, particularly since on naturalistic grounds the "linguistic evidence" is far more compelling, not to speak of the fact that data do not come categorized in such ways. Whatever it means, the distinction might allow a revision of his notion of "reification," though apparently not of language. See Chapter 3 of this volume for specific references and discussion.

4 For fuller discussion, see comments on Searle's presentation of these views in Chomsky 1990; also those of Ned Block and others. The objections are left unanswered in his response or the subsequent book, Searle (1992).

5 For a recent exposition, see Quine 1990; for more extensive discussion of an (essentially identical) earlier version, see Chomsky 1987, and Chapter 3 in this volume.

5   LANGUAGE AS A NATURAL OBJECT

1 The target of the derisive comments is Colin McGinn's *The Problem of Consciousness* (McGinn 1991). McGinn points out the fallacy of the argument. See also McGinn 1993; Chomsky 1975.

2 For some comment on his misinterpretation of the computational theories to which he alludes, and of the nature of semantics, in which he expects to find a solution to the "crisis," see Chomsky 1993a.

3 Note that this interpretation of such studies differs from some that appear in the philosophical literature. The term "I-language" was introduced to overcome misunderstanding engendered by the systematic ambiguity of the term "grammar," used both to refer to an I-language and to the linguist's theory of it. Thus Jones's knowledge of his I-language (grammar, in one sense) is nothing like some linguist's (partial) knowledge.

4 In cases of language development that were studied carefully, there had been normal language exposure up to 19 or 20 months, then a long period before onset of training (in the most successful case, almost four years). Though confirming evidence is lacking, it is reasonable to suspect that early exposure

may be crucial, particularly in the light of recent discoveries about very early language acquisition. See C. Chomsky 1986; Mehler and Dupoux 1994.

5 I put aside, here and below, the further assumption that these relations hold of objects in a public language. This notion is unknown to empirical inquiry, and raises what seem to be irresolvable problems, so far unaddressed. For discussion, see Chomsky 1993a, and Chapter 2 above.

6   LANGUAGE FROM AN INTERNALIST PERSPECTIVE

1 That Putnam and Davidson differ is not entirely clear, since Putnam does not indicate what he means by "language" while Davidson spells out a notion modeled on formal language that is surely not Putnam's; Davidson's conclusion would, however, seem to exclude whatever is intended. Internalist linguistics would also be excluded unless we understand "people" to include their faculties, states, etc.

2 Burge is describing what he takes to be "psychology as it is," but the context indicates that more is intended. On the assumption, see later in the chapter.

3 These motives lie behind Putnam's important paper (1975), as he reiterates in Putnam (1992).

4 A footnote is omitted. The statement about emptiness of thought seems much too strong, but put that aside.

5 A questionable term, since Putnam seems to have dropped the implicit requirement that the "experts" to whom we defer even speak our language; the social aspect therefore disappears, and we are back to "same substance" considerations.

6 Irrelevantly here, it could be that a technical notion of *reference* should be introduced in the study of the syntax of mental representations, much as relations among phonetic features are introduced into phonology.

7 It does not follow, however, that "meaning alike for us merely means, if anything, that we are communicating successfully" (Quine cited in Dreben 1992: 305). Similarly, sounding alike for us does not merely mean that we are communicating successfully. In both cases, there is a good deal more to say about what is "alike" in terms of shared properties of language and mind, when we depart from Quine's anti-naturalist behaviorist strictures.

8 These observations, familiar in the study of language, should be distinguished from Davidson's conclusion that "there is no such thing as a language" in the sense generally assumed by "philosophers and linguists," "no such thing to be learned, mastered, or born with" (Davidson 1986b: 446). However, Davidson has a very different notion of *language* in mind; and though he is surely right, in thinking that "there is no such thing," the argument for that conclusion or about the notions of the empirical study of language is flawed. He observes correctly that, in actual communication, all sorts of conjectures are used in a "passing theory," which is a psychological particular. It does not, however, follow that there is no use for "the concept of a language," for a "portable interpreting machine set to grind out the meaning of an arbitrary utterance," etc. (1986b: 445). That would be like arguing that there is no jet stream, because of the chaotic elements in weather patterns. For some comment, see Chapter 2 of this volume.

9 The discussions in the literature about "what Marr meant" are somewhat strange; what matters is what a scientist does, not what he may have had in mind. For what seems to me an accurate account of Marr's actual theory, see Egan (no date).

10 The proposals reported in Bradley (1994) have been undermined, but the problem remains of accounting for prevailing asymmetries ranging from the "molecular handedness" of amino acids and DNA through location and orientation of organs.

7 INTERNALIST EXPLORATIONS

1 On some analogies, and a number of issues bypassed much too quickly here, see Chomsky (1995a).

2 John Searle and I have discussed these issues for some years. We apparently agree on the incoherence of monism, dualism, materialism, etc. (compare Searle 1992: 25; Chomsky 1968: 98), and on the essential accuracy of eighteenth-century conceptions of mind–body of the kind just mentioned. But not on how to account for the properties of language; see below.

3 Note that I do not agree that the choice lies between interpreting "*grasp* and *understanding* as conscious states" or as "mere training-induced reaction patterns" (Gaifman (1996: 387) endorsing a view that he attributes to Michael Dummett). Understanding (of (1), S, etc.) appears to involve states and processes that fall under neither category.

4 On how it is accessed, there are various ideas. For critical discussion of some of these and a "late insertion" alternative, see Halle and Marantz 1993. I will ignore all such matters here.

5 Stich (1996: 38f.) reporting – not advocating – standard formulations, which he distinguishes from (I-)linguistics and the "proto-science" of reference.

6 Note that there is no contradiction in accepting Wittgenstein's cautionary remarks on these matters along with quite strong conclusions about invariants of sound and meaning.

7 Thomas Reid is the best known of those who argued in the manner of modern ordinary language philosophy that the conception of an idea as "the object that the mind contemplates" is based on a misinterpretation of surface grammar; his argument could be extended to thought, belief, and other cases. On ideas as objects of thought or modes of mind in seventeenth- and eighteenth-century thought, see Yolton (1984), who argues that Reid and other commentators have misread the tradition; see below.

8 In the earliest work of the kind considered here, it was assumed that an I-language generates "markers" at the several linguistic levels (phonetic, word, phrase structure, etc.), each "representing" PHON(E) as a predicate holding of it. Thus PHON(E) *is a . . .* , where . . . is its phonological (word, phrase structure, etc.) "representation" (for details, see Chomsky 1955/1975). PHON(E) (hence indirectly, markers at all levels) could be taken to "represent" utterances in a similar way. Since utterances are associated with states of speakers, the predication could be construed as holding of these, the course taken by Bromberger and Halle (1996), discussing phonological levels in terms of intentions of speakers (understood as supervening on brain

states). Their purpose is to compare competing theories, a good reason for more careful foundational work, which has otherwise rarely been undertaken.

9 For similar reasons, while the thesis of "autonomy of syntax" has been vigorously rejected, it has never been defended, to my knowledge; nor formulated in any intelligible way by its opponents.

10 For similar reasons, a theory of T-sentences runs into problems when object and metalanguage differ, so that informativeness of nonhomophonic T-sentences does not provide good grounds for justifying the approach. Whatever its merits, which are real, it leaves untouched the question of how language engages the world, much of the heart of the traditional theory of meaning. See also Fodor 1990.

11 Not to be confused with it is postulation of semantic (or phonetic) Values as mental entities, with (LI, Value) relations that have formal properties of *refer* and *denote* in their technical sense. That has to be assessed alongside of postulation of other syntactic objects. It seems to me appropriate (though unconventional) to construe much work in natural-language semantics in these terms.

12 One might, perhaps, understand some structuralist proposals along these lines, but that would be a dubious interpretation, I think.

13 The quotes are from Cudworth (1838: 425), but the point of view is general; and also influential at least in the Kantian version; see Chomsky 1966: 67–8.

14 Adapting Aristotelian notions and applying them broadly to lexical semantics, Moravcsik (1975; 1990) takes the factors to be "constituents, structure, function, and agency." For some comment, see Chomsky 1975; for elaboration of similar ideas, see Pustejovsky 1995.

15 I am overlooking irrelevant terminological differences.

16 Searle argues further that postulation of unconscious rules is illegitimate, but on grounds that seem to me without merit; see Chomsky (1990). His *reductio* using the analogy of a "vision faculty" is not relevant because the principle he rightly rejects lacks any explanatory force.

17 There has been serious work with a vaguely similar flavor, both traditional and modern. See Jackendoff (1994: Chapter 14 and sources cited).

18 I will put aside questions of accuracy of attribution where not relevant.

19 The observation is familiar; see, for example, Strawson 1952: 189.

20 For some experimental work concluding that H_2O content is only weakly correlated with judgments about what is water, or even prototypical water, see Malt 1994; Braisby *et al.* (1996) review various ideas and experimental work on such matters, and present findings of their own which, they argue, "show that natural kind terms are not employed in an essentialist manner." Understanding is limited, hence confidence in interpretation of data.

21 There are many interesting insights on such cases in papers by Tyler Burge, among them 1986b; 1989. It is not entirely clear to me if and, if so, where we differ substantively about them. For one interpretation, see Mercier 1992.

References

Almog, Joseph (1991) "The what and the how." *Journal of Philosophy* 5: 225–44.

Angell, C. Austen (1995) "Formation of glasses from liquids and biopolymers." *Science* 267: 1924–1935.

Atlas, Jay (1989) *Philosophy without Ambiguity*. Oxford, Clarendon Press.

Austad, Steven (1994) "Communication complexity and modality in non-human primates." In Carleton Gajdusek, Guy McKhann and Liana Bolis, eds., *Evolution and Neurology of Language: Discussions in Neuroscience*, X.1–2, pp. 89–93.

Austin, John (1962) *How to do Things with Words*. Oxford, Clarendon Press.

Baillargeon, Renée (1993) "How do infants learn about the physical world?" MS, University of Illinois.

Baker, Lynne Rudder (1987) *Saving Belief: A Critique of Physicalism*. Princeton University Press.

Baker, Lynne Rudder (1988) "Cognitive suicide." In R.H. Grimm and D.D. Merrill, eds, *Contents of Thought*. Tucson, AZ, University of Arizona Press.

Baldwin, T.R. (1993) "Two types of naturalism." *Proceedings of the British Academy* 80: 171–99.

Barinaga, Marcia (1994) "Neurons tap out a code that may help locate sounds." *Science* 264: 775.

Bilgrami, Akeel (1987) "An externalist account of psychological content." *Philosophical Topics*.

Bilgrami, Akeel (1992) *Belief and Meaning*. Blackwell, Oxford.

Bilgrami, Akeel (1993) "Discussion." In Noam Chomsky *et al. Language and Thought*. London, Moyer Bell, pp. 57–68.

Bradley, David (1994) "A new twist in the tale of nature's asymmetry." *Science* 264: 908.

Braisby, Nick, Bradley Franks and James Hampton (1996) "Essentialism, word use, and concepts." *Cognition* 59: 247–74.

Brock, William (1992) *The Fontana/Norton History of Chemistry*. New York and London, Norton.

Bromberger, Sylvain (1992a) "Types and tokens in linguistics." In S. Bromberger, *On What We Know We Don't Know*. University of Chicago Press, pp. 170–208.

Bromberger, Sylvain (1992b) *On What We Know We Don't Know*. Chicago, University of Chicago Press.

Bromberger, Sylvain (1996) "Natural kinds and questions." In Matti Sintonen, ed., *Essays on Jaakko Hintikka's Epistemology and Philosophy of Science.* Poznan, Studies in the Philosophy of Science and the Humanities.

Bromberger, Sylvain and Morris Halle (1996) "The Content of Phonological Signs," MS, MIT.

Brook, Andrew (1994) *Kant and the Mind.* Cambridge University Press.

Burge, Tyler (1986a) "Individualism and Psychology." *Philosophical Review* 95: 3–45.

Burge, Tyler (1986b) "Intellectual Norms and Foundations of Mind." *Journal of Philosophy* 83: 697–720.

Burge, Tyler (1986c) "Cartesian error and the objectivity of perception." In Philip Pettit and John McDowell, eds., *Subject, Thought and Context.* Oxford, Clarendon Press, pp. 117–36.

Burge, Tyler (1989) "Wherein is language social." In A. George, ed., *Reflections on Chomsky.* Blackwell, Oxford, pp. 175–91.

Burge, Tyler (1992) "Philosophy of language and mind." *Philosophical Review* 101: 3–51.

Carey, Susan (1985) *Conceptual Change in Childhood.* Cambridge, MA, MIT Press.

Chomsky, Carol (1986) "Analytic study of the Tadoma method: Language abilities of three deaf-blind subjects." *Journal of Speech and Hearing Research* 29: 332–47.

Chomsky, Noam (1951/1979) *Morphophonemics of Modern Hebrew.* University of Pennsylvania Master's Thesis. New York, Garland Publishing. (Revised version of 1949 BA thesis.)

Chomsky, Noam (1955/1975) *Logical Structure of Linguistic Theory.* Plenum, New York; excerpted from unpublished 1955/56 MS.

Chomsky, Noam (1957) *Syntactic Structures.* The Hague, Mouton.

Chomsky, Noam (1964) *Current Issues in Linguistic Theory.* The Hague, Mouton.

Chomsky, Noam (1965) *Aspects of the Theory of Syntax.* Cambridge, MA, MIT Press.

Chomsky, Noam (1966) *Cartesian Linguistics.* Harper and Row, New York.

Chomsky, Noam (1968) *Language and Mind.* Harcourt Brace Jovanovich, New York. Extended edition 1972.

Chomsky, Noam (1969) "Some empirical assumptions in modern philosophy of language." In S. Morgenbesser, P. Suppes and M. White, eds., *Philosophy, Science and Method: Essays in Honor of Ernest Nagel.* New York, St Martin's Press, pp. 260–85.

Chomsky, Noam (1975) *Reflections on Language.* Pantheon, New York.

Chomsky, Noam (1977) "Questions of form and interpretation." In Noam Chomsky, *Essays on Form and Interpretation.* North Holland, New York, pp. 25–59.

Chomsky, Noam (1980) *Rules and Representations.* Oxford, Blackwell.

Chomsky, Noam (1981a) *Lectures on Government and Binding.* Dordrecht, Foris.

Chomsky, Noam (1981b) "Principles and parameters in syntactic theory." In N. Hornstein and D. Lightfoot, eds., *Explanations in Linguistics.* London, Longman, pp. 123–46.

Chomsky, Noam (1986) *Knowledge of Language*. New York, Praeger.

Chomsky, Noam (1987) "Reply" [to reviews of his 1986 by A. George and M. Brody]. *Mind and Language* 2: 178–97.

Chomsky, Noam (1988a) *Language and Problems of Knowledge: The Managua Lectures*. Cambridge, MA, MIT Press.

Chomsky, Noam (1988b) "Language and Problems of Knowledge." *Synthesis Philosophica* 5: 1–25.

Chomsky, Noam (1990) "Accessibility 'in Principle'." *Behavioral and Brain Sciences* 13: 600–1.

Chomsky, Noam (1991a) "Linguistics and adjacent fields: a personal view." In A. Kasher, ed., *The Chomskyan Turn*. Oxford, Blackwell, pp. 3–25.

Chomsky, Noam (1991b) "Linguistics and cognitive science: problems and mysteries." In A. Kasher, ed., *The Chomskyan Turn*. Oxford, Blackwell, pp. 26–53.

Chomsky, Noam et al. (1993a) *Language and Thought*. London, Moyer Bell.

Chomsky, Noam (1993b) "A minimalist program for linguistic theory." In K. Hale and J. Keyser, eds., *The View from Building 20*. Cambridge, MA, MIT Press, pp. 1–52.

Chomsky, Noam (1995a) "Language and Nature." *Mind* 104: 1–61.

Chomsky, Noam (1995b) "Bare Phrase Structure." In G. Webelhuth, ed., *Government and Binding Theory and the Minimalist Program*. Oxford, Blackwell, pp. 383–439.

Chomsky, Noam (1995c) *The Minimalist Program*. Cambridge, MA, MIT Press.

Chomsky, Noam (1998) "Minimalist inquiries: the framework." MS, MIT.

Churchland, Patricia (1994) Presidential address of the APA Pacific Division, March 1994.

Churchland, Paul (1979) *Scientific Realism and the Plasticity of Mind*. Cambridge University Press.

Churchland, Paul (1981) "Eliminative materialism and the propositional attitudes." *Journal of Philosophy* 78: 67–90. Reprinted in Scott Christensen and Dale Turner, eds., *Folk Psychology and the Philosophy of Mind*. Hillsdale, NJ, Erlbaum, 1993.

Churchland, Paul (1994) Review of Searle, 1992, *London Review of Books*, 12 May.

Clark, Andy and Annette Karmiloff-Smith (1993) "The cognizer's innards." *Mind and Language* 8: 487–530.

Cohen, Leonore (1941) *From Beast-Machine to Man-Machine*. Oxford University Press.

Cudworth, Ralph (1838) *Treatise concerning Eternal and Immutable Morality*. American edition of *Works*, ed. T. Birch.

Darwin, C. (1859/1968) *The Origin of Species by Means of Natural Selection*. Edited by J.W. Burrow. Harmondsworth, Penguin.

Davidson, Donald (1980) "Psychology as philosophy." Reprinted in *Essays on Actions and Events*. Oxford University Press, pp. 229–39.

Davidson, Donald (1984) *Inquiries into Truth and Interpretation*. Oxford University Press.

Davidson, Donald (1986a) "A coherence theory of truth and knowledge." In E. Lepore, ed., *Truth and Interpretation*. Oxford, Blackwell, pp. 307–19.

Davidson, Donald (1986b) "A nice derangement of epitaphs." In E. Lepore, ed., *Truth and Interpretation*. Oxford, Blackwell, pp. 433–46.

Davidson, Donald (1990a) "The structure and content of truth." *Journal of Philosophy* 87: 279–328.

Davidson, Donald (1990b) "The second person." MS, University of California, Berkeley.

Davies, Martin (1991) "Individualism and perceptual content." *Mind* 100: 461–84.

Dennett, Daniel (1988) "When philosophy encounters artificial intelligence." *Daedalus* 1998 = *Proceedings of the American Academy of Arts and Sciences* 117: 283–95.

Dennett, Daniel (1991) Review of McGinn (1991). *TLS* 10 May.

Descartes, René (1649/1927) Letter (to Morus). In R.M. Eaton, ed., *Descartes Selections*.

Devitt, Michael and Kim Sterelny (1989) "Linguistics: what's wrong with 'the right view'." *Philosophical Perspectives* 3: 497–531.

Dijksterhuis, E.J. (1986) *Mechanization of the World Picture*. Princeton University Press.

Dobbs, Betty Jo and Margaret Jacob (1995) *Newton and the Culture of Newtonianism*. Humanities Press, New York.

Dreben, Burton (1992) "Putnam, Quine and the facts." *Philosophical Topics* 20: 293–315.

Dummett, Michael (1986) "A nice derangement of epitaphs: some comments on Davidson and Hacking." In E. Lepore, ed., *Truth and Interpretation*. Oxford, Blackwell, pp. 459–76.

Dummett, Michael (1991) *The Logical Basis of Metaphysics*. Cambridge, MA: Harvard University Press.

Dummett, Michael (1993) *The Seas of Language*. Oxford, Clarendon Press.

Earman, J., ed. (1992) *Inference, Explanation and Other Philosophical Frustrations*. Berkeley, CA, University of California Press.

Edelman, Gerald (1992) *Bright Sun, Brilliant Fire*. New York, Basic Books.

Egan, Frances (no date) "Computation and content." MS, Rutgers.

Epstein, Samuel (1999) "UN-principled syntax and the derivation of syntactic relations." In Samuel Epstein and Norbert Hornstein, eds., *Working Minimalism*. Cambridge, MA, MIT Press.

Evnine, Simon (1991) *Donald Davidson*. Stanford University Press.

Fodor, Jerry (1975) *The Language of Thought*. New York, Crowell.

Fodor, Jerry (1983) *The Modularity of Mind*. Cambridge, MA, MIT Press.

Fodor, Jerry (1987) *Psychosemantics*. Cambridge, MA, MIT Press.

Fodor, Jerry (1990) *A Theory of Content*. Cambridge, MA, MIT Press.

Fodor, Jerry (1994) *The Elm and the Expert*. Cambridge, MA, MIT Press.

Fodor, Jerry and Ernest Lepore (1992) *Holism: A Shopper's Guide*. Oxford, Blackwell.

Frege, Gottlob (1892/1965) "Über Sinn und Bedeutung." *Zeitschrift für Philosophie und Philosophische Kritik* 100: 25–50. Reprinted in part as "On sense and nominatum" in Ernest Nagel and Richard Brandt, eds., *Meaning and Knowledge: Systematic Readings in Epistemology*. Harcourt, Brace & World, New York, pp. 69–78.

Friedman, Michael (1993) "Remarks on the history of science and the history of philosophy." In P. Horwich, ed., *World Changes: Thomas Kuhn and the Nature of Science*. Cambridge, MA, MIT Press, pp. 37–54.

Gaifman, Haim (1996) "Is the 'bottom-up' approach from the theory of meaning to metaphysics possible?" *Journal of Philosophy* 93: 373–407.

Galilei, Galileo (1632) *Dialogues on the Great World Systems*, as translated by Thomas Salusbury, 1661.

Gay, Peter (1970) *The Enlightenment: An Interpretation*. London, Weidenfeld and Nicholson.

Gibson, Roger (1986) "Translation, physics, and facts of the matter." In E. Hahn and P.A. Schilpp, eds., *The Philosophy of W.V. Quine*. La Salle, Open Court, pp. 139–54.

Gleitman, Lila (1990) "The structural sources of verb meanings." *Language Acquisition* 1: 3–55.

Goodman, Nelson (1978) *Ways of Worldmaking*. Hassocks, Harvester Press.

Gould, Stephen J. (1982) *The Panda's Thumb*. New York, Norton.

Griffin, Donald (1994) "Animal communication as evidence of animal mentality." In Carleton Gajdusek, Guy McKhann and Liana Bolis, eds., *Evolution and Neurology of Language: Discussions in Neuroscience* X.1–2, pp. 67–71.

Hagoort, Peter, Colin Brown and J. Groothusen (1993) "The syntactic positive shift (SPS) as an ERP-measure of syntactic processing." *Language and Cognitive Processes* 8: 439–83.

Hagoort, Peter and Colin Brown (1994) "Brain responses to lexical ambiguity, resolution and parsing." In Charles Clifton *et al.*, eds., *Perspectives on Sentence Processing*. Hillsdale, NJ, Erlbaum, pp. 45–80.

Halle, Morris and Alec Marantz (1993) "Distributed morphology and the pieces of inflection." In K. Hale and S.J. Keyser, eds., *The View from Building 20*. Cambridge, MA, MIT Press, pp. 111–76.

Harman, Gilbert (1980) "Two quibbles about analyticity and psychological reality." *Behavioral and Brain Sciences* 3: 21–2.

Haugeland, John (1979) "Understanding natural language." *Journal of Philosophy* 76: 619–32.

Herbert of Cherbury (1624) *De Veritate*. Translated by M.H. Carré, University of Bristol Studies No. 6, 1937.

Higginbotham, James (1985) "On semantics." *Linguistic Inquiry* 16: 547–93.

Higginbotham, James (1989) "Elucidations of meaning." *Linguistics and Philosophy* 12: 465–517.

Hobbes, Thomas (1889) *The English Works of Thomas Hobbes*, Vol I. Edited by William Molesworth.

Holton, Gerald (1996) "On the art of scientific imagination." *Daedalus = Proceedings of the American Academy of Arts and Sciences* 125: 183–208.

Huarte, Juan (1575) *Examen de Ingenios*. Translated by Bellamy, 1698.

Humboldt, Wilhelm von (1836/1988) "Über die Verschiedenheit des Menschlichen Sprachbaues. Berlin. Translated by Peter Heath as *The Diversity of Human Language-Structure and its Influence on the Mental Development of Mankind*. Cambridge University Press.

Hume, David (1740/1978) *A Treatise of Human Nature*. Edited by L.A. Selby-Bigge. Second edition revised by P.H. Nidditch. Oxford, Clarendon Press.

Hume, David (1748/1975) *An Enquiry concerning Human Understanding*. Edited by L.A. Selby-Bigge; third edition revised by P.H. Nidditch. Clarendon Press, Oxford.

Hume, David (1841) *The History of England: From the Invasion of Julius Caesar to the Revolution in 1688*. London, 6 volumes; T. Cadell.

Jackendoff, Ray (1994) *Patterns in the Mind*. New York, Basic Books.

Jacob, François (1974) *The Logic of Living Systems: A History of Heredity*. Translated by Betty E. Spillmann. London, Allen Lane.

Jacob, Margaret (1988) *The Cultural Meaning of the Scientific Revolution*. Philadelphia, PA, Temple University Press.

Jacob, Margaret (1991) *Living the Enlightenment: Freemasonry and Politics in Eighteenth-Century Europe*. Oxford University Press.

Jaeger, H.M. and Sidney R. Nagel (1992) "Physics of the granular state." *Science* 255: 1523–31.

Jenkins, Lyle (1999) *Biolinguistics: Exploring the Biology of Language*. Cambridge University Press.

Jerne, Niels Kaj (1985) "The generative grammar of the immune system (Nobel lecture)." *Science* 229: 1057–9.

Jespersen, Otto (1924) *The Philosophy of Grammar*. London, Allen & Unwin.

Kant, Immanuel (1783) *Prolegomena to any Future Metaphysics*.

Kayne, Richard (1994) *The Antisymmetry of Syntax*. Cambridge, MA, MIT Press.

Kenny, Anthony (1984) *The Legacy of Wittgenstein*. Oxford, Blackwell.

Koyré, Alexandre (1957) *From the Closed World to the Infinite Universe*. Baltimore, Johns Hopkins Press.

Kripke, Saul (1972) *Naming and Necessity*. In Donald Davidson and Gilbert Harman, eds., *Semantics of Natural Language*. Dordrecht, Reidel, pp. 253–355.

Labandeira, Comrad C. and J. John Sepkoski (1993) "Insect diversity in the fossil record." *Science* 261: 310–15.

La Mettrie, J.O. de (1747) *L'Homme-Machine*. Critical edition, A. Vartanian, ed., Princeton University Press.

Lange, Friedrich Albert (1925) *The History of Materialism*. London, Kegan Paul.

Larson, Richard and Gabriel Segal (1995) *Knowledge of Meaning*. Cambridge, MA, MIT Press.

Lasnik, Howard (1989) *Essays on Anaphora*. Dordrecht, Kluwer.

Lepore, Ernest, ed. (1986) *Truth and Interpretation: Perspectives on the Philosophy of Donald Davidson*. Oxford, Blackwell.

Lewis, David (1983) "Languages and language." In David Lewis, *Philosophical Papers*, vol. I. Oxford University Press, pp. 163–88.

Lewontin, Richard (1990) "The evolution of cognition." In D.N. Osherson and E.E. Smith, eds., *An Invitation to Cognitive Science*, vol. 3. Cambridge, MA, MIT Press, pp. 229–46.

Lewontin, Richard (1994) MS, Harvard.

Llinás, Rodolfo (1987) "'Mindness' as a functional state of the brain." In Colin Blakemore and Susan Greenfield, eds., *Mindwaves: Thoughts on Intelligence, Identity and Consciousness*. Blackwell, Oxford, pp. 339–58.

Locke, John (1690/1975) *An Essay Concerning Human Understanding*. Edited by P. Nidditch. Oxford, Clarendon Press.

Lormand, Eric (1996) "How to Be a Meaning Holist." *Journal of Philosophy* 93: 51–73.

Lyons, John (1977) *Semantics*, 2 vols. Cambridge University Press.

Malt, Barbara (1994) "Water Is Not H_2O." *Cognitive Psychology* 27: 41–70.

Marr, David (1982) *Vision*. New York, W.H. Freeman.

Marshall, John (1990) Foreword to Yamada (1990).

Marshall, Jonathan (1989) "On making representations." In C. Brown, P. Hagoort and T. Meijering, eds., *Vensters op de Geest*. Utrecht, Stichting Grafiet.

McGinn, Colin (1991) *The Problem of Consciousness*. Oxford, Blackwell.

McGinn, Colin (1993) *Problems in Philosophy*. Oxford, Blackwell.

Mehler, Jacques and Emmanuel Dupoux (1994) *What Infants Know*. Oxford, Blackwell.

Mercier, Adèle (1992) "Linguistic competence, convention and authority: individualism and anti-individualism in linguistics and philosophy." PhD dissertation, UCLA.

Mijuskovic, Ben Lazare (1974) *The Achilles of Rationalist Arguments*. Martinus Nijhoff.

Miller, George and Noam Chomsky (1963) "Finitary models of language users." In R.D. Luce, R. Bush and E. Galanter, eds., *Handbook of Mathematical Psychology*, vol. II. New York, Wiley, pp. 419–91.

Moravcsik, Julius (1975) "Aitia as Generative Factor in Aristotle's Philosophy." *Dialogue* 14: 622–36.

Moravcsik, Julius (1990) *Thought and Language*. London, Routledge.

Mountcastle, Vernon (1998) "Brain science at the century's ebb." *Daedalus*, Spring 1998 = *Proceedings of the American Academy of Arts and Sciences* 127: 1–36.

Nagel, Thomas (1993) "The mind wins!" Review of Searle (1992) *New York Review*, 4 March. Reprinted (1995) as "Searle: why we are not computers" in T. Nagel, *Other Minds*. Oxford University Press, pp. 96–110.

Neville, Helen, J. Nicol, A. Barss, K. Forster and M. Garrett (1991) "Syntactically based sentence processing classes: evidence from event-related brain potentials." *Journal of Cognitive Neuroscience* 3: 151–65.

Passmore, John (1965) *Priestley's Writings on Philosophy, Science and Politics*. New York, London: Collier-MacMillan.

Pateman, Trevor (1987) *Language in Mind and Language in Society*. Oxford University Press.

Peirce, Charles Sanders (1957) "The logic of abduction." In Vincent Thomas, ed., *Peirce's Essays in the Philosophy of Science*. New York, Liberal Arts Press, pp. 235–55.

Penrose, Roger (1989) *The Emperor's New Mind*. Oxford University Press.

Piattelli-Palmarini, Massimo (1986) "The rise of selective theories: a case study and some lessons from immunology." In W. Demopoulos and A. Marras, eds., *Language Learning and Concept Acquisition: Foundational Issues*. Norwood, NJ, Ablex, pp. 117–30.

Popkin, Richard (1979) *The History of Skepticism from Erasmus to Spinoza*. Berkeley, CA, University of California Press.

Pustejovsky, James, ed. (1993) *Semantics and the Lexicon*. Dordrecht, Kluwer.

Pustejovsky, James (1994) "Coercion and cocomposition." MS, Brandeis.
Pustejovsky, James (1995) *The Generative Lexicon*. Cambridge, MA, MIT Press.
Putnam, Hilary (1975) "The meaning of 'meaning'." In *Philosophical Papers, vol. 2: Mind Language and Reality*. Cambridge University Press, pp. 215–71.
Putnam, Hilary (1978) *Meaning and the Moral Sciences*. Routledge & Kegan Paul.
Putnam, Hilary (1986a) "Meaning holism." In E. Hahn and P.A. Schilpp, eds., *The Philosophy of W.V. Quine*. La Salle, Open Court, pp. 405–26.
Putnam, Hilary (1986b) "Meaning and our mental life." In Edna Ullmann-Margalit, ed., *The Kaleidoscope of Science*. Dordrecht, Reidel, pp. 17–32.
Putnam, Hilary (1988a) *Representation and Reality*. Cambridge, MA, MIT Press.
Putnam, Hilary (1988b) "Much ado about not very much." *Daedalus*, 1988 = *Proceedings of the American Academy of Arts and Sciences* 117: 269–81.
Putnam, Hilary (1992) "Replies." *Philosophical Topics* 20: 347–408.
Quine, Willard (1960) *Word and Object*. Cambridge, MA, MIT Press.
Quine, Willard (1969) "Reply to Chomsky". In Donald Davidson and Jaakko Hintikka, eds., *Words and Objections: Essays on the Work of W.V. Quine*. Dordrecht, D. Reidel, pp. 302–11.
Quine, Willard (1972) "Methodological reflections on current linguistic theory." In Donald Davidson and Gilbert Harman, eds., *Semantics of Natural Language*. Reidel, Dordrecht, pp. 442–54.
Quine, Willard (1981) *Theories and Things*. Cambridge, MA, Harvard University Press.
Quine, Willard (1986) "Reply to Gilbert H. Harman." In E. Hahn and P.A. Schilpp, eds., *The Philosophy of W.V. Quine*. La Salle, Open Court, pp. 181–8.
Quine, Willard (1987) "Indeterminacy of translation again." *Journal of Philosophy* 84: 5–10.
Quine, Willard (1990) *Pursuit of Truth*. Cambridge, MA, Harvard University Press.
Quine, Willard (1992) "Structure and nature." *Journal of Philosophy* 89: 5–9.
Ramberg, Bjorn (1989) *Donald Davidson's Philosophy of Language*. Oxford, Blackwell.
Reid, Thomas (1785) *Essays on the Intellectual Powers of Man*. Edinburgh, John Bell.
Rhum, Michael (1993) "Understanding 'belief'." *MAN* 28.4, December.
Romaine, Suzanne (1994) *Language in Society*. Oxford University Press.
Rorty, Richard (1986) "Pragmatism, Davidson and truth." In E. Lepore, ed., *Truth and Interpretation*. Oxford, Blackwell, pp. 333–55.
Scheffler, Israel (1955) "On synonymy and indirect discourse." *Philosophy of Science* 22: 39–44.
Schiffer, Stephen (1987) *Remnants of Meaning*. Cambridge, MA, MIT Press.
Schofield, Robert (1970) *Mechanism and Materialism*. Princeton University Press.
Schweber, Silvan (1993) "Physics, community and the crisis in physical theory." *Physics Today*. 46: 34–40.
Searle, John (1980) "Minds, brains and programs." *Behavioral and Brain Sciences* 3: 417–24.
Searle, John (1992) *The Rediscovery of the Mind*. Cambridge, MA, MIT Press.
Segal, Gabriel (1987) "In Deference to Reference." PhD dissertation, MIT.

Smith, Barry (1992) "Understanding language." *Proceedings of the Aristotelian Society*, pp. 109–41.

Smith, Neil (1999) *Chomsky: Ideas and Ideals*. Cambridge University Press.

Smith, Neil, Ianthi-Maria Tsimpli and Jamal Ouhalla (1993) "Learning the impossible: the acquisition of possible and impossible languages by a polyglot *savant*." *Lingua* 91: 279–347.

Soames, Scott (1989) "Semantics and semantic competence." *Philosophical Perspectives* 3.

Spelke, Elizabeth (1990) "Origins of Visual Knowledge." In D.N. Osherson, S.M. Kosslyn and J.M. Hollerbach, eds., *An Invitation to Cognitive Science*, vol. II. Cambridge, MA, MIT Press, pp. 99–127.

Stich, Stephen (1983) *From Folk Psychology to Cognitive Science*. Cambridge, MA, MIT Press.

Stich, Stephen (1996) *Deconstructing the Mind*. Oxford University Press.

Strawson, Galen (1994) *Mental Reality*. Cambridge, MA, MIT Press.

Strawson, Peter (1950) "On Referring." *Mind* 59: 320–44.

Strawson, Peter (1952) *Introduction to Logical Theory*. London, Methuen.

Stryker, Michael (1994) "Precise development from imprecise rules." *Science* 263: 1244–5.

Thackray, Arnold (1970) *Atoms and Powers*. Cambridge, MA, Harvard University Press.

Tremblay, Mireille (1991) "Possession and Datives." PhD dissertation, McGill University.

Turing, Alan (1950) "Computing Machinery and Intelligence." *Mind* 49: 433–60.

Uebel, Thomas, with comments by Christopher Hookway (1995) *The Vienna Circle Revisited*. Centre for the Philosophy of the Natural and Social Sciences, London. DP 6/95.

Ullman, Shimon (1979) *The Interpretation of Visual Motion*. Cambridge, MA, MIT Press.

Waldrop, M. Mitchell (1990) "Spontaneous order, evolution and life." *Science* 247: 1543–5.

Weisskopf, Victor (1989) "The origin of the universe." *Bulletin of the American Academy of Arts and Sciences* 42.

Wellman, Kathleen (1992) *La Mettrie: Medicine, Philosophy and Enlightenment*. Chapel Hill, Duke.

Wheeler, John (1994) *At Home in the Universe*. New York, American Institute of Physics.

Witherspoon, Gary (1977) *Language and Art in the Navajo Universe*. Ann Arbor, MI, University of Michigan.

Wright, Crispin (1989) "Wittgenstein's rule-following considerations and the central project of theoretical linguistics." In A. George, ed., *Reflections on Chomsky*. Oxford, Blackwell, pp. 233–64.

Yamada, Jeni (1990) *Laura*. Cambridge, MA, MIT Press.

Yolton, John (1983) *Thinking Matter*. Minneapolis, MN, University of Minnesota Press.

Yolton, John (1984) *Perceptual Acquaintance*. Minneapolis, MN, University of Minnesota Press.

Index

abduction 80

ability, distinguished from knowledge 50–2, 97–8

abstract *see* concrete–abstract dimension

access: to consciousness 93–8, 141, 147 – in principle 96–8, 141, 143

acoustic phonetics 174

acquisition 6–8, 181; and concept formation 61–6; "initial state" as a device for 4–5; innateness and selectivity x–xi, 121–2; labelling of innate concepts 61–2, 65; and lexical access 121–2; and sensory deficit 121–2; *see also* child language acquisition; Language Acquisition Device (LAD)

adjacency 11, 121

agency, and objects 21–2

agreement 14

algorithms 113, 147, 159

Almog, Joseph 42

analytic–synthetic distinction xiv, 46–7, 61–5

anaphora 39, 140

animal, man and 3

animate–inanimate dimension 126

anthropological linguistics 6

anthropology 136

anti-foundationalism 76–7

arbitrariness, Saussurean 27, 120

argument-structure 11

Aristotle 187, 204n

articulatory phonetics 174

articulatory–perceptual systems 28, 120, 123–6, 180

artifacts, capacities of 114

Artificial Intelligence 200n

assertability conditions 109

assignment of derived constituent structure 199n

association 92, 93

Atlas, Jay 151

"atomic" units 10

atomism, physical 111

auditory cortex 158

Austin, John 45, 132

authority: deference to 155; first-person 142–3

autosegmental 40

Baker, Lynne Rudder 153–4

Baldwin, T.R. 79–80, 81, 144

Barinaga, Marcia 158

Bedeutung (Frege) 130, 131–2

Beekman, Isaac 110

behavior, causation of 72, 95

behaviorism 46–60, 80, 92, 93, 101, 103

belief systems: and the language faculty xiv, 63–4, 129; lexicon and 32; and the terms of language 21–2, 137, 148–9

beliefs: absence of term in other languages than English 119; attribution of 91, 119, 135, 146–7, 153–4, 200n; convictions about the nature, as *a posteriori* or *a priori* 89; different about the same subject 149, 192–3; false 33, 43; fixation 63–4; individuation of 165, *see also* I-beliefs justification

intelligibility, in scientific discourse 151–2
intention 62, 91, 125, 137, 180; referential 130–1; *see also* conceptual–intentional systems
"intentional laws" 166
intentional terminology 113–15
intentionality: Brentano on 22; naturalistic inquiry and 45, 132
interests 125, 128, 137
interface: between language faculty and other systems of the mind 123; legibility conditions at the 10–12; levels 10, 28, 39, 173–5; location of the 174; phonetic and semantic representations at the 10–12, 160, 173–4; properties 124–6; weakest assumptions about relations 10, 128–9
interface condition, requires erasure of uninterpretable features 14–15
internal processes, correlation with distal properties 162
internal relational structure 22
internalism vii, xiv, xv, 15, 125; critique of 162; defined 134; form of syntax 129
internalism–externalism issues 148–63
internalist approach 33–4, 38–45, 134–63, 164–94; legitimacy of inquiries that go beyond 156; and other domains of psychology 158–9; to differing beliefs 193; to language-world relations 15–16
internalist linguistic theory (T) 142–3, 146
internalist semantics 34, 38–9, 45
interpretation, language and xiii–xiv, 46–74
interpretations, assignment of 160–1
"interpreter", Davidson on the 29, 56, 67–70, 102
intuitions 44, 70, 84, 119, 130, 135, 138, 161, 197n
intuitions: limits of xiv–xv; as subject of linguistic study 171–2; and technical terms 148–9

intuitive categories, meaninglessness for science 161–3
intuitive judgements: about statements 40–2; as data to be studied as evidence 171–2; different 64; forced with ordinary expectations withdrawn 172
invented forms 181
invented system, designed to violate principles of language 121

Jacob, François 139
Jacob, Margaret 108, 110
Jakobson, Roman 140
James, Henry 47, 90
Japanese: anaphora in 140; evidence from about referential dependence 53–4, 58, 102; importance for study of English xv, 53–4, 58, 102; right-headed 93
Jerne, Niels Kaj 65
Jespersen, Otto 73

K, as constant knowledge of language 51
K-ability 51
Kant, Immanuel 112, 182; method of transcendental argument 165
Kayne, Richard 123, 131
Kekulé von Stradonitz, August 111
Kenny, Anthony 50, 197n
knowing-how 51–2
knowledge: distinguished from ability 50–2, 97–8; nature of 170; nature of tacit xiii
knowledge of language vii, ix, xiv, 50–2; and cognition x, 73; defined 73; in English usage 170; as the internal representation of generative procedure in the brain 50–2; as learned ability 50; partial 48–9, 99–100, 146; uniform among languages 126; *see also* innateness
Kripke, Saul 37, 141–2; *Naming and Necessity* 41
Kripke's puzzle 191

psychological mechanisms 117–18
psychology: internalist 143; invented
    technical term 153; and software
    problems 105
psychology vi, vii, 1, 80, 136, 138,
    154, 160, 181, 202n
psychosemantics 165
"public language" 30, 32–3, 37, 38,
    40, 127, 131–2, 136, 148, 155–8,
    187–8
purposes 136–7
Pustejovsky, James 128
Putnam, Hilary xiii, 19, 41, 152,
    156–7; on alleged facts 136; on
    Bohr 43; Chomsky's critique of
    19–45; critique of "MIT
    mentalism" 184–9; division of
    linguistic labor 71, 187–8; on
    impossibility of explanatory models
    for human beings 19–20; on
    intentionality 45; on languages
    and meanings as cultural realities
    157–8; rejection of the "innateness
    hypothesis" 65, 66–7; "The
    Meaning of Meaning" 41–2;
    Twin-Earth thought experiment
    40–1, 148–9, 155; on water 127–8

quantifiers 11, 124
quantum theory 111
Quine, Willard xiii, 46, 57, 61,
    101, 141; coordinate structure
    constraint 55–6; displacement
    of clicks study 55, 58, 140;
    distinction between "fitting" and
    "guiding" 94–5; epistemology
    naturalized 46–7, 80, 81; on
    extensional equivalence 132; on
    grammaticality 63; indeterminacy
    of translation 132, 140, 147;
    "naturalistic thesis" 92–3, 144; no
    fact of the matter 58, 59; radical
    translation paradigm 52–5, 101–2;
    "revision can strike anywhere"
    66–7, 188

R ("refer") relation 38–40; and R-
    like relation 41–2

rational inquiry, idealization to
    selected domains 49–50
reduction viii, xiv, 82, 87, 106,
    144–5
reference 2, 148; as an invented
    technical notion 148–50, 152–3;
    causal theory of 41; choices about
    fixing of 67; cross-cultural
    similarities 171; fixation of 42, 44,
    128; notions of independent 137;
    in philosophy of language 16–17;
    problem of relation 37–42; the
    "proto-science" of 171; in the
    sciences 152; semantics and
    130–2; as a social phenomenon
    relying on experts 188; social-co-
    operation plus contribution of the
    environment theory of specification
    of 41–2; specification of 41–2;
    technical notion of 202n;
    transparence of relation 39–40;
    as a triadic relation 149–50; two
    aspects of the study of 171; use of
    term 36, 130, 188; usefulness of
    concept 38–45, 181
referential dependence 47, 50, 126,
    180–1, 196n
referential properties, debate on
    24–5
referential use of language 180–1
reflection: evaluation by 166;
    operations of the mind which
    precede 170
regulative principle 46, 52
Reid, Thomas 80, 182, 196n, 203n
reification 92–3, 94, 201n
relatives 181
representations: "informational" with
    intentional content 195n; as
    postulated mental entities xiii,
    159–60; two levels of phonetic and
    logical xi–xii, 173
rhyme, relations of 174
Richards, Theodore 111
rigidity principle 94
Romaine, Suzanne 156
Rorty, Richard 46–7, 52, 61, 63
Royal Society 110